The United States Ballistic Missile Defence: International Chaos or Deterrence?

Neha Kumar

KNOWLEDGE WORLD
KW Publishers Pvt Ltd
New Delhi

KW Publishers Pvt Ltd
NEW DELHI: 4676/21, First Floor, Ansari Road, Daryaganj, New Delhi 110002
Email: mail@kwpub.in/knowledgeworld@vsnl.net Tel.: +91.11.23263498 / 43528107
MUMBAI: 15 Jay Kay Industrial Estate, Linking Road Extn., Santacruz (W), Mumbai 400054
email: mumbai@kwpub.in Tel.: +91.22.26614110 / 26613505

www.kwpub.in

ISBN 13: 978-93-80502-03-8

Published by Kalpana Shukla, KW Publishers Pvt Ltd
4676/21, First Floor, Ansari Road, Daryaganj, New Delhi 110002

Printed and Bound in India

Cover design by Anoop Kamath

Dedicated

to

My Parents

Contents

Acknowledgements

This book is the result of support and cooperation of many individuals, institutions and libraries. At the completion of this work I am indebted to many.

First and foremost, I express my deep and profound sense of gratitude to my father, CA Kishore Kumar and my mother Mrs Indira Kumar for their guidance, inexhaustible patience and constant encouragement. I am, indebted to my father for helping me in channelising my thoughts and in giving them a definite form and shape. He acts as a guide, editor and critic of my work.

I am thankful to the academic faculties of Jawaharlal Nehru University, School of International Studies (SIS), which taught me research methodology and international theories in detail. I am also obliged to Prof R R Submarbanium for suggesting me to choose this topic. I am thankful to my supervisor, Dr Swaran Singh, for all his guidance and kind help.

I am obliged to my generous colleagues and seniors at United Service Institution of India (USI). I am especially thankful to Brig (retd) Arun Sehgal and Comde (Retd) Rajiv Swahney for providing me a platform and opportunity to write this book. I am also thankful to my senior Dr Sudha Raman who helped me in finding a publisher for this book.

I am also thankful to Capt B N Tiwari for helping me and for engaging me in long discussions and giving me valuable insights about the military viewpoint, thinking and percepts. I am grateful to him for his constant assurance and support during my studies. Without his encouragement this book won't have been possible. I am also grateful to my sister Manisha for listening me patiently and helping me out whenever I had a problem during the year of writing this book.

I am also obliged to the staff of Jawaharlal Nehru University library, Institute of Defence Studies and Analysis (IDSA) Library, Col Pyara Lal Memorial Library, USI, American Centre Library. Their kind cooperation and permission to use library facilities has made this work possible.

Neha Kumar

Abbreviations

ABM	Anti Ballistic Missile
ABMT	Anti Ballistic Missile Treaty
ABL	Airborne Laser
ACV	Armored Combat Vehicles
ASAT	Anti Satellite Weapon
ASCM	Anti Ship Cruise Missile
ATTU	Atlantic to Urals Zone
BMD	Ballistic Missile Defence
BMDO	Ballistic Missile Defence Organisation
CBM	Confidence Building Measures
CFE	Conventional Armed Forces in Europe
CIA	Central Intelligence Agency
CMD	Cruise Missile Defence
CPP	Chinese Communist Parties
CTBT	Comprehensive Test Ban Treaty
DIA	Defence Intelligence Agency
DoD	Department of Defence
EKV	Exoatomespheric Kill Vehicle
EW	Early Warning Radar
FAS	Federation of American Scientists
FATA	Federally Administered Tribal Areas
FC	Frontier Constabulary
GAO	General Accounting Office
GCS	Global Control Systems
GMD	Ground Based Midcourse Defence
HEU	High Enriched Uranium
IAEA	International Atomic Energy Agency
ICBM	Intercontinental Range Ballistic Missile
ICOC	International Code of Conduct against Missiles
INF	Intermediate Range Nuclear Force Treaty
ISI	Inter-Services Intelligence
IRBM	Intermediate Range Ballistic Missile
JU	Jammat-ud-Dawa
KRL	Khan Research Laboratories

LeT	Lashkar-e-Toiba
LEU	Low Enriched Uranium
LWR	Light Water Reactor
LOW	Launch on Warning
MAD	Mutual Assured Destruction
MDA	Missile Defence Agency
MEL	Mobile-Erector-Launchers
MIT	Massachusetts Institute of Technology
MTCR	Missile Technology Control Regime
NATO	North Atlantic Treaty Organisation
NCRI	National Council of Resistance of Iran
NIE	National Intelligence Estimate Report
NPT	Non Proliferation Treaty
NMD	National Missile Defence
NWFP	North-West Frontier Province
PSI	Proliferation Security Initiative
RMSI	Regional Maritime Security Initiative
SDI	Strategic Defence Initiative
SEATO	South East Asia Treaty Organisation
SRBM	Short Range Ballistic Missile
SSBN	Ballistic Missile Submarine
SSBM	Surface to Surface Ballistic Missile
START	Strategic Arms Reduction Treaty
STSS	Space Tracking Surveillance System
SLV	Space Launch Vehicles
TEL	Transporter-Erector-Launchers
TMD	Theatre Missile Defence
TLE	Treaty Limited Equipment
UCS	Union of Concerned Science
UAV	Unmanned Aerial Vehicles
UNSC	United Nation Security Council
WTO	World Trade Organisations
WMD	Weapons of Mass Destruction
ZBM	Zero Ballistic Missile

1

Deterrence and Ballistic Missile Defence in Cold War Period

Introduction

Deterrence has dominated the scene of international relations since the end of World War II. From the end of World War II to throughout the Cold War, US and Russia threatened each other with the use of nuclear weapons but never used them. It was clearly understood that mutual nuclear deterrence was largely responsible for the 'long-term peace' between the two superpowers.[1] Nuclear weapons were regarded as instruments for prevention of war rather than for destruction. [2]

The credibility of nuclear deterrence depends on their effective delivery, most importantly, on ballistic missiles.[3] Here emerges the issue of Ballistic Missile Defence (BMD) which aims at destroying ballistic missiles carrying Weapons of Mass Destruction (WMD) in space, before they reach their destination. This means a massive reduction in the adversary's credibility towards nuclear deterrence. As a result, the adversary tries to develop offensive weapons or counter-measures to strengthen its deterrence power.[4] This has led to the debate on whether BMD stabilises or destabilises the deterrence theory.

Defining 'Deterrence'

The term 'Deterrence' could be defined as discouraging the enemy from taking action by giving various military and economic incentives as well as threats. Deterrence is relevant in war and is aimed at prevention of escalation of conflict. It has been defined by the US Department of Defence(DoD) as "Prevention of action by fear of the consequences. Deterrence is a state of mind brought about by the existence of credible threats of unacceptable counteraction".[5] In military parlance, it means preventing the enemy from taking armed action by giving similar kinds of military threats. Deterrence means to compel the enemy in a situation of conflict and to act or react in the light of the existing dispositions, which constitute an effective threat.

Thomas Schelling defines deterrence as, "persuading a potential enemy that he should in his own interest avoid certain course of activity".[6] Deterrence involves a cost-benefit analysis, and works by convincing the enemy that the cost of taking action will outweigh the benefits. The decision to either go to war or maintain peace is taken keeping in view the consequences involved in a particular action, and any government is not likely to go to war unless it foresees considerable advantage by doing so.[7]

Deterrence depends on the credibility of threat, which means the enemy should be capable enough to retaliate under certain conditions. This capability should be combined with communication, and the enemy should be given clear messages about how the threats could be mutually beneficial. Therefore, capability and credibility are two important components of deterrence. Capability depends on military force while credibility depends on effective communications to convince the enemy that threat is real. [8]Prof William Kaufmann has mentioned in 1954:

> Essentially, deterrence means preventing certain types of contingencies from arising. To achieve this objective, it becomes necessary to communicate in some way to a prospective antagonist what is likely to happen him, should he create a situation in question. The expectation is that, confronted with this prospect, he will be deterred from taking the action that is regarded as inimical at least so as other less tolerable alternatives are open to him. [9]

This clearly means that enemy has to be persuaded that the deterrer has the capacity to act, 'that in acting he could inflict costs greater than the advantages to be won from attaining the objective; and that he really would act as specified in the stated contingency.' In addition to communication, deterrence also depends on public opinion. Deterrence will be credible 'only to the extent that important segments of public opinion in domestic and allied countries support it.' Finally, deterrence depends on cost, 'there must be some relationship between the value of the objective sought and the costs involved in its attainment.'[10] According to Scott Sagan, credibility depends on wide range of options including the perceived interests at stake, one's reputation for following through on threats, the legitimacy of the conflict and the so called 'audience costs' of backing down.[11]

Roy E Jones has mentioned some important ways to make deterrence 'credible.' He mentioned that if the adversary has the capacity to retaliate on large scale to a nuclear attack, the credibility will depend on the belief that deterrer is prepared to act irrationally in extreme circumstances. This means, under specified circumstances, deterer will carry out first strike against an adversary even if it means to bring full scale retaliatory attack from the other side. Further, practical steps should be taken so as to limit the damage and to ensure that first strike would not result into 'suicidal attack.' This can be done by building up forces to such a scale that adversary's first blow could be destroyed or could nearly destroy the retaliatory forces of an enemy. This could consist of the capability to destroy the retaliatory forces of an enemy in mid flight.[12]

During the Cold War, deterrence is believed to have prevented the escalation of conflict between two nuclear superpowers. Soviet Union feared that if it carried out an attack on the US, retaliation by the US forces could cause large-scale unrest and possible dissolution of the Soviet empire. Any aggression by Soviet Union could also bring the Western Alliance together or mobilise the West, which could either reduce its own security or greatly increase the cost of maintaining its position in the arms' race. The same was feared by the US. This prevented a nuclear war between the US and the Soviet Union during the Cold War.[13] Nuclear powers were aware of the fact that exchange of nuclear weapons will result into there own total or partial destruction. The assumption on which deterrence of cold war period was based is that if these weapons were used between the two leading military powers neither of them would emerge from the conflict without facing a political and social destruction.

It is important here to note the distinction between deterrence and defence. Gleen Synder provided explanation for this, 'Essentially, deterrence means discouraging the enemy from taking military action by posing to him a prospect of cost and risk that outweighs his prospective gain. Defence means reducing our own prospective costs and risks in the event that deterrence fails.'[14]The US often tries to combine both the concepts due to theoretical problems in the concept of deterrence [15] and this led to a debate whether defence is positively or negatively related to deterrence. Defence makes other countries cautious and this led to the rise of security dilemma.[16]

Deterrence: Pre and Post Nuclear Era

The concept of 'deterrence' is not new. The concept of 'balance of power', which was adopted in the 18th and 19th centuries, was similar to the concept of 'deterrence'. The core logic of the balance of power was that the military capabilities available to any combination of power should be sufficiently balanced so that full-scale conflict will appear profitless.[17] The root idea of the balance of power was that only force could counter the effect of force and that stability, predictability and regularity could only occur when the forces were in equilibrium. This concept of 'balance of power' could be compared with the concept of 'chandelier' which remains stable if the weights attached to it are distributed in such a way that the forces they exert are in equilibrium. The chandelier would lose stability if one of its weights became heavier without being compensated for it. This could be compared to a state that becomes stronger due to economic or military advantages. The chandelier would also become unstable if two weights move together without any compensatory movement elsewhere. Therefore, marginal conflicts were fought during this period so as to achieve marginal adjustments in the balance of power, something which diplomacy has failed to secure.[18]

With the introduction of nuclear weapons, the concept of 'balance of power' was replaced by the concept of 'deterrence'. The difference between pre-nuclear deterrence and post -nuclear deterrence is that pre-nuclear deterrence was stabilised not by technological weapons but by shifting of diplomatic alliances. During this period, the aim was to ensure that a state had as many players with it as it were numbered against. Nevertheless, this concept failed and resulted in World War I and World War II. The reason for its failure was the limited nature of destruction by potential armed conflict. Countries were willing to take that kind of risks during this period due to small amount of destruction involved in war.[19] The concept of 'deterrence' changed with the introduction of air power. Politicians and military heads realised the importance of air power and the possibility of strategic bombing towards deterring the enemy. During the 1920s and 1930s, it was felt that directly attacking and destroying the population centre of the enemy could prevent the disastrous event of World War I.[20]

British Prime Minister David Lloyd George said "the bomber will always get through, unstoppable by any defensive measures, causing immense damage to physical infrastructure and public morale".[21] This reinforced the concept of 'deterrence'. The fear of immense danger to infrastructure and civilian life proved far more potent in preventing the enemy while considering the option of war. However, these assumptions proved wrong during World War II and excessive attacks on population centres increased the enemy's will to resist attacks. This proved that the use of bombers was insufficient to deter the enemy.

The advent of nuclear weapons transformed the entire discourse on war since nuclear weapons were regarded as a "means to deter" and not "means to achieve victory" in war. The nuclear bombings on Hiroshima and Nagasaki witnessed complete destruction of life and property within a few minutes, which was not possible by the use of conventional weapons. Nuclear weapons were different from any other weapons used during the Cold War because of their large-scale impact and the speed at which they could cause destruction. Conventional weapons took large amounts of time to inflict damage and gave politicians ample time to review the situation and start negotiations for damage control or to terminate the war before irreparable damage was done. On the other hand, nuclear weapons threatened complete destruction within a few seconds, causing irreparable damage. Therefore, there was little scope for political negotiations in the case of a nuclear war. The aim of the war such as territorial limits of the aggressor and aggressed or freedom become meaningless in the advent of large scale of destruction caused by thermonuclear weapons.[22]

Bernard Brodie mentioned two propositions which make nuclear weapons different from other weapons. The first proposition is that nuclear weapons are not just another destructive weapon added to the already existing list of weapons. It is something which threatens to make the rest of the list unimportant. The second proposition is that it is wholly vain to expect scientists or engineers to develop any counter or 'answer' to atomic bomb.[23]He also mentioned that with ordinary explosives it was physically impossible for agents to smuggle into another country, either prior to or during hostilities, a sufficient quantity of materials to blow up more than a few specially chosen objectives. However, few pounds of U-235 or plutonium are sufficient to blow a major part of city.[24]

Nuclear weapons were used by the US and it dropped atomic bombs on the Japanese cities of Hiroshima and Nagasaki. Thereafter, nuclear weapons became the first category of weapons that appeared non-usable. Also, during the initial years when nuclear weapons were first used, hardly anything was known about their impact and potential. The reasons behind the use of nuclear weapons on Japan were:

- The US was the only nuclear country at that point of time and therefore there was no fear of retaliation or question of deterrence.
- The nuclear bomb was used mainly as a warning signal to Soviet Union rather than to defeat Japan. Scholars like Alprovitiz said that Japan was almost defeated at that time and would surrender, even if nuclear weapons were not used. [25]

When Soviet Union acquired nuclear weapons in 1949, the equations changed completely. Now there was a fear of retaliation by Soviet Union against the US, which could cause large-scale destruction. Nuclear weapons had also raised the costs of war. This led to the introduction of the concept of 'nuclear deterrence', which made war obsolete.

Similarly, Bernard Brodie in his famous book, *The Absolute Weapon* wrote, "The chief purpose of our military establishment has been to win wars. From now on its chief purpose must be to avert them. It can have no useful purpose".[26] Henry Kissinger wrote, "The nuclear age turned strategy into deterrence, and deterrence into exotic exercise." Similarly, Kenneth Waltz came up with his famous theory of 'more may be better' and said:

> Nuclear weapons and an appropriate doctrine for their use may make it possible to approach the defensive-deterrent ideal, a condition that would cause the chances of war to dwindle. Concentrating attention on destructive power of nuclear weapons has obscured the important benefits they promise to states trying to coexist in a self-help world. If weapons are not well suited for conquest, neighbours have more peace of mind. According to the defensive-deterrent ideal, we should expect war to become less likely when weaponry is such as to make conquest difficult, to discourage pre-emptive and preventive war, and to make coercive threats less credible.[27]

Waltz mentioned four ways in which nuclear weapons made war totally obsolete:

> First, wars can be fought in the face of deterrent threats, but the higher the stakes and the closer a country moves toward winning them, the more surely that country invites retaliation and risks its own destruction. States are not likely to run major risks for minor gains. Wars between nuclear states may escalate as the loser uses larger and larger warheads. Fearing that states will want to draw back, not escalation but de-escalation becomes likely. War remains possible. But victory in war is too dangerous to fight for. If states can score only small gains because large ones risk retaliation, they have little incentive to fight.
>
> Second, states act with less care if the expected costs of war are low and with more care if they are high. In 1853 and 1854, Britain and France expected to win an easy victory if they went to war against Russia. Prestige abroad and political popularity at home would be gained if not much else. The vagueness of their plans was matched by the carelessness of their acts. In blundering into the Crimean War they acted hastily on scant information, pandered to their people's frenzy for war, showed more concern for an ally's whim than for the adversary's situation, failed to specify the changes in behaviour that threats were supposed to bring and inclined towards testing strength first and bargaining second. In sharp contrast, the presence of nuclear weapons makes States exceedingly cautious. Think of Kennedy and Khrushchev in Cuban missile crisis. Why fight if you can't win much and might lose everything?

> Third, the question demands a negative answer all the more insistently when the deterrent deployment of nuclear weapons contributes more to a country's security than does conquest of territory. A country with a deterrent strategy does not need the extent of territory required by a country relaying on a conventional defence in depth. A deterrent strategy makes it unnecessary for a country to fight for the sake of increasing its security, and this removes a major cause of war.
> Fourth, deterrent effect depends on both on one's capabilities and on the will one has to use them. The will of the attacked, striving to preserve its own territory, can ordinarily be presumed stronger than will of the attacker striving to annex someone else's territory. Knowing this, the would-be attacker is further inhibited.

The presence of nuclear weapons on the international conflict scenario brought about a major shift in war policies. Possession of nuclear weapons made wars limited. Deterrence strategies that created caution all around the globe, thus reducing the possibility of wars, were formed.

Nuclear weapons also affected the prospective damage inflicted on the enemy: it was proportionate to adversary's expected gains in war, after those gains discounted for the many uncertainties of war. The US developed nuclear weapons so as to win World War II and then used them to gain strategic advantage over perceived enemies. This led to the outcome of war or negotiations about it in the favour of the US. The fear of irreparable damage prevented war and escalation of conflict in the Cold War period.

Weapons of Mass Destruction and Missiles

The use of missiles to deliver nuclear weapons or WMD was to further re-enforce the credibility of nuclear deterrence. Missiles were found to be capable of delivering WMD far and wide into the territories of the enemy state. The importance of missiles was realised by the use of V-2 rockets by Germany during World War II. The German V-1 and V-2 programmes against the United Kingdom forced approximately 1,450,000 people to evacuate London. The British Air Ministry conducted studies in 1944 which stated that the costs incurred by the allies to defend against the V-1 threat were four times greater than those incurred by Germans to carry out the defensive attacks.[28] The introduction of missiles changed the war scenario. Nations could now strike deep inside the enemy territory. Missiles had the capability to destroy civilian and industrial installations within minutes.

In evaluating V-2 rockets, R.V. Jones, Chief of British Royal Air Force scientific intelligence during World War II said:

> Our own politicians had been carried away with the threat: for some psychological reason, they seemed far more frightened by one tone of explosive delivered by rocket than by five tons delivered by aircraft. The reason was that no weapon yet produced has a comparable romantic appeal. Here is a 13 ton missile which traces out a flaming ascent to heights hitherto beyond the reach of man, and hurls itself 200 miles across the stratosphere at unparallel speed to descend with target. One of the greatest realisations of human power is the ability to destroy at distance.[29]

Initially, it was believed that there was no way to escape from a missile attack, and no way to defend industrial and civilian population from missile attacks. The WMD, especially nuclear weapons, were only of limited use unless States developed capabilities to carry them on missiles. Missiles were revolutionary because even if they did not carry any WMD, they could inflict large-scale damage by creating psychological fear and causing damage on enemy territories by its debris. This created the dilemma of choosing between deterrence or defence. The question that arose was: what would be the consequences in case of failure of deterrence?

Before such technological developments, there were three important functions of military: to punish the enemy, to deny it territory, and to mitigate damage. Deterrence was accomplished by convincing the enemy that its territorial plans would be frustrated and costs inflicted on it during the course of war would be more than gains achieved. However, nuclear weapons along with missiles increased the relative importance of prospective cost in deterring the enemy and reduced the importance of frustrating the aggressor. As a result, nuclear powers now had to exercise the choice between the objectives of deterrence and defence, since the relative proportion of 'punishment capacity' to 'denial capacity' had become a matter of choice.[30] As a result, the US realised the importance of Ballistic Missile

Defence (BMD) in preserving itself against ballistic missiles and thus strengthening its deterrence in the missile age. Throughout the Cold War, there were negative and positive relationships established between BMD and deterrence.

Let us began by outlining what is BMD. At the most simple level, the aim of BMD is to identify approaching missiles and to destroy them before they reach their target. In doing so, the BMD works in three phases. The BMD systems have their unique set of leverages and limitations at each of these three phases, which are:

Boost Phase Defences

Boost Phase is the first phase of missile flight when the booster rocket motors are burning and accelerating the missile to high altitude and speed. In case of ballistic missiles, this phase lasts for 3-5 minutes and in the case of short-range missiles, it lasts for 1-2 minutes. The advantage of destroying approaching missiles in this phase is that it would destroy the missiles before they have time to dispense with their warheads, especially if these are multiple warheads. The debris of missiles will also fall in the territory of hostile state.[31]

After initial detection and tracking by the radar, kinetic kill vehicle is launched which would collide with the approaching missile. Powerful lasers, such as air borne lasers, could also be used for this purpose. Several such programmes are under development.[32] The advantage during this phase is that this is the only phase during which ballistic missile motors are burning, leaving distinct signature plume, which makes detection and interception easier.[33] The problem with the boost phase is that it must be located near the enemy missile launch and in its very initial stage because the boost phase lasts only for 3-5 minutes. Therefore, the interceptor does not have much time to cover distance. This shortcoming makes it impossible to prepare defences against states which are not located near the border.[34] Detection during boost phase would be difficult if rockets were launched from remote locations or on cloudy days because infrared detection satellites may not detect their heat signatures immediately.[35]

Midcourse Phase Defences

Midcourse is the period when warheads start separating from the missile structure. For chemical and biological weapons, the canisters separate from the deployment forum. It is the longest phase of missiles and lasts for up to 20 minutes in ballistic missiles.[36] To kill missiles during this phase would require Exoatmospheric Kill Vehicle (EKV), which consists of a miniaturised package of sensors, computers and thrusters. It is launched on top of the interceptors, travels up to 140 miles and destroys warheads through sheer collisions.[37] During this phase, intercepts take place outside the earth atmosphere and provide the largest opportunity to intercept missiles. As this phase lasts for 20 minutes, few interceptors are needed to defend larger areas. However, the long period of time also provides attacker to deploy counter-measures.[38] The detection and discrimination of decoys from the actual warhead represent the problem in mid course defence.[39]

Terminal Phase Defences

Terminal phase is the period when the warheads start re-entering the earth atmosphere. It lasts for as little as 30 seconds. The re-entry of the missile bodies, warheads and decoys are of course slowed down due to air resistance.[40] Terminal defences are useful in protecting small or high value targets and are not suitable for larger countries like the US. Since these defences work only in the last minutes of missile stage, they must be based near the city or small region which they intend to protect.[41] The premium here remains on time. Therefore, such a defence would require large and impractical number of terminal defence sites. [42]

Relationship Between BMD and Deterrence

Ever since the emergence of the concept of 'nuclear deterrence', the US has adopted many variants of the deterrence policy, such as massive retaliation, flexible response, and Mutual Assured Destruction (MAD) so as to maintain the credibility of its nuclear deterrent. These are often combined with the concept of BMD in the negative and positive sense so as to strengthen deterrence posture of the US. James Schlesinger, former Secretary of Defence for President Ford, said that the goal of military might of the US and its allies during the Cold War period was to create effective posture of deterrence that precluded outright military assault by the Soviet Union. He remarked that at the heart of the deterrence theory laid the credibility of the strategies and forces to respond in the event of direct military assault. He said that without credibility, deterrence would be nothing more but a façade.[43] The following table illustrates the ends, ways and means of deterrence during the Cold War:

Table 1.1: Cold War Strategies: Ends-Ways and Means

Ends	Ways	Means
United States Security	Massive Retaliation, Flexible Response, Mutual Assured Destruction	Atomic Weapons and Thermonuclear Weapons
European Security	Treaty Diplomacy like SALT I , SALT II, ABM treaty	Delivery Triad: Bombers, ICBM and Submarines
Stop Soviet Aggression		Anti Ballistic Missile Systems

Source: http://www.iwar.org.uk/military/resources/nuclear/Durr_C_W_02.pdf

All these deterrence policies had positive and negative relationships with BMD (see Annexure I). During the period of Cold War, this evaluation of their relationship can be divided into four phases:

Phase 1: Negative relationship between Massive Retaliation and BMD, 1954-1961

Phase II: Positive relationship between Flexible response and BMD, 1961-1972

Phase III: Restricting deployment of BMD and establishment of MAD, 1972-2001

Phase IV: Revival of relationship with President Reagan's Strategic Defence Initiative, 1983

Negative Relationship Between Massive Retaliation and BMD, 1954-1961

Massive Retaliation was the first systematic nuclear doctrine of deterrence that was evolved at the end of World War II. The Eisenhower administration decided to take a 'New Look' towards the security problems of the US. Former US President Harry Truman had viewed the nuclear weapons as instruments of terror and weapons of last resort while President Eisenhower viewed nuclear weapons as weapons of first resort.[44] He approved a new planning document (NSC-162/2) and announced the policy of Massive Retaliation.[45] According to this policy, the US would not constrain itself to meet communist military probe with the local conventional counterforce, as it had done during the war in Korea. President Eisenhower and Secretary of State John Foster Dulles were convinced that threat to use nuclear weapons had ended the stalemate. Therefore, the same policy could be applied to prevent future conventional wars.[46] Instead, the US would retaliate instantly and massively against the major communist powers, even if it had limited communist aggression. This meant that the US would not rest on conventional weapons so as to stop Soviet aggression and instead would retaliate with nuclear weapons. Secretary of Defence for President Kennedy, Robert Mc Namara, explained this in the following words:

> The cornerstone of our strategic policy continues to be to deter deliberate nuclear attack upon the US or its allies. We do this by maintaining a highly reliable ability to inflict unacceptable damage upon any single aggressor or combination of aggressors at any time during the course of a strategic nuclear exchange, even after absorbing a surprise first strike. This can be defined as assured destruction capability. Assured Destruction is the very essence of the whole deterrence concept. We must possess an actual assured destruction capability, and that capability also must be credible... If the US is to deter a nuclear attack, on itself or on its allies, it must possess an actual and a credible assured destruction capability.[47]

To formulate such a capability, the US had to possess second-strike forces which would be able to absorb the first-strike of the enemy and in turn inflict damage on the enemy forces. Such capabilities would make the enemy first-strike capability suicidal.[48] McNamara said:

> When calculating the force required, we must be conservative in all our estimates of both a potential aggressor's capabilities and his intentions. Security depends upon assuming a worst plausible case, and having the ability to cope with it. In that eventuality we must be able to absorb the total weight of nuclear attack on our country,

> - on our retaliatory forces, on our command and control apparatus, on our industrial capacity, on our cities, and on our population and still be capable of damaging the aggressor to the point that his society would be simply no longer viable in 20th century terms. That is what deterrence of nuclear aggression means. It means certainty of suicide to the aggressor, not merely to his military forces, but also to his society as a whole.[49]

The aim of massive retaliation was to reduce the dependence of the US on the ground forces and conventional weapons and to replace it by nuclear threat. The author of the US policy of containment, Secretary John Foster Dulles, outlined the heart of Massive Retaliation on 12 January 1954 before the Council of Foreign Relations. He said "The US would deter communist aggression by depending primarily upon great capacity to retaliate instantly by means and places of our own choosing".[50] A column in *New York Times* on 16 January 1954 said that the US was saying to China and USSR as clearly "as governments ever say that in the event of another proxy war or bushfire war in Korea, Indochina, Iran or elsewhere, the US would retaliate instantly with atomic weapons against the USSR and Red China." Thus, massive retaliation raised the cost of war which outweighed the gains from aggression.[51] The concept of massive retaliation appeared as a strategic component of a new US national security policy, the rationale for force structure of the New Look Policy and the guiding principle of the American nuclear strategy for almost a decade[52].

There were broadly three reasons for the adoption of the US strategy of massive retaliation:

- The President believed that nuclear weapons presented real and usable military options.
- The members of the President Administration publicised their willingness to use nuclear weapons in any conflict in the belief that this would deter large and small-scale communist aggression.
- Concentration on nuclear weapons would decrease the military spending on other weapons which President Eisenhower considered necessary for economic well- being.[53]

The nascent formulation of BMD was opposed to the concept of Assured Destruction. The concept of assured destruction was based on the first-strike capability. However, BMD would degrade the first-strike capability of the Soviet Union. The BMD would destabilise the relationship of the USSR and the US by undermining assumed Soviet intention to maintain Americans as hostage for deterrence purposes. The Soviet Union would always react to these damage limitation programmes by enhancing its offensive capabilities. In such a case, the US BMD programme would provide dynamics for offensive-defensive arms race.[54]

Flexible Response and its Positive Relationship with BMD: 1961-1972

The strategy of massive retaliation came under criticism by several proponents of limited war and the Kennedy administration decided to introduce the doctrine of "Flexible Response." During 1960s, the US strategic nuclear deterrence policy was to deter an attack against the US and its allies by having the capability to wipe out the enemy's first-strike capability.[55]It was felt that it was impractical for the US to use its nuclear weapons against the limited attack by the Soviet Union. If the US chose to do so, it would be followed by the Soviet Union inflicting a nuclear attack on the US. Thus, the US would risk its own cities by launching a nuclear war in response to a relatively smaller nuclear probe. The doctrine of Massive Retaliation was regarded as politically and military inflexible as it did not reserve nuclear weapons for response to a direct Soviet nuclear attack. As a result, in case of the Soviet Union aggression, the US was left with only two options: whether to respond massively or to do nothing. Nuclear response was very unlikely to be regarded as legitimate, especially against small military attacks of the Soviet Union.[56]

The doctrine of massive retaliation could not be applied if both the adversaries had second-strike capability. Carrying out nuclear attack in case of limited attacks by the Soviet Union would mean one's own destruction. Under such conditions, the cost of implementing threat was greater than the cost of not doing so, thus making threat incredible.[57] On the other hand, if the US could respond in a controlled manner against the military targets of an adversary, the enemy calculations might be altered. [58]

The underlying assumption was that there was a stable nuclear balance between the US and Soviet Union. Therefore, nuclear war was very unlikely and both sides were deterred by each other by simply possessing nuclear weapons. As nuclear war was out of the question, enemies would try to gain ground by initiating limited war. Under limited war, the US would be hesitant to use nuclear weapons because the Soviet Union could then retaliate with its own nuclear weapons. Therefore, there was a need to change the doctrine so as to prevent the US from 'suicidal policies'.[59] In fact, the US was never able to resolve the dilemma, i.e., simultaneously worrying that too much reliance on MAD would lack credibility and too much confidence in fighting a 'limited conflict' against Soviets while increase the chance of war.[60]President Kennedy was opposed to this doctrine of US massive retaliation and said:

> Under every military budget submitted by this administration, we have been preparing primarily to fight the one kind of war we least want to fight and are least likely to fight. We have been driving ourselves into a corner where the only choice is all-or-nothing-at-all, world devastation or submission, a choice that necessarily causes us to hesitate on the brink and leaves the initiation in the hands of our enemies.[61]

The other criticism of the massive retaliation doctrine was that it ignored the importance of conventional weapons and ground forces in deterring attack. Moulton said:

> The most serious consequence of the Dulles manifesto of massive retaliation probably was the major deemphasize on adequate conventional ground forces to deal with conflict situations which would likely emerge once mutual deterrence becomes recognised fact of international life. Official policy had involved training and equipping local forces to provide the first line of defence, with American nuclear forces as second line.[62]

The other reason for the shift in policy was the launch of Sputnik on 4 October 1957, which alarmed the US about threats of ballistic missiles. Although the US was trying to possess Intercontinental range of Ballistic Missiles (ICBM) since the end of World War II, the first US ICBM missile was not operational till 1958.[63] The Gaither Committee was appointed to look into the matter of 'missile gap' and it stated that unless the US stepped up its programme of intercontinental strategic forces, the Soviet Union would have a large strategic force and would have the capability to carry out first-strike attack and would be able to destroy all American strategic capability.[64] This provided a new boost to the concept of combining BMD and deterrence. Specially, the US Air Force said that the US should have the capability to destroy the Soviet ICBM. It was said that finite deterrence does not offer sufficient forces to deter limited acts of aggression, attacks on the US allies and surprise attack on the US.[65]

As a result of the technological development in weaponry and delivery vehicles, it was feared that the US could be actually inferior to the Soviet Union. In a famous article, published in 1959, Albert Wohlstetter questioned the ability of the US to respond to the Soviet Union surprise attack. It was felt that having powerful deterrence posture was not enough and that there must be ability to survive first-attack and to retaliate accordingly. The capability of the US to survive first-attack was doubted as the American strategic forces and bombers were dangerously exposed to the Russian attack and survivability became an important concern of the US. Thus, it was realised that it was important to combine BMD with deterrence posture of the US to limit the damage [66]

Gradually, the doctrine of flexible response replaced the 'suicide or surrender dilemma' of Eisenhower massive retaliation strategy by providing a genuine alternative to nuclear retaliation in case of a Soviet Union conventional attack.[67] A flexible response was expected to help the US to maintain strategic nuclear forces so as to meet with conventional threats. The idea of this doctrine was to combine the basic tenet of massive retaliation with the flexibility of the overall defence posture. To quote Donald Snow:

> First in order to serve as a maximum deterrent to nuclear war, US strategic retaliatory forces must be visibly capable of fully destroying the Soviet society under all conditions of retaliation. Second, in the event that war was forced on the US, its strategic offensive and defensive forces should have the power to limit the destruction to the nation's cities and population to the maximum extent possible.[68]

The flexible response was expected to reduce the US dependence on nuclear weapons and introduce multiple options to deal with the conflict. According to President Kennedy, the idea of flexible response was:

> to deter all wars, general or limited, nuclear or conventional, large or small – to convince all potential aggressors that any attack would be futile – to provide backing for the diplomatic settlement of disputes- to insure the adequacy of our bargaining power for an end to the arms race.[69]

Flexible response assisted the US to prepare and fight a wide variety of wars. This doctrine accepted the ground rules laid down by the enemy for any given conflicting situation and to answer its move by a wide variety of options available. It was thought that the nuclear war would not be beneficial to the US.[70] The aim of initiating flexible response in the US deterrence policy was to have various options so that the US could pick up the tactics which were best suited for the given conflicting situation.

McNamara had done a remarkable work by introducing 'no cities doctrine'. This doctrine meant that the US would not attack Soviet cities. Instead, it would attack Soviet military capabilities. Flexible response/No Cities doctrine consisted of offensive and defensive strategies. Offensive Strategy meant destroying Soviet military installations and to disable most of its forces before they could be used. McNamara said Americas should respond by attacking the Soviet Union strategic forces, such as bomber bases, missile sites and other installations associated with long-range nuclear forces so as to limit Soviet power. Defensive strategies involved defending the US from Soviet weapons that might escape counterforce attack. As a result, the US started building such weapons that could intercept and destroy incoming bombers and missiles.[71] There were two steps taken to reduce the causalities. The first was to strengthen the civil defence programme of the country so as to minimise civilian causalities. Installing blast shelters did this. Secondly, there was an effort to provide active defence to the US by installing BMD.[72] Thus, flexible response/No cities doctrine established a positive relationship between deterrence and BMD. Prominent nuclear expert Kahn said:

> It was the purpose of surveying US forces to limit destruction of the US targets so that projected losses were within a theoretical realm of acceptability, thus allowing for the maintenance of the US retaliatory capabilities. Defensive systems mean ABM (Anti-Ballistic Missile Treaty) systems, air defence and civil defence. Offensively the doctrine called for a portion of the US retaliatory capabilities to be targeted against Soviet strategic systems-be they bombers, submarines or missile sites.[73]

From Flexible Response to MAD: Return to Negative Relationship

It was hoped that the combination of offensive and defensive strategies by the US would prove to be destabilising and would speed up the offensive-defensive race of weapons. The Soviet Union might think that the defensive capabilities of the US endangered its deterrence and might result in first-strike by the US. Presuming this, the combination of the US defensive and offensive forces gave the US the capability to strike first and to destroy many Soviet nuclear forces and defences. Under such conditions, USSR would take preemptive actions and would decide to strike first.[74] US Secretary of Defence Harlond Brown said in 1979:

> In the interests of stability, we avoid the capability of eliminating the other side deterrent, insofar as we might be able to do so. In short, we must be quite willing- as we have been for some time- to accept the principle of mutual deterrence, and design our defence posture in light of that principle.[75]

The ABM system led to action-reaction phenomenon and arms race. McNamara said, "If we were to deploy a heavy ABM system throughout the US, the Soviets would clearly be motivated to so increase their offensive capability as to cancel out our defensive advantage." Therefore, each side would become conscious for maintaining its first- strike capability.[76]

Also, both the US and USSR discovered that BMD would be very expensive and ineffective against an opponent which could deploy counter-measures in order to penetrate or overcome the defences.

Developing complete defence against the ballistic missile attack was considered impossible. Policy makers believed that missile defence could not provide an alternative to the concept of deterrence.

Another reason for giving away the idea of defence was that if the US deployed defence to protect its territories, it would be followed by the Soviet Union. The circumstances where both the superpowers had defences would create a lot of dilemma. First, any improvement in offensive forces would provide coercive power to the state. The country that first obtained the technology to penetrate the defence of the other side would be at an advantage. Second, defences could increase the feasibility of conventional wars. Superpowers would fear conventional warfare as it could escalate into nuclear warfare. However, if such fear was removed, they would not hesitate to go to war. World War I and II demonstrated that these conventional wars could be very devastating. Therefore, defences would increase the probability of conventional war while neutralising the possibility of nuclear war.[77] Also there were other doctrinal reasons also for the shift in the US policy of 'flexible deterrence' to 'Mutual Assured Destruction.'[78]

This led to a shift of the US deterrence policy from flexible response to MAD and its codification in the Anti Ballistic Missile (ABM) treaty. The ABM treaty formally established deterrence as the underlying strategic policy of the US and Soviet Union. Both the countries adhered to not deploying ABM systems for defending their territories, thus establishing a state of mutual deterrence.[79]

The ABM treaty of 1972 permitted the US and Soviet Union to deploy two ABM systems. This number was further reduced to one ABM system in 1974. Both sides could deploy one ABM system either at its national capital or at the ICBM silo launcher site. This treaty banned development, testing and deployment of sea-based, air-based, mobile land-based ABM systems. The pretext behind this treaty was that neither side would be capable of protecting itself from nuclear attacks by using ABM systems. Therefore, both sides would retain high confidence in their retaliatory capacity. The assumption was that attack by one side could lead to escalation of conflict and ultimately, use of nuclear weapons. The use of nuclear weapons would produce catastrophic results for both the US and USSR. This fear prevented war between the two adversaries. This is known as the concept of Mutual Assured Destruction (MAD) and has remained the basis of the US deterrence policy till 2001. Lawrence Freedman has skillfully explained the concept of MAD:

> The underlying assumptions of the theory of MAD were that, for the foreseeable future, the offence would be able to maintain the advantage over the defence. Because of this, all one could do to prevent the other from inflicting crippling devastation was to threaten retaliation. The lesson drawn form this assumption for the purpose of force planning was that one need only ensure a sufficiency of offensive forces to assure destruction after allowing for all feasible improvements in the first-strike capabilities of either side. The lesson drawn for arms control was that, every improvement in one side's defence provided no extra security but merely a spurt to the offence of the other, once both sides ceased making defensive moves forces could stabilise at current levels.[80]

Revival of Relationship with the coming of Star Wars: 1983

The above study concludes that the concept of MAD was introduced in the US nuclear deterrence policy by placing restrictions on the development and deployment of BMD systems. However, this arrangement was again suspected by President Ronald Reagan in his Star War speech. President Reagan had expressed his doubts on the effectiveness of deterrence, under MAD, in preventing war. He had supported introduction of the BMD so as to strengthen deterrence. He began the whole debate again, which was subsequently settled by the ABM treaty. He sought to reformulate the concept of deterrence by proposing Strategic Defence Initiative (SDI). He said:

> What if free people could live secure in the knowledge that their security did not rest upon the threat of instant US retaliation to deter a Soviet attack, that we could intercept and destroy strategic ballistic missile before they reached our own soil or that of our allies.[81]

If we closely analyse, it were the circumstances prevailing at that time which drove the US to abandon the MAD doctrine. The US regarded the USSR as an 'untrustworthy adversary.' Reagan administration felt that USSR was using arms control as means to provide a false sense of security to the West. Despite, arms control treaties; Soviet Union continued to develop its military forces. Also, they could easily cheat west as Soviets never agreed for intrusive-onside inspection.[82] The US was also gathering information that Soviet Union was developing hit and kill capabilities which would threaten the survivability of the US silo based ICBMs (Lawrence 1987: 60).

President Reagan said:

> For 20 years the Soviet Union has been accumulating enormous military might. They didn't stop when their forces exceed all requirements of a legitimate defensive capability. Ant they haven't stopped now. During the past decade and a half, the Sviets have build up a massive arsenal of a new strategic nuclear weapons that can strike directly at the US. As an example, the US introduced its last new intercontinental ballistic missile, the Minute Man III in 1969, and we're now dismantling our even older Titan missiles. But what has the Soviet Union done in these intervening years? Well, since 1969 the Soviet Union has built five new clases of ICBM's and upgraded these eight times. As a result, their missiles are much more powerful and accurate that they were several years ago, and they continue to develop more, while ours are increasingly obsolete. [83]

Therefore, the US felt that its offensive forces were not effective in maintaining deterrence. This concern led the US President to question: What if deterrence collapsed? The answer was that if the deterrence failed without any shield, it would cause the death of millions of the US population.[84] It was thought that the SDI would provide a shield to the US and would protect the US from the after effects of nuclear attacks.

Throughout the period in 1970s and in early part of 1980s, concern was raised on the implications and the possibilities of attack by Soviet Union on the fixed land based Minuteman ICBM force. It was said that any surprise attack on the US ICBM force would deny the option to the US to respond or retaliate. It was assumed that

- Such an attack by Soviet Union would be experienced as limited in nature
- Under such circumstances, the only available option to the US will be to surrender in front of the USSR or to suffer attacks on its own cities

- As the US would not opt for its annihilation, it will surrender before the Soviet Union
- Soviet Union will rely on options of (a) (b) (c) for having decisions in its own favor.

Under such situations, it was believed that SDI can perform four important functions. First, the development of full scale population defence over the US would bring end to the concept of MAD, which would in effect, will render nuclear weapons 'impotent and obsolete.' Second, the development of SDI would make the nuclear weapons of Soviet Union obsolete and this was perhaps the real goal of Secretary of Defence Weinberger and other defence analysts of the US. Third, if successfully deployed, SDI would protect the US strategic retaliatory force and its command, control and communication networks, in addition to protecting population. This would have definitely enhanced deterrence of the US. Fourth, SDI might be helpful in providing limited protection to the US cities against small-scale nuclear attacks, such as an unauthorised or accidental Soviet launch or a deliberate attack. Therefore, it was believed that SDI would help in enhancing deterrence:

> Successful SDI ....would not lead to abandonment of deterrence but rather to an enhancement of deterrence and an evolution in the weapons of deterrence through the contribution of defensive systems that threaten no one. We would deter a potential aggressor by making it clear that we could deny him the gains he might otherwise hope to achieve rather than merely threatening him with costs large enough to outweigh those gains.

It was said that SDI would protect land based missiles and command and control centres against a Soviet first strike. It would also deter Soviet Union from engaging in any kind of nuclear operations against the US, thus strengthening the US deterrence. Reagan administration spelt out the new policy for implementing its plan of SDI, as mentioned below:

- In his speech, President Reagan made it clear that the ultimate goal of his policy is to eliminate the threat posed by nuclear weapons. After few days, he offered an alternative in which 'the great nations of the world will sit here like people facing themselves across a table with a cache of cocked guns, and no one knowing whether someone might tighten the finger on the trigger.'

- President Reagan wanted to turn off the concept of Assured Destruction and he mentioned that it is people and not weapons which need to be protected and weapons not people should be threatened.
- The objective was to provide total and not partial protection. However, the focus was only on ballistic missiles. This aimed at having total protection. The argument given for this was that ballistic missiles are most critical tests and if they could be stopped, than slower moving forces will be less challenging.
- At the same time, President Reagan also mentioned that ABM treaty will be respected because it permitted research on ABM systems. He also realised that deployment of ABM system were years away.[85]

The reality was far removed from this. The technologies of SDI were too ambitious and it would not have been possible for SDI to defend an attack. Hoffman provided the answer for this. He said there could be range of strategic Soviet attacks on the US military targets that were co-located with population centers. He said that if SDI was sufficiently effective to prevent the Soviets from hitting the military targets, and if the US retained the capability to hit back at Soviet cities in retaliation, it would deny the USSR to achieve specific military targets and would contribute powerfully in deterring attack.[86] Therefore, SDI was considered essential for the preservation of US deterrence.

Therefore, it was soon realised that it is very difficult to join various technology and to develop a perfect system. It was also feared that Soviet Union might also develop defensive capability against the US. This would give rise to a situation in which adversary would deploy both an effective defensive system and highly accurate counterforce weapons to destroy the other's side nuclear weapons resulting into highly instable condition. If deployed, SDI would also raise the fear of conventional warfare between superpowers. It was the fear of nuclear escalation which was preventing nuclear power states to engage them in conventional war. Once such fear is removed, superpowers will not hesitate to go for conventional war. In sum, SDI was considered as destabilising. Drell mentioned:

> An effective but imperfect ABM on one side would exacerbate the risk of war because the side that did have an ABM might calculate that it would be better off if it struck first and used the ABM defence to deal with the weakened response...Similarly, the side that did not have ABM might calculate that its situation would be better if it struck first and avoided being caught trying to retaliate with a weakened force against the ABM defence.

The policy of SDI was also criticised as it can force Soviet Union to have preemptive strike against the US. If one side achieve SDI, it is obvious that other side will be at disadvantage. The other side would have advanced notice of this shift in the strategic balance and might be tempted to preempt before the shift had become absolute. It is also possible that as Soviet Union would not be able to strike the military targets, it would focus on cities. It is true that Soviet Union was not interested in counterforce targeting at that time, yet its possibility cannot be ruled out.[87]

Therefore, BMDs continued to prevail in the debates of the US nuclear issues during the Cold War but deterrence continued to be at the centre of the US nuclear strategy. The Cold War deterrence theory was quite effective because the US and Soviet Union acquired nuclear systems that would withstand the attacks while the planned missile defence systems seemed too porous to reduce significantly the other side second-strike capability. Under such conditions, MAD was the concept used to describe the reality of the Cold War period.[88]

The reason for such a strong dependence on deterrence was that leaders of both sides were rational and were governed by the cost-benefit analysis. President John Kennedy and National Security Adviser McGeorge Bundy mentioned in a 1969 Foreign Affairs article:

> In the light of certain aspects of retaliation there has been literally no chance at all that any sane political authority, in either the US or in Soviet Union, would consciously choose to start a nuclear war. The proposition is true for the past, present and future. For sane men on both sides, the balance of terror is overwhelmingly persuasive.[89]

As the nuclear balance of terror became an important part of maintaining strategic stability, the question was how to maintain this strategic stability throughout the Cold War period. The answer to this was to maintain strategic nuclear retaliatory capability and to eschew strategic offensive or defensive capabilities that could destabilise the balance of terror by limiting the damage that might result from nuclear power exchange. Such capabilities included BMD. Thus, Cold War concepts remained mainly against the deployment of BMD and relied on deterrence posture.[90]

Therefore, it is clear that defence has played a subsidiary role in nuclear strategy and primary role was taken up by deterrence. However, deterrence raises its own conceptual problems and to address these issues, policy makers and defence analysts often shift towards the policy of defence. The approach holds that to deter nuclear attacks, the US should have the capability to threaten Soviet Union. At the same time, it was repeatedly recognised that there is need to deter Soviet Union attack in case of failure of deterrence.[91]

The MAD also remains the main feature of the US deterrence policy, even much after the end of Cold War. However, after the Cold War, the US faced new challenges in the form of rogue states and terrorist groups. The US feels that these rogue states are impossible to deter by any conventional form of deterrence. After the 9/11 attacks, it becomes crystal clear that new threats are coming not from the states but from non-state actors. As a result, the US has begun to revise its debates and decisions to deploy BMD so as to preserve deterrence and to deal with these new threats. However, debate has also started whether these are really threats, and how they have promoted the deployment of US BMD, or whether these threats have been exaggerated.

Another concern is that the US withdrawal from the ABM treaty has led to the fall of MAD, which was basis of the US deterrence policy. The questions raised are whether BMD is supplemented by the US deterrence posture, complemented by deterrence or will it lead to complete degradation of the US deterrence policy due to the counter-measures employed by other states to deal with BMD. These questions are dealt in the following pages.

2

Post-Cold War Challenges to Deterrence

Introduction

The fall of USSR resulted in the end of cold war. The threat paradigm of the US shifted from known enemies during the Cold War to more generalised, global set of potential competitors, adversaries and circumstances which did not fall or fit into the traditional pattern of nation-states. Therefore, the traditional concept of deterrence could not be applied to them.[1] It was felt that the US's cold war deterrence policy could no longer prevent two main threats: rogue states and non-state actors.

There were three watershed events in the post-Cold War period, which raised doubts on the credibility and reliability of US deterrence doctrines. This resulted in the US policies on deterrence being reviewed and the need to include BMD. These three events were:

- Gulf War I and the use of missiles by Iraq
- 9/11 terrorist attacks on the US
- Proliferation of WMD to rogue states

In September 2002's National Security Strategy, the Bush administration acknowledged that the threat environment was radically different, and had changed the complete scenario as compared to the Cold War period.

New deadly challenges have emerged from rogue states and terrorists. None of these contemporary threats rival the sheer destructive power arrayed against us by the Soviet Union. However, the nature and motivations of these new adversaries, their determination to obtain destructive power hitherto available only to the world's strongest states, and the greater likelihood that they will use weapons of mass destruction against us, make today's security environment more complex and dangerous.[2]

Reasons for Proliferation of Ballistic and Cruise Missile

There are various reasons why states get attracted towards developing missiles:

- Clearly, the US has advanced high-tech air-power as compared to other states. This was obvious during the Gulf War I and in the Kosovo war. As a result, other states considered missiles as the counter-option. Air power is more accurate as compared to missiles. However, air power required intensive research and development, involving huge investment. Countries like Egypt and Syria invested many dollars on traditional air power weapons but could not compete with the US. On the other hand, missiles required less investment and research as compared to air power. Missiles also offered political leverage as they could damage the economic infrastructure of developed nations and result in large number of causalities.
- Precision strike missiles could strike high value military targets without creating much damage to the civilian population. Hence, these could be important instruments to deter an enemy.
- There has been no effective defence established against these missiles. The performance of Patriot missiles was not very satisfactory during the 1991 Gulf War. Even today, the technology of BMD is not fully reliable.[3]

Due to these reasons, US adversaries regard missiles as an important instrument to deter the US and European states.

Missile Threats to the US

The National Intelligence Estimate Report (NIE) 1995 acknowledged that developing of ballistic missiles was in its mature stages. It was said that states that had already acquired ballistic missiles were in the process of modernising their arsenals. On the other hand, emerging ballistic missile states continued to increase the range, reliability and accuracy of their missile systems, posing a threat to US forces, allies and interests throughout the world. Earlier, the US has faced threat from SRBM especially from Scud.[4]

The US considers the following points to gain access and to determine the threat levels from other states and their missiles:

Current Missile Capabilities of States: These capabilities include assessment of range, payload of deployed systems as well as availability of missile launchers. (TEL or MEL). It is also important to have the knowledge of system reliability, system response time and TEL/MEL range.

Estimates of Warhead Type: It includes information about warheads available to the adversaries like chemical, nuclear or biological weapons. Absence of such warheads does not mean absence of threats. Conventional warheads could also be used to cause considerable damage to densely populated areas.

Missile Infrastructure: Information about missile infrastructure will provide clues about objectives of programme and how quickly these could be achieved. It includes information about direct support facilities such as those intended for design, production and testing as well as supporting industries and infrastructure.

Missile related Exports or Imports: Information on exported material would help to comprehend the success and failure of programmes. Information about the type and scope of foreign, technical and service imports, the ability of programme to assimilate these imports and shift in resources towards a particular programme is useful, too.

Military and Operational Factors: This includes training for missile units, combat experience of missile and supporting units and command and control systems and the impact of deployed system on military operations.

Threat Assessment: Beyond technical factors, political motives and intentions of states should be kept in mind. This analysis would include state missile behaviour, including its use or threat to use missile systems and use of flight tests to send missile signals.[5]

By this assessment, Defence Intelligence Agency (DIA), Central Intelligence Agency (CIA) and the Rumsfeld Commission formulated the following ballistic missile threats for the US. In 1999, DIA observed that there was strategic nuclear threat from Russia, China and rogue states. Russia continued to rely on nuclear weapons to upset the conventional balance. China was prioritising its modernisation programme. This report said that China had invested massively in several nuclear programmes and upgraded its command and control structure. This report also mentioned that rogue states like North Korea and Iran would develop ICBM capability in a few years. The DIA also said that all these missiles could be armed with WMD.[6] Similarly, CIA, in 2000, acknowledged that there was a missile threat from Russia, China, North Korea and Iran.[7] Missile threats to the US are discussed here in detail:

Persian Gulf War I and use of Missiles by Iraq

The Persian Gulf War I in 1990 was the first post-Cold War challenge to the US deterrence. During this period, Iraq invaded Kuwait despite US threats of retaliation. This was the true manifestation of the 'missile war'. On 17 January 1991 and 26 February 1991, Iraq fired about 90 modified Scud missiles at its targets in Israel. This represented the fundamental change in the nature of war and domination of the missile power.[8] The US realised missiles were no longer the property of big and industrialised states. It was found that missiles could be accumulated and used by technologically and economically backward countries like Iraq, too. The absence of any rational calculation on the part of these states has made the situation worse. Even after the US made it clear that it would not tolerate territorial aggression in the region, Saddam Hussein was not at all deterred.[9] Iraq did not hesitate to attack Israel with ballistic missiles despite US's immediate retaliation.[10] After Gulf War I, Saddam Hussein was widely depicted as an implacable foe. During Gulf War I, it was believed that deterrence had failed from the outset as Iraq seized Kuwait despite of US warning. Saddam Hussein represented the class of 'non deterable threats'.[11] Thus, it was thought that the US needed more strategies with better technologies to deter rogue states.[12]

Thus, Gulf War I made it clear that some countries in the Middle East were trying to acquire WMD. After Gulf War, a spokesman from Iran declared, "No country in the world has the right to come here and to make decision about the future of Islamist countries." To prevent interference in the region, WMD were regarded as 'the poor man's nukes', providing third world countries with weapons of terror. These weapons are inexpensive and technologically less complex. Gulf War I also saw the importance of missiles.[13] Barry Schneider and Larry Fink said Mobile missiles can avoid detection even when a superpower trains all its intelligence gathering capabilities on the task of finding and counting them.[14]

It was the Gulf War I which altered the thinking of the US. The concept of "Rogue State" emerged in the mind of the US. According to the US, these states possess a large military establishment, a sustainable supply of modern weapons and a desire to accumulate WMD. They could have hegemonic inclinations towards states in their regions or could harbor ambitions that could jeopardise the US interests. The US list of rogue states consists of North Korea, Iran, Iraq, Syria and Libya. The purpose of identification of rogue states was not to prepare full-scale war against them but to prepare the US to deal with these new threats.[15] The BMD was considered as one of the option which can neutralise the nuclear and missile threat coming from rogue states.

It was felt during Gulf War I that these states would not use WMD for revenge or war. Rather, these states will try to obtain intercontinental ballistic missiles as 'strategic weapons of deterrence and coercive diplomacy'. Rogue States assumed that if the US becomes vulnerable to direct attacks by WMD, they could limit the US freedom of action in their regions of interests. Even the US accepted that if Iraq possesses ICBM and nuclear facility, they might have adopted a different way to deal with them.[16] The *Proliferation: Threat and Response* mentioned:

> From the perspective of the leader of a state, ballistic missiles are an effective instrument- and weapon of choice- to threaten the rear of the US and coalition forces in the face of the US air superiority. Missiles are much less expensive than acquiring and maintaining a world class air force competitive with the US military aviation; missiles with low profile infrastructure and mobile launchers are much less vulnerable than aircraft to US offensive operations; missiles are easier to control than other means of deep strike; and when armed with high explosive, missiles have considerable psychological effect when used against urban targets.[17]

Gulf War I also brought to the notice about two important aspects of deterrence theory:

- Iraq launched Scud missile attacks against Israel and Saudi Arabia on 17 Jan 1991. These missiles resulted into insufficient causalities. However, Iraq used these missiles due to their political value, just like; the Germany used V-1 and V-2 rockets during Second World War to have political advantage. These attacks showed fearlessness of Saddam Hussein and his willingness to act against the US and its coalition force.[18] Although, the US deployed Patriot missiles for the interception of missiles but they achieved little success. Also, it was difficult to locate the mobile launchers. As a result, policy makers were forced to reconsider the debate of deterrence and defence.[19] It also shows that proliferation of missiles continued despite of all the international action against proliferation activities. It is impossible to halt the dissemination of basic scientific and technical knowledge or to place all countries under suspicion.[20]
- Iraq did not use chemical weapons against Israel or the coalition forces despite of its repeated warning. However, it is not very clear whether it was due to the technological problem of placing chemical warheads on Scud missiles or the fear of nuclear retaliation by the US and Israel. The available literature on the subject often points to the second as more plausible reason. In such case, it shows that one aspect of nuclear deterrence was workable and nuclear weapons could be an important part of the US policy.[21]

Gulf war I also led many western countries, especially the US, to feel that there are some countries who wish to have regional expansion without the direct intervention of great powers and international community. It was also considered as an attempt of direct intimidation of the western countries by radical countries. Therefore, the Gulf War I resulted in a renewed emphasis on BMD. The BMD were introduced for the first time in combat during the Persian Gulf War. The US Patriot TMD engaged Scud missiles launched by Iraq at Israel and Saudi Arabia. During war, Patriot was assessed as the most effective way to deal with Scud missiles but later it was discovered that it was not as effective as it was believed to be. After war, the US intensified its efforts to improvise and build BMD.[22]

The Rumsfeld Commission

A Commission was appointed under Secretary of Defence Donald Rumsfeld to assess the ballistic missile threat to the US. This report concluded that proliferation of missiles was amplifying throughout the world and there could be near term threat to the US homeland, the US forces deployed abroad and the US friends and allies. Following four main conclusions were drawn by the Rumsfeld Commission:

- Concerted efforts by the number of overtly or potentially hostile nations to acquire ballistic missiles with biological and nuclear payloads pose a growing threat to the US, its deployed forces, and its friends and allies.
- The threat is broader, more mature and evolving more rapidly than has been reported in estimates and reports by the intelligence community.
- The intelligence community's ability to provide timely and accurate estimates of ballistic missile threats to the US is eroding.
- The warning times the US can expect of new, threatening ballistic missile deployment are being reduced. Under some plausible scenarios...the US might have little or no warning before operational deployment.[23]

The Commission said:

> Newer ballistic missile and weapons of mass destruction development programmes no longer follow the pattern initially set up by the US and Soviet Union. These newer programmes require neither high standards of reliability, missile accuracy and safety nor large number of missiles and therefore can move ahead more rapidly.[24]

The testing of the North Korea *Taepo-Dong* missile affirmed the claims of the Rumsfeld Commission that rogue states were serious in developing ballistic missile capabilities. Although the test was a failure, it showed that North Korea was engaged in the development of long-range missiles. North Korea is estimated to have 750 ballistic missiles, including some 600-800 Scud missiles and approximately 150-200 medium range ballistic missiles.[25] South Korean intelligence indicated that DPRK is developing rocket engines that could have a range of 6,700 kms. Similarly, Iran has made concrete progress in ballistic missiles and it claims to have conducted a successful missile test of Shahab-3. Iran also claimed to have conducted a successful test of a long-range missile on 27 November 2007 called 'Aurosh'. In Feb 2009, Iran successfully launched a satellite in space and this technology could be converted into acquiring long range missiles. The ballistic missile programmes of other states like Syria and Libya are also of great concern to the US.[26]

As a result, the US nuclear deterrence policy is in danger. The reason is that under the control of the rogue states, these weapons have become tools of intimidation and military aggression against their neighbours. These weapons will allow rogue states to blackmail the US and its allies. Such states view these weapons as the best means to overcome conventional superiority of the US.[27]

Even long after the end of the Cold War the world is still at threat. The danger of nuclear weapon proliferation is greater than before. Threats from rogue states are also greater than the threats from Soviet Union. In the Cold War period, nuclear states took some responsibility for nuclear weapons and it was known that neither superpower was going to make a calculated strike against the other. However, today, weapons lie in the hands of dangerous states that will not hesitate in using these weapons against the US.[28]

It is hardly expected that the Cold War doctrines of deterrence will be effective in the post-Cold War period due to the complexity of the situation, such as presence of many actors, deep-rooted conflicts with long history and asymmetric confrontation involving non-state actors such as terrorist groups. The Cold War nuclear confrontation was dichotomous, symmetrical and ideological based on thorough calculation and rigorous logic and both the US and Soviet Union shared some responsibility of superpower and fear of global catastrophe, which enabled highly technical and rigorous handling of the deterrence situation. However, the post-Cold War conflict is fought over all kinds of issues such as territory, personality cult and religion. In such a situation, the logic of mutual deterrence is replaced by human factors such as distrust, revenge, pride, miscalculation and misinterpretation.[29] The basic concept has totally changed, creating more fear and chaos in the international arena.

Therefore, after Cold War, it was said that the US could not deter rogue states. Whenever these states fear fall of their regime, they may also use all weapons available to them. This shows failure of deterrence.[30] The US deterrence would be debilitating because nuclear weapons or missile capabilities of rouge states would alleviate the US capability to interfere in regional conflicts. Let us examine this in the present political situation. North Korea could deter the US from interfering in a future Korean War by threatening attacks on South Korea or places crucial to reinforcement operation. Fear of large number of causalities for the US would be sufficient to deter the US from interference. Threat of nuclear weapons to US allies would deny the US forces basing rights.[31] The post-Cold War crisis with Iraq, Serbia and North Korea proves that the US deterrence policy did not work. Deterrence of regional challengers may not follow the same pattern as that of the Cold War. Rouge states have unfamiliar goals and values. Under such conditions, deterrence may fail.[32] This show that US deterrence power is under attack by rouge states and therefore it needs BMD to deter its adversaries

9/11 Terrorists Attacks on the World Trade Center

On 11 September 2001, the post- Cold War security bubble finally burst. It made it clear that the US and its allies have failed to invest in an 'A list' of security problems, which could affect their way of life, position in the world and survival. This 'A list' of future security challenges contained the following four major items:

- Collapse of Soviet Union
- Growth of Beijing military and economic power
- Proliferation of weapons of mass destruction
- Prospect of growing terrorism.[33]

After taking charge, Bush's strategy revolved around the first two. However, in the aftermath of the attacks on the World Trade Center and Pentagon on 11 September 2001, terrorism occupied the center stage in the US policies.[34] The 9/11 attacks on the US have reinforced question marks on deterrence as it has demonstrated to the US that they will have to deal with people that cannot be deterred by conventional methods of deterrence. Large-scale military capabilities of the US do not deter the Al Qaeda. Even after 9/11, Al Qaeda continues to attack the US and its allies around the world. The US has tried regime change in the case of Afghanistan by its military force, but could not eliminate terrorists. To put it simply, the Al Qaeda and other terrorist groups have not been deterred by anything that the US has done so far.[35] US Secretary of Defence Donald Rumsfeld said:

> We have entered an era of enemies without country or conscience, which operate in small cells scattered across the globe. Yet our forces continue to be arranged essentially to fight large armies, navies, and air forces. The world has changed, and so must we.[36]

Since 11 September 2001, the US has learnt that the world has many actors who conceivably do things which civilised nations may term unthinkable, such as destruction with the use of WMD. The danger posed by these weapons, particularly, when in the hands of terrorist groups or rogue states, means that the US must adapt to the security capabilities to meet the threats of today and tomorrow. The time has come to move beyond the framework of MAD, and to accrue deterrence with defensive and offensive measures as well.[37]

The events of September 11 have proven that international terrorists are more organised, more capable and ruthless. They are willing to sacrifice themselves and are indifferent to the killings of innocent people.[38] President Bush asserted that while the Iron curtain no longer existed, it was still a dangerous world, particularly with WMD in the hands of the world's least responsible states. For the first time in the history of modern terrorism, by their suddenness, the scale of destruction, the disorganisation and the cost caused; the attacks on the WTO and Pentagon unleashed a level of violence comparable in their effect to military operations. Over 30 years, international terrorism has caused the death of 500 people annually. The 9/11 marked the arrival of mass terrorism with destruction capability hitherto thought to belong with states.[39]

The dilemma of credibility of deterrence in case of non-state actors is that these groups are willing to attack civilian populations and to escalate this to the level of high conflict. These groups are motivated by the ideologies of religion and apocalyptic beliefs. For example, the Al Qeda is acting in the name of religion. They think in suicidal terms and are willing to endure significant costs and destruction to achieve their objective.[40] Traditional concepts of deterrence are not seen as working against terrorists whose avowed tactics are wanton destruction and the targeting of innocents; whose so-called soldiers seek martyrdom in death and whose most potent protection is statelessness. The overlap between states that sponsor terror and those who pursue WMD themselves compel the US to take action.[41]

The other problem is that terrorism embodies many instruments, many groups and no central command. During the Cold War, there was only one state which the US had to deter, i.e., USSR. As a result, there was one single ideology which was successful to deter them. On the other hand, there is no single method to deter various unorganised terrorist groups who have different means and ideologies to achieve their objectives.[42]

Some experts believed that not only states but also terrorist groups have the wherewithal to launch ballistic missile attacks. This may not be true for long-range missiles but can well hold for short-range missiles. There have been reports of well-organised terrorist groups who are trying to acquire short-range missiles, especially those terrorists that are sponsored by rogue states. For example, the Hezbollah used anti-ship cruise missiles (ASCMs) during the conflict in Lebanon in 2006. Following the September 11 attack, the US made it clear that it would also hold accountable any state that harbours and supports terrorists responsible for the latter's act. If such states have ballistic missiles in their arsenals, they conceivably could retaliate against a unilateral or multilateral action by launching a missile attack on the US territory, especially when the US were distracted by a major conflict in another area of the world. Military prudence dictates that the US should have a missile defence capability to defend America.[43]

Missile Threats from China and Russia

Besides the threat coming from rogue states and terrorist groups, the US also faces missile threats from China and Russia. These countries are also accused of advancing proliferation of missiles technology to countries of the Middle East such as Iran, Syria, Libya, Pakistan etc. China has been active in modernisation of its forces since a decade. The relationship between China and the US is also not very good over the issue of Taiwan. According to Department of Defence(DoD):

> China has the most active ballistic missile programme in the world. It is developing and testing offensive missiles, forming additional missile units, qualitatively upgrading certain missile systems and developing methods to counter BMD. PRC modernisation efforts build upon current capabilities that encompass ballistic missiles to target the US as well as Japan and other regional US allies.

China acquired 30 DF-5 and DF-31 intercontinental missiles, approximately 100 intermediate range ballistic missiles and 100 short-range rockets. [44] The Office of the Secretary of Defence of the US said that between 650-730 SRBMs are deployed opposite to Taiwan and one hundred missiles would be added every year.[45]

As a part of modernisation of ballistic missiles, China is developing DF-31 which is capable of targeting the West Coast of the US and further DF-31 A would also be able to reach the US continent. These missiles will be mobile and thus require less launch preparation time as compared to old liquid fuel missiles possessed by China. The effort of the US to develop BMD has further provided a push for China's ballistic missile programme. China is trying to develop multi-independent missile warhead. China is also developing Julang 2 SLBMs. According to the US Air Force National Intelligence agency, 'Julang 2 has a range of up to 9,600km which will for the first time, allow Chinese to target portion of the US from operating areas located near Chinese coast.'[46]

The assessment of the US on the military power of the People Republic of China has mentioned that since 2000, China has shifted from a largely vulnerable, strategic deterrent based on liquid fueled intercontinental range ballistic missiles fired from fixed locations to more survivable and flexible strategic nuclear force. This is manifest by the development of DF 31 and DF 31A – both are road worthy and mobile, solid propellant systems. The development of such forces along with the development of new class of nuclear powered ballistic missile submarine (SSBN), submarine launched ballistic missile (SSBM) in 2009-2010 will enable it to form credible sea based deterrence and will give Chinese leaders a greater flexibility and options for strategic strike than previously available. Under such circumstances, China will be able to inflict huge damage to the US forces.[47]

China is becoming a super power not only in the region but also in the world. However, the US believes that China is a rational state and would use its forces only to deter the US action in Taiwan Strait. The US feels that Chinese missiles could limit the US's pursuit of interests in Asia. Further, China also has a record of proliferation of missiles, which is not conductive to the interests of the US.

The relationship between Moscow and Washington is not as tense as it was during the Cold War though Russia still maintains its ballistic missiles on high alert. The poor command and control system of Russia add to fear of accidental attacks on the US. Russia is also against the BMD programme of the US. As a result, Russia began development of new missiles like Topol M. Russia has also claimed to develop RS-24 missile, which is MIRV and capable of penetrating missile defence of the US. Thus, the US is facing threat from Russia.

Threat Coming from Electromagnetic Pulse (EMP)
Congress testimony has described the EMP threat in the following words:

> When the detonation occurs at…greater than about 40 kilometres, the gamma rays…encounter the atmosphere…interact with air molecules to produce positive ions and recoil electrons…The Earth's magnetic field interacts with the…electrons and causes charge acceleration, which further radiates electromagnetic energy. EMP is produced by these charge separation and charge acceleration phenomena, which occur in the atmosphere in a layer about 20km thick and about 30km above the earth's surface. . [48]

In general, EMP is caused by the interaction of high energy nuclear radiation with atoms in the atmosphere. When a nuclear bomb is exploded at high altitude, it will interact with Earth ionosphere and magnetic field to produce EMP. Such kind of attack will produce direct and indirect effects in the electrical currents. Direct currents are due to shocking of electronics and stressing of electrical systems while indirect effects are due to damage of electronic controls. A successful EMP attack will disturb all electrical systems bringing nation to standstill. The EMP induces high voltage and currents in antenna and voltage connected to electrical systems which will stop their operations. The long line networks like electric power grid and telecommunication systems receive and propagate the largest EMP currents making them unable to work. There are thirteen interdependent critical structures (Food, Agriculture, Water, Public Health, Emergency Services, Government, Defence Industrial base, Information and Telecommunication, Energy, Transportation, Banking and Finance, Chemical Industry and Hazardous material, Postal and Shipping) depends on proper function of electrical devices and computer systems. Beside this, EMP attack will also make recovery of a nation difficult bringing it to a standstill for many days. It may be possible that an adversary first hinder all communication and network systems by EMP attacks and than attack the US with WMD. Under such conditions, the US would not be able to retaliate due to high dependence of its economy and defence forces on the electrical equipments and computers.

There are three types of EMP produced, as mentioned below:

Nuclear High Altitude Electromagnetic Pulse (HEMP): This is produced by exploding nuclear bombs above the altitude as done by the US in 1962. Generally, countries which have nuclear weapons and delivery systems can effectively produce HEMP

High Power Microwave (HPM): HPM consists of a class of directed energy devices that emit electromagnetic rays at high frequencies. By changing the power, frequency and distance to target, HEM can produce effects that would disturb electrical appliances.

Electromagnetic Bombs by Use of FCG: Electromagnetic bombs or E-bombs are another effective way to produce EMP. They use conventional explosive to destroy a pre-charged electric circuit in a way that produce a desired electromagnetic wave. FCG is the most mature e-bomb technology which is used for this purpose.[49]

There are various countries including Russia and China who can use EMP weapons against the US. Russia has not only mentioned about EMP threat but has also given threat of exercising this option in 1999 when the relations between the US and Russia were tense due to NATO campaigning in Yugoslavia. A bipartisan delegation from the House Armed Services Committee of the US Congress met in Vienna with their Russian counterparts on the Duma International Affairs Committee, headed by Chairman Vladimir Lukin with the objective of reducing tension between the two countries. It is during this meeting that the Russian counterpart threatened that "If we really want to hurt you with no fear of retaliation, we would launch an SLBM and detonate a single nuclear warhead at high altitude over the US and shut down your power grid and communication for six months or so."[50]

Despite of all Russian claims about reduction in size of nuclear arsenals, it still maintains capability to launch EMP attacks. Dr Lowell Wood, the member of the Congressional Commission on EMP has also mentioned that:

> Soviet strategic strike forces characteristically have featured weaponry well-suited to efficient EMP generation over exceptionally wide areas. That EMP strike component exists today in the Russian strategic order-of-battle, moreover likely at its maximum Cold War strength. I can very confidently predict that it will be one of the last features of Soviet strategic nuclear weaponry to be retired from the Russian strategic force structure.[51]

Similarly, China could also exercise EMP threat so as to isolate Taiwan. It is possible that China launch EMP attack on the US so that it cannot retaliate and give chance to China to take Taiwan forcibly. Similarly, North Korea could also exercise EMP threat so as to achieve its own national interests while destroying the US capability to retaliate.

The EMP weapons have different characteristics which encourage the adversary to have such weapons. First, EMP weapons do not rely on the in depth knowledge of the system they strike and affect all the electronic systems without any prejudice. Second, EMP weapons are effective in all weather conditions. Third, they are area weapons with scalable footprints. One EMP weapon can affect the area as big as a tennis court or as big as the US. Fourth, they produce persistent and lasting effects by destruction of electrical components. Fifth, in order to protect the entire system from EMP attacks, the computer systems need to be hardened from end-to-end which is a costly and complex issue. As a result, presently, there is no defence against these attacks. Sixthly, EMP attacks do not kill people directly. In fact it can disable the military capability of the US and can serve an economic and military aim.[52]

The BMD is one of the ways to protect the US from EMP attacks. The BMD can intercept and destroy the missiles before they are detonated above the earth surface. Deploying a missile defence architecture that can intercept a missile early in flight would prevent the US from such circumstances in which their retaliatory capability is reduced. It is one of threat associated with the proliferation of nuclear and missile systems and therefore could be dealt with deployment of BMD systems.

The Growing Threat of Missiles

In 1972, only nine states possessed ballistic missiles. In 1990, 16 states got ballistic missiles. By the end of 2006, this rose to 25 states leading to the fear that they can be passed on to terrorist groups due to weak command and control structure. Similarly, the number of states that possess medium, intermediate or intercontinental ballistic missiles has increased from five to nine. These states are getting technological and financial assistance from Russia and China. The US intelligence community said that with the continued foreign assistance, Iran could be able to develop ICBM, capable to reach the US and all regions of Europe before 2015.[53] Thus, it is essential to take adequate steps to deal with threat coming from missiles.

Measures Taken by the US to Deal with Missile Threats

Clearly, proliferation of WMD represents a threat to the US deterrence policy. The US felt that the Cold War concepts of deterrence and containment are insufficient to deal with rogue states and terrorist groups seeking WMD. President Bush declared:

> For much of last century, America's defence relied on the Cold War doctrines of deterrence and containment. In some cases, those strategies still apply. But new threats also require new thinking. Deterrence-the promise of massive retaliation against nations-means nothing against shadowy terrorist networks with no nation or citizens to defend. Containment is not possible when unbalanced dictators with WMD can deliver those weapons on missiles or secretly provide them to terrorists groups. [54]

Therefore, the US brought an effective strategy to counter WMD as a part of its National Security Strategy.[55] The US strategy against WMD proliferation consists of three pillars: "Counter proliferation to combat WMD use; strengthening non proliferation regimes; and ability to respond to WMD attacks." The main constituents of counter proliferation are: interdiction, deterrence and defence.[56] The idea was that such a joint exercise against interdiction will act as deterrence against the proliferators.[57]

The following were introduced by the US as the part of the interdiction.

Proliferation Security Initiative (PSI)

Proliferation Security Initative (PSI) is a loose consortium of 80 states dedicated to interdict the transportation of WMD and ballistic missiles. Each member commits it for interdicting transfer or transport of WMD to states and non-state actors, to exchange information about suspected proliferation activity and to act appropriately against suspected transportation of WMD at sea, ashore and aloof.[58] The objective and working of PSI is mentioned in "Statement of Interdiction" issued by 11 states in September 2003.[59]

The US suspects that in 2002, a North Korea freighter, *So San,* was transporting WMD from East Asia to Middle East. As *So San* approached the coast of Yemen, the US asked Spain to stop the ship and to request the board to inspect the crowd. During inspection, Spain found that parts of Scud missiles were hidden in the ship. Later, Yemen admitted that missile parts were scheduled to be delivered to it.[60] This shows proliferation of WMD through various channels of sea and air and absence of any international measures to deal with it. The PSI was formed particularly to check on transfers of WMD from rogue states or terrorist groups which are not part of any proliferation regime.

Regional Maritime Security Initiative (RMSI)

After 9/11, the US was alarmed about ungoverned maritime trade. It was acknowledged that sheer number of cargos, and the speed and efficiency of its international nature could be easily utilised by terrorist groups for their nefarious purposes and for proliferation of WMD.[61] It was also detected that unguarded seas could lead to 'maritime terrorism' which would not be conductive to international peace and security. It was found that liquefied petroleum gas could be employed by the terrorists as floating bombs which can disable ports. It was also feasible for terrorists and rogue states to smuggle 'dirty bombs' and 'dirty nukes' through container ships. Terrorists could also target commercial ships in the seas, leading to havoc and loss of life and properties.[62]

To solve the problem of ungoverned seas, United States made a proposal to the international community of Regional Maritime Security Initiative (RMSI). It was made to look after maritime security initiatives. It emphasises on information sharing, providing cueing of emerging threats contributing security of the seas and creating an environment hostile to the terrorist and other criminal activity.[63]

UN Security Council Resolution 1540

The UN Security Council Resolution 1540 was adopted in 2004 so as to enforce effective measures against the proliferation of WMD and their means of delivery into the hands of the non-state actors or terrorist groups. There was a concern about 'system of abstinence' and to strengthen them by norms and instruments. All states have the three primary obligations under UNSC 1540 relating to such items: to prohibit support to non-State actors seeking such items; to adopt and enforce effective laws prohibiting the proliferation of such items to non-State actors, and prohibiting assisting or financing such proliferation; and to take and enforce effective measures to control these items, in order to prevent their proliferation, as well as to control the provision of funds and services that contribute to proliferation.[64]

There are three important aspect of the UN Resolution 1540. First, it considers state as a legitimate holder of WMD and mentions that non- state actors have no such rights and they must be denied access to such things. Even the state which does not have respectable expertise, technology and materials is problematic. Secondly, the resolution states that all countries should follow norms of non-proliferation and should be parts of multilateral arms control regimes. Thirdly, in order to ensure compliance, the resolution mentions that the states are requested to submit report on implementation of new founded Committee of the Security Council, which would further report to the UNSC.[65]

Therefore, the main aims of introduction of these regimes are to keep check on rogue states' and terrorist states' proliferation of WMD. This indicates that the US has clearly understood that the main threats to its national interests are coming from non-state actors.

Limitations of these measures and the US move towards the BMD Programme

It was found that PSI and RMSI faced several limitations and it was difficult to stop proliferation of missiles. Such types of regimes require universal participation of states, which is not practical. The aim of such a regime is to stop transfer of WMD by ships or aircraft. The success depends on universal participation. Both PSI and RMSI are 'informal non-organisational', acting on partial intelligence, with no independent budget or coordinating principles.[66] Therefore, these regimes met with limited success vis-à-vis proliferation of WMD to rogue states or to non-state actors.

Similarly, UN resolution 1540 has several limitations. The state adhering to UN resolution 1540 must strengthen its domestic laws so as to stop proliferation of WMD. However, there has been lack of such provisions and efforts on the part of states. Besides this, there has been absence of enforcement measures.[67] As a result of this, the US felt that there have been limitations in the international control on ballistic missiles and other WMD, and therefore it is necessary to move towards BMD so as to deal with the problem of ballistic missile proliferation.

Difference Between Old and New Threats and Withdrawal of the US from ABM Treaty

From the above analysis, we can see that there are following differences in dealing with these new threats:

- Leaders of rogue states and terrorist groups may feel less constrained in their use of force and may be more prone to taking risks, as compared to the Cold War period. Rogue states and non-state actors have shown such willingness to take substantial risks, even if such gambles involved a major sacrifice of the lives of their people and affecting the treasure of their nation's adversary.

- Past deterrence postures were dependant on the mutually understood diplomatic vocabulary and established communication channels; this may not exist with rogue states and non-state actors. The miscalculations, misinterpretations and misunderstandings might result in potential catastrophic destruction during the acute regional crisis.
- The US and its allies may not understand the fundamental political and military values within the potential aggressive governments well enough to implement effectively deterrence by offensive threats alone.[68]

During the Cold War, the US developed secure, effective and reliable communications with the USSR so as to control accidents which could lead to escalation. Both sides developed mutual understanding by negotiating arms control treaties, such as, ABM treaty. Whereas, the conditions to develop effective communication among the US and adversaries could not be established with rogue states like Iran and North Korea or with terrorist groups.[69]

Another reason given that deterrence would not be effective against terrorist groups is because they do not have any 'return address' against which the US could retaliate or they may completely miscalculate the consequences of their own actions so as to make the deterrence threat ineffective. Besides, terrorist groups want to provoke political authorities to take drastic actions so as to 'expose' them and to underdetermine their popular support. In such a case, terrorist groups might want for harsh retaliation, and use nuclear weapons.[70] President Bush, during his West Point speech, declared:

> For much of the last century, America's defence relies on the Cold War doctrines of deterrence and containment. In some cases, those strategies still apply. But new threats also require new thinking. Deterrence-the promise of massive retaliation against nations-means nothing against shadowy terrorist networks with no nation and citizens to defend. Containment is not possible when unbalanced dictators with WMD can deliver those weapons on missiles or secretly provide them to terrorist allies. We cannot defend America and our friends by hoping for the best. We cannot put our

faith in the words of tyrants, who solemnly sign non-proliferation treaties, and than systematically break them.[71]

Also, there is a doubt that whether the mathematical equation of deterrence could be applicable in real world as it is not possible to predict human behaviour. Payne summarises the folly of trying to use mathematical formulas of computer models to predict human behaviour:

> "Stable" deterrence never is the sure result of any constellation of forces. The specific details of time, place, culture, ideology, religion, domestic politics, leadership goals, motivations, health and even personality-what may be called local conditions-can be decisive in determining if and how deterrence operates, whether a leadership chooses between aggression or conciliation.
> These local conditions have led numerous decision makers in past to surprising acts of aggression that 'should' not have taken place if they were prudent, 'rational' evaluation of their own best interest assumes in balance of power thinking, Think for example of the Japanese attack on Pearl Harbor and Hitler's declaration of war on the US in 1941, Soviet emplacement of missiles in Cuba in 1962, Chinese attacks on the Sino-Soviet border in 1969, the Arab states' attack on Israel in 1973, the Argentinean invasion of the Falklands in 1982 and Iraqi missile strikes in 1991.'

With the proliferation of nuclear weapons, there is risk of nuclear attacks which make it necessary for the US to change its nuclear posture.

Therefore, there exist a large number of differences in the Cold War and post-Cold War deterrence concepts. The characteristics of cold war concept of nuclear deterrence are in many ways different from the post cold war period, as mentioned in Table 2.1:

Table 2.1 : Cold War Nuclear Deterrence v/s Post Cold War Nuclear Deterrence

Characteristics of Cold War Nuclear Deterrence	Characteristics of Post Cold War Nuclear Deterrence
There was a bipolar, long term competition between the two nuclear states and their allies.	There is multi polar security environment involving threats coming from unstable regimes.
There was a large number of nuclear arsenals in the hands of the US and USSR.	There are varied inventories of nuclear weapons ranging from emerging capabilities to sophisticated threats.
Sophisticated command, control and communication systems were maintained so as to avoid any miscalculations.	There is weak and in fact the non existence of command and control structure due to poor technological conditions and financial problems
There was continuous maintenance of strategic stability by negotiation of arms control treaties.	There is non existence of arms control treaties between such states. In fact, there is collaboration among states and non state actors in proliferation of nuclear capabilities and weapon capabilities
There was a crisis management procedure and mechanisms to avoid or to contain accidental launches or weapons system testing.	There is little protection against accidental launch by rogue states.
Both the sides also maintain relative transparency in fielding forces through arms control agreements.	There are limited communications and hot lines established between the nuclear adversaries.
There was open discussion regarding nuclear doctrine and both parties were well aware that where the 'red lines' lie.	There are no open discussions on nuclear doctrines. In fact, some states do not have any nuclear doctrines to describe their intentions and motives.

There was mutual rationality postulating that neither side would ultimately risk the destructive consequences of nuclear war.	States are exploring possibilities of having first strike against the adversaries. There is presence of non-deterrable actors.

Source: Hafta, Robert P; Hichkad, Ravi R; Johnson, Dona J and Pratt, Philip W, "Deterrence and Defence in the Second Nuclear Age" http://www.docstoc.com/docs/5207546/Deterrence-and-Defense-in-The-Second-Nuclear-Age, Assessed on 14 May 2009.

Therefore, the traditional concept of deterrence has been challenged and fear of breakdown of deterrence arises. Derek D.Smith in his book *Deterring America: Rogue States and the Proliferation of Weapons of Mass Destruction* has mentioned various instances where deterrence could actually break. The most important of it are mentioned below:

- *Asymmetries of interests encouraging weaker state to go for war against stronger states*: Derek D. Smith has mentioned that there are many examples from history where weaker state launched an attack against the stronger state. There are various factors playing in the minds of state which induce them to take action against powerful states. Sometime, weaker state feels that asymmetries of interest are in their favour which can provide them success in war. In the present context, a weaker state possessing WMD might feel that it can easily deter the US, particularly, when its interests are at stake. Taking example from the game theory, it is assumed that there is one driver as a convict on a death row alone while other driver is with a family. In such circumstances, there will be an inherent advantage to the side which has 'nothing to loose.' Here, the US is regarded as a family man who cannot afford to loose in a conflict. A state, whose most important interests are at stake, would not hesitate to strike at the US.
- *Problem of identifying aggressor*: Traditional concept of deterrence does not tell that what needs to be done when the vital interests of states are actually in conflict. Richard Betts mentioned, 'The logic of deterrence is clearest when the issue is preventing unprovoked and unambiguous aggression...Deterrence is less reliable when

> both sides in a conflict see each other as the aggressor...Such situations are ripe for miscalculation.' For example, the US regard possession of WMD in the hands of rogue states as a grave threat to its security and if the US poses a challenge to such a rogue state, the other state will regard it as a aggression against it. In such conditions, deterrence might fail.[72]

In addition to this, the three main operational requirements for stable deterrence are absent in post cold war period. First, there should not be a preventive war during the transition period when one state has nuclear weapons and other state is building but it has not yet achieved a nuclear capability. The country which already has nuclear weapons must not attack its rival in a preventive war so as to avoid risks and costs later. During the first stage, i.e. period when a state is trying to have a nuclear weapon, the preemptive strike could be exercised without the fear of retaliation. However, the question is whether such strike is so deep as to destroy development of nuclear weapons completely? In case it did not, then country struck could resume its nuclear development and may pose risk to the adversary. When the state has achieved even a rudimentary nuclear capability, it is not feasible to exercise preemptive attack on it. Second, both the states should develop not just the capability to inflict some level of unacceptable damage but should also have sufficient defence for second strike. Third, nuclear arsenal must not be prone to accident or unauthorised use.[73]

If analysed, these requirements of deterrence have not been fulfilled. The first requirement of preemptive strikes against the country which is trying to obtain nuclear weapon is quite visible. The US carried out attacks against the Iraq as it was accumulating WMD. Similarly, Israel carried out strike on Syria for destroying its development of nuclear facilities. Second, although the US has capability to retaliate, the same cannot be said about the new nuclear states. They are still developing such capabilities. Third, the accidental launch of nuclear states due to poor command and control structure in cold war period cannot be ruled out. The last two points have direct relevance to deterrence. It cannot be understood that if the new nuclear states do not possess the capability to retaliate, how they can threaten the US deterrence which prompted the US to have BMD. It is mainly the fear that these states would develop such capabilities in future which forced the US to opt for BMD. The US also feared that these states could exercise first nuclear strike against the US without the fear of retaliatory capability of America. Therefore, the US opts for BMD programme. In such a case, the deterrence of opposite state is threatened by the US BMD programme and will eventually end up in the arms race. The threat of the unauthorised use of the nuclear weapons also results into the US BMD programme. Therefore, it can be stated that traditional concept of deterrence is not working and the US need BMD capability to deal with new threats.

This led to withdrawal of the US from the ABM treaty and declaration to develop BMD. President Bush stated that, "I have concluded that the ABM treaty hinders our government ability to develop ways to protect our people from future terrorist or rogue state attacks."[74]

In the words of President Bush:

> The 1972 ABM treaty was signed by the US and the Soviet Union at a much different time, in a vastly different world. One of the signatories, Soviet Union, no longer exists and neither does the hostility that once led both our countries to keep thousands of nuclear weapons on hair-trigger alert, pointed to each other. The grim theory was that the neither side would launch nuclear attack because it knows that other side would respond, thereby destroying both.
>
> Today, events of September 11 made all too clear, the greatest threat to both our countries came not from each other, or any big power in the world, but from terrorist groups who strike without warning or rogue states who seek WMD. Therefore, we must have flexibility to develop effective defence against those attacks. Defending America is my biggest priority and as commander-in-chief, I cannot and will not allow the US to remain in the treaty that prohibits us from developing effective defences.[75]

The US has adopted a mix of offensive and defensive forces in order to deter regional aggressors. The US's policy for deterring regional aggressors is based on the US combination of policy of deterrence through denial of benefits and deterrence through the threat of retaliation. The goal of the US is not to replace the policy of deterrence of retaliation by deterrence of denial but rather to add another tool for preserving its deterrence.[76]

Therefore, the US amalgamates the policy of defence so as to prevent itself from these new threats. The US felt that there is need to devalue missiles as tools of extortion and aggression, undermining the confidence of adversary that threatening missile attack would blackmail the US. Thus, missile defence would add critical dimensions to our deterrence.[77] The US has mentioned that deterrence remains a policy goal but is no longer the organisational principle for dealing with nuclear threats.[78] Although some scholars believe that the development of BMD would not add to the US deterrence or protect the US homeland against the terrorist attacks. The reason is that terrorist will find some other way to attack the US. The terrorist needs to kill few people and to frighten large population.[79] George W. Bush claims that the BMD is a system designed to defend against 'rogue states' and terrorists. However, the efficacies of a BMD for such purposes are negligible. It would not have prevented the 9/11 attacks.[80] It is also interesting to note that how an attack that did not involve ballistic missiles perpetrated by people who do not have ballistic missiles underscored the threat of ballistic missile. No rogue states have missiles capable of hitting the continental United States. The missile test of North Korea was a failure and shows that technology is not developed to strike the US.[81]

There are other arguments also like development of counter-measures, offensive-defensive weapons race etc which would not help in strengthening of the US deterrence policy. The other questions raised are whether terrorist groups and rogue states possess the capability to launch attack on the US, as successful missile attacks require successful technologies. This has given rise to the debate whether the logic of deterring terrorist attacks and rogue states missile attacks is really strengthening the US deterrence policy or not.

One of the major shifts during this period was that the Bush administration was finding means to deter not only military attacks of the states but also the attacks by the terrorist groups and rogue states which are considered as non-deterrable. There was a strong desire on the part of the US to strengthen its deterrence posture against the terrorist groups and rogue states. Therefore, the reason given for adopting missile defence was non applicability of traditional concept of deterrence in post-cold war period. However, the Bush administration never gave up concept of deterrence. There are 22 official documents of the US which mentioned that deterrence is an important part of the US strategy. This gives an impression to Russia and China that the US is adopting mix of offensive and defensive weapons which may endanger their security. As a result, other countries like Russia, China, India and Pakistan are likely to upgrade or expand their own nuclear weapons missile delivery capabilities. Rogue states will also develop counter-measures to harm the US interests.[82] This has given rise to debate on positive and negative relationship between BMD and deterrence. These are discussed in detail in the next chapter.

3

BMD and Deterrence

Introduction

The withdrawal of the ABM treaty and the decision to develop a BMD system so as to prevent the US from new threats has led to a debate on the continued linkage between deterrence and BMD. The ABM treaty has established the concept of MAD, which made an equation of mutual vulnerability as the basis of the deterrence policy of the US during whole of the Cold War period. The US withdrawal has led to a complete fall of MAD and it was thought that the BMD establishment would make the concept of deterrence irrelevant. However, according to the US, BMD would provide more credibility to deterrence. President Bush's speech in the White House summarises the rationale behind the building of the BMD by the US:

> A terrorist regime that can strike America or our allies with a ballistic missile is likely to see this power as giving them free rein for acts of aggression and intimidation in their own neighbourhoods. But with missile defences in place, the calculus of deterrence changes in our favour. If this same terrorist regime does not have confidence that their missile attack would be successful, it is less likely to engage in acts of aggression in the first place. We would also have more options for dealing with their aggression if deterrence fails... Missile defence also strengthens our counter-proliferation efforts... By deploying effective defences, we reduce incentives to build ballistic missiles--because rogue regimes are less likely to invest in weapons that cannot threaten free nations...Missile defence also helps us dissuade nations from developing nuclear weapons. Through our missile defence partnerships with nations in Asia and

> Europe and the Middle East, we can help friends and allies defend against missile attack. These defences will build their confidence. And these defences will make it less likely that they will feel the need to respond to the nuclear ambitions of Iran and North Korea by developing nuclear weapons of their own.[1]

The President concluded by articulating the clear strategic benefit of deploying a missile defence system.

It is important here to clarify the difference between deterrence and defence. Deterrence means discouraging the enemy from taking military action by posing costs and risks which would outweigh its gains. Defence means reducing costs and risks in the event that deterrence fails. Deterrence works on the intentions of the enemy whereas defence reduces the ability of the enemy to inflict damage.[2]

Some experts in this field say that BMD could make deterrence more volatile and destabilise the whole region. This chapter will try to look at how BMD could affect the deterrence policy of the US.

Three Basic Schools of BMD Debate

Sean Clark has classified three schools of BMD debate, as mentioned below:

Opposed School

This school is totally opposed to the development and deployment of BMD systems due to four main reasons. First, this school is completely opposed to the BMD programme as it believes that withdrawal from the ABM treaty would completely upset the strategic balance. This school believes that the ABM treaty allowed each side to have enough nuclear weapons so as to ensure their opponent's termination. Thus, the ABM treaty preserved a strategic balance. With the deployment of the BMD, this equilibrium would get upset and will bring strategic stability to end, endangering further the US deterrence policy.

Secondly, this school believes that the deployment of BMD would result in the proliferation of nuclear weapons and offensive missiles. Offensive weapons are less expensive than BMD and could be accumulated in large numbers so as to overwhelm defensive systems. This school is also unconvinced that BMD would be effective given the previous performance of the Patriot missile defence. As a result, US deterrence would be reduced by deployment of offensive weapons and would not add to its security.

Thirdly, this school is opposed to BMD programme due to its technical failures. In 1991, Patriot system fared poorly against Iraqi Scud missiles. Several operational tests of BMD also faced failures. Also, BMD is unable to deal with the counter-measure technology.

Fourthly, this school is opposed to BMD programme as they believe that BMD deployments bring heavy expense and danger of cost inflation. This deployment of the two-site, 250 interceptors and GMD system will alone cost an estimated $ 58 billion. The Congressional Budget Office (CBO) estimates that a Space-Based Laser (SBL) constellation of 24 laser-armed satellites would cost up to $ 100 bn over the years 2002 to 2025.

Limited BMD Programme

This school rejects the core logic of the ABM treaty and concept of MAD. They believe that rogue states pose risk, willing to use WMD and could not be deterred. This has been proved by North Korea *No-Dong* missile test in 1998. This school believes that the US should go for BMD programme despite of all technological hurdles and international political ramifications.[3]

The rest of this chapter will deal with the positive and negative relationship between the BMD and deterrence.

Various Deterrence Relationships

Deterrence relationships between the various states and the US could be divided into three parts:

Established Deterrence Relationships: An established relationship is characterised by a high level of institutionalisation (formal or informal), primarily between two states or alliances. This kind of relationship could lead to estimation of future actions between the states, like, the relationship between the US and Russia or the US and China. History suggests no failure of deterrence in this category.

Semi-established Deterrence Relationships: Under this, the competition and mutual understanding among the states are in their formative stages. Some institutional measures have been established but the learning curve has not yet generated nuclear regulatory rules and procedures that are acceptable to all parties. The failure of deterrence is very less in such cases.

Non-established Deterrence Relationships: This is a situation in which there are different types of capabilities that could establish deterrence relationships but there is absence of historical and procedural interactions between the parties about the meaning of stability or regulatory rules for relationship. Such as relationship between Iran and the US. Such relationships are prone to failure.[4]

Whether the missile defence threatens the deterrence of other state or not also depends upon the technical performance of the BMD. Dean Wilkening has mentioned in his paper that it is assumed that there is probability of 0.80 that in an attack no warhead gets through the BMD and there is probability of 0.50 that no warhead leaks through the BMD. The NMD basically prevents limited range of missile attacks by the US and Russia as well ICBM attacks of possible rogue states in the future. Russia and China are saying a lot about degradation of their deterrence posture by the US BMD capabilities. However, determining the level at which a defence poses a threat to nuclear deterrence of other powers depends on how many weapons the attacker believe can penetrate the missile defence for deterrence to be workable. If holding a handful of targets at risk is sufficient for deterrence, BMD possess no threat to the deterrence of other states. However, if the adversary wants to hold wide range of targets at risks, BMD will be an obstacle to it. [5]

The positive relations between BMD and Deterrence

President Bush has stated, "We need new concepts of deterrence that rely both on offensive and defensive forces. Deterrence could no longer base on threat of nuclear retaliation. Defences can strengthen deterrence for reducing the incentive of proliferation."[6] Similarly, Secretary of State Colin Powell said, "You keep enough weapons so that you will be able to deter anyone else who is planning strike against you".[7] It was found that cold war conflict was based on two linked systems of cooperative endeavour- a managed system of deterrence and a managed system of abstinence. A managed system of deterrence means a situation in which states continue to use nuclear weapons so as to curb enmity and to maintain stability, but in a manner which is increasingly controlled and rule bound. The system of managed abstinence refer to a situation whereby other non nuclear states abandoned their sovereign right to develop and hold nuclear weapons and use such technology only for peaceful civilian purposes. Such states are usually under the nuclear umbrella of great powers. Both the systems have certain features which are explained below:

System of Deterrence

System of Deterrence involved:

- Nuclear hardware, deployed by nuclear powers with extensive command and control systems and hotlines installed to have communication in crisis.
- Both the states do understand the practices as expressed in the deterrence theories propounded by Brodie, Schelling and others. Both the states also took into account the nuclear deterrence theory as mentioned in nuclear doctrine of how nuclear and conventional forces could be deployed and managed to ensure vulnerability and restrain.
- Both the nuclear states also maintain bilateral arms control treaties which engage both the parties in dialogue and reduce the chances of misconceptions about each other arsenals.[8]

System of Abstinence

System of Abstinence included:

- The nuclear umbrella was kept over the allies of the US and USSR which incorporated them into NATO or in Warsaw Pact. Such kind of arrangement made allied forces feel reasonably secure despite their lack of nuclear weapons.
- There was an instrumental mechanism to verify states renucations through rigorous accounting and inspections of materials and technologies used for civilian purpose and to prevent export of weapons related to materials meant to use for civilian purpose.[9]

These two systems prevented threats and fear of nuclear escalation during cold war period. However, the situation is completely different in the post cold war period. As mentioned above, there were only two nuclear power state who maintained effective command and control systems, fully understood nuclear deterrence theory and also maintained bilateral arms control treaties to maintain strategic balance. In post cold war period, many states either developed or trying to develop nuclear weapons despite their technological backwardness. This includes India, Pakistan, North Korea and Iran. While India poses no threat to the US; Pakistan, North Korea and Iran have poor command and control structure. These states do not understand fully the formulation of deterrence theory. These three states nurse anti-American feeling and bilateral treaties are out of question. Also, end of cold war resulted into fragmentation of USSR and also of Warsaw Pact. The States which were earlier secure under USSR nuclear weapons now feel necessary to develop nuclear weapons. Therefore, the circumstances of the present world are totally different from the cold war period since the traditional concept of deterrence was made only to deal with bilateral nuclear powers. It is not fit for dealing with multilateral nuclear powers in the international community.

Therefore, it was felt that there is need to make changes in the cold war concept of deterrence which could no longer be applicable. As a result, it was felt necessary to change the deterrence doctrine and to include following things:

- Maintain sufficient deterrence in the face of possible conflict with Russia, adjusting the level of sufficiency to the Russian strategic offensive and defensive potential
- To have available, adequate space based, air borne, electronic and human intelligence gathering in order to identify and locate, if possible, before operation deployment and proliferation of threats.
- To equip themselves with the capacity to destroy adversary's sites while keeping collateral damage minimum. This capacity can include dual capable delivery systems, stealth aircraft, cruise missiles or very accurate ballistic missiles, combining penetration and precision capacity.[10]

The US does try to have all these concepts of deterrence. While first point about Russia makes some sense, the other two points have created large debates. While the US is capable enough to gather intelligence about possible deployment of missiles by a particular state, it is not able to stop them from doing so. Like the recent case of North Korea in 2009. The US and the rest of the international community were well aware that North Korea is about to test missile and international community gave lot of warnings. However, nothing deterred North Korea to have this test. The third point refers to the US preemptive attacks. However, preemptive attacks have created lot of debates and adversial states are trying to develop nuclear and missile capability to protect themselves from such attacks and to keep the US away from their regional matters.

Therefore, the US finally concludes that there is no way under which they can shun development of BMD for complementing their deterrence. According to the US, BMD could play two important roles vis-à-vis deterrence. First, BMD might discourage an enemy to acquire ballistic missiles, which could threaten the US and its allies. Some states have acquired or are trying to acquire ballistic missiles because they know that the US has no defence against them and they expect that if they have capability to threaten the US with limited capability, the US would withdraw its forces and support from the region. Missile Defence would undermine this calculus by removing free ride of ballistic missiles. Secondly, even if these states acquire ballistic missiles, the US would be in a position to deter their use in conflict. A rational leader would have to decide whether to threaten or to attack the US by balancing the costs and benefits of such action. The offensive weapons in the hands of the US would only allow it to raise the costs of such actions by threatening costly and unacceptable damage on the adversary, if it attacked with ballistic missiles. With the missile defence, the US could also reduce the potential benefits of such actions by intercepting attacking missiles. Even an imperfect defence could raise doubt in the mind of the enemy so as to discourage attacks.[11]

The traditional concept of deterrence ignores the role of modern technology. The traditional concept of deterrence focuses only on prevention of threats arising from nuclear weapons. However, today the concerns for the security must consider capabilities that are beyond nuclear weapons. Modern technology has made possible advances in weaponry that were not feasible during US-USSR standoff. There have been developments in technologies like precision guided weapons, conventionally armed earth penetrators, conventionally armed ballistic missiles and hit to kill BMD. This requires more than just threat of nuclear retaliation. This is one of the reasons behind the US decision to combine both nuclear weapons and BMD.

The effectiveness of the NMD in preventing deterrence is explained beautifully with the help of 'challenger-defender model. There are two players in international conflicts, the challenger and the defender. NMD could be effective only under condition: when the defender is soft, i.e., prefers concessions to war, and the challenger is hard, i.e., prefers war to concessions. If the defender's missile defence is effective, its costs in war get reduced, as a result it would not prefer to back out from war. This means that the threat of the defender is credible. In such a situation, the defender would not suffer costs while the challenger will have to do so. Classical deterrence theory states that high costs of war make nuclear wars obsolete. In such a way, effective BMD would be effective in preventing war and thus strengthening deterrence. The NMD would have a stabilising effect on deterrence by reducing the cost of the defender, thereby improving the defender's credibility.[12]

Deployment of BMD would have an effect on the extended deterrence also. President Bush has called for a new framework, based on deterrence that relies both on offensive and defensive forces, the strategic adjustment of extended deterrence and US-Japan relationship.[13] The BMD would give complete security to the US. Therefore, the US would be more willing to interfere in regional conflicts. By reducing the risk of retaliation against United States, missile defence would increase the credibility of extended deterrence.[14] BMD capability would give the US a much better chance to intervene in regional conflicts. The US fears death and destruction wrought by even small nuclear attacks on itself as being far worse than the consequences of not intervening in conflicts. During the Cold War, Mac George Bundy said that a decision that could lead to attack by even one bomb would be a 'catastrophic event'. Charles Glaster and Fetter observe that the US interests in the regional disputes "are not truly vital, making it hard to justify pursuing foreign policies that increase the probability of attacks with weapons of mass destruction on the US cities." Due to this, NMD deployment has been favoured as it would not only strengthen the US extended deterrence but also prove important for the achievement of the US vital interests in the regional affairs.[15]

Some military experts state that NMD would strengthen the credibility of the US extended deterrence, which would lead its allies to give the issue close attention.[16] Under Secretary for Defence Walter Solcombe said that US Missile defence would further complement deterrence by enhancing US ability to fulfil its global security commitments to its allies by rendering useless any ballistic missile equipped with WMD, thereby reinforcing US commitments to its allies.[17]

National Policy also mentions the concern of meeting these new threats on Ballistic Missile Defence Fact Sheet, 2003:

> The deployment of effective missile defences is an essential element of the US broarder efforts to transform our defence and deterrence policies and capabilities to meet the new threats we face. Defending the American people against these new threats is the Administration's highest priority.[18]

It is said that deployment of missile defence and protection of NATO cities and allies would strengthen the US nuclear deterrence. It would give the US a greater chance to navigate crisis with more steadiness and even prevent adversaries from acquiring ballistic missiles. In this case, an enemy would fear operational defeat of his attack as well as threat of NATO retaliation. Thus, it would strengthen deterrence of its allies and US.[19] Also, defences would help to deter an attack from the enemy because enemy would have less confidence about its ability to carry out successful attack. Defences would also complicate the attacks and will raise the cost of carrying out effective delivery of weapons.[20]

Some scholars believe that there is always a risk of escalation associated with deterrence. However, no such risk has been associated with missile defence. If missile defence is deployed in the post-Cold War context, threats of ballistic missiles and WMD in regional conflicts are supposed to be countered by missile defence.[21] It is also said that deployment of missile defence would add additional layer of credibility to US power, and they may remove necessity for Washington to launch nuclear weapons.[22]

Similar thoughts have been expressed by the Nuclear Posture Review (NPR):

> Advances in defencive technologies will allow US non-nuclear and nuclear capabilities to be coupled with active and passive defences to help provide deterrence and protection against attack, preserve US freedom of action and strengthen the credibility of US alliance commitments.[23]

It is also argued, that there is always a risk of failure of deterrence and occurrence of nuclear war. Robert Jervis has given two situations under which states would be compelled to have total nuclear war. First, Clausewitz believed that the friction of modern war that causes armies to drift towards more and more escalation would increase sustainability in nuclear war. The destruction caused by even a small nuclear attack would place high pressure on the civilian government to retaliate in kind. This would also disturb the communication and command networks which are necessary for imposition of cease fire. Second, limited nuclear war is a possibility. Also, the US has mentioned that it will use its limited nuclear weapons against China in case of Taiwan conflict. It is difficult to see that how a limited nuclear war can be terminated. To cease a limited nuclear war before it could become a total war; a state has to accept its defeat at the hands of other after it has already absorbed some amount of destruction and while it still has the capability to inflict destruction to the other party. It is hard to imagine that such a state will take initiative to accept defeat, particularly when, it has capacity to destroy the other nation.[24] It is here the concept of missile defence comes when it is possible to have failure of deterrence.

Some scholars say that deployment of US missile defence would make US nuclear deterrence vulnerable because it would evoke the other side to strengthen offensive nuclear missile capabilities. Nevertheless, some scholars dismiss this as the Cold War thinking. Missile defence, if combined with substantial disarmament of offensive capabilities, would facilitate further disarmament, ultimately enhancing conversation from offensive to defensive. Japan, for instance, has agreed to respond to North Korea's missile programme by deploying TMD instead of developing nuclear weapons. Thus, BMD in regional crisis would not make US deterrence less viable.[25] There are those who say that missile defence is not affecting deterrence in a negative way. Eighty percent of Russian nuclear forces could survive the US first-attack and possess the ability to penetrate US missile defence. Thus, missile defence does not eliminate second-strike capability.[26] Some proponents insist that defence and retaliatory deterrence are complementary responses to new threat but defences can negate potential of regional adversaries and render attack not only fatal but also futile.[27] Some scholars support limited NMD system. Defences must be balanced against deterrence. Defences offer some insurance, if deterrence fails but defences can undercut deterrence if they overreach their potential or aggravate global or nuclear threat.[28]

The BMD and Deterrence: Continued Negative Relationships

The other view is that missile defence is introducing new uncertainties in global nuclear deterrence and increasing instability in the system. If country A believes that it has perfect defence against country B, than country B may also believe that it has lost its deterrence capability against country A. Instead, if both countries have 500 nuclear warheads capable of attacking each other, both are likely to believe that other side would be deterred. If A introduce defensive system with 100 anti-missile interceptors, country B will believe that its missile force would be impotent and would increase its deliverable warheads from 500 to 2000 in order to restore deterrent capability. Thus any defensive system would make deterrence more precarious.[29]

Going back to the 'challenger-defender' model, the NMD would undermine deterrence if the challenger is extremely dissatisfied with the NMD system as it would destroy the capability to retaliate and to attack the defender. Under such conditions, the challenger will look forward to various other alternatives, such as strengthening deterrence by building offensive forces.[30]

There is another group of experts who believe that giving Missile Defence to third party, United States is sending wrong signals. For instance, Europeans fear that "US might create a self-fulfilling prophecy, by addressing concerns that traditional deterrence might fail, US pursuit of NMD would ensure that it will definitely fail."[31]

The arguments made by the proponents of NMD that missile defence is needed to deter rogue states because they value regime survival above all is not true. The reason being that hope of the individuals to secure their place in new governments might remove the reckless attempt of the rogue states to take their countries to nuclear war. The devastating consequences of the US nuclear retaliation for rogue state nuclear strike would realise the worst nightmare of an unpopular regime, massive instability and a total breakdown of political control. It is also important to note that the US could render far greater destruction on these adversaries than rogue states could cause. If a rogue state uses its nuclear arsenal to maximum effect, it would not have anything in reserve for bargaining and will be exposed to full US retaliation.[32]

One French expert mentions how NMD sometime stand for "No more deterrence." A limited anti-missile defence of US territory, far from being inconsistent with the creation of a stable deterrent posture against third countries, might strengthen the credibility of a retaliatory threat by removing the prospect of a cheap shot at the United States. Moreover, such a defence would not alter the mutual vulnerability of the large nuclear powers to one another that is the foundation of the traditional view of nuclear deterrence. In both these senses, defences should be seen not as an alternative to deterrence, but as an additional element to strengthen deterrence.[33]

There are also reports which say that the US is exaggerating the threat of the missile attacks of rogue states and terrorist groups. The technology of the rogue states is not sufficient to carry out a successful attack on the US. For example, Iran still has to develop successful stage separation technology; it needs to develop a propulsion system for an ICBM. The current propulsion system of Iran's Shahab 3 and Shahab 4 are not sufficient for ICBM. Similarly, North Korea's No-Dong test in 1998 was unsuccessful. It was found that No-Dong could carry a payload of 100-200 kg, which means that this payload is considerably less than the amount needed to carry nuclear weapons. This also means that this missile could carry only a small quantity of chemical and biological weapons, which are not sufficient to inflict large number or mass-casualty.[34] The situation in which an adversary is unthreatening from its own perspective, the building of defensive measures of the US could be seen as offensive gesture. The leader of rogue states might believe that the US seeks to protect itself because it seeks to attack.[35] Under such conditions, the adversary would also try to build its offensive forces so as to prevent it from any future attacks. This would result into arms report and thus degradation of the US deterrence.

Proponents of missile defence often said that by developing missiles, states are deterring the US from interfering in their regional conflicts. However, there is no reason that the US should be deterred from interfering in the regional issues if one takes an example from cold war period. During cold war, it was argued that the stability of mutual deterrence made it impossible to have full scale conventional war despite of the huge nuclear holdings by both the superpowers. The same could be applied to the US and the potential nuclear regional power. No state is as rational as assumed by the US. In fact, they are clever enough to find out the ways to deter the US for the achievement of their national interests.[36]

It is also said that deploying missile defence would push hostile states and movements to use other forms of attacks. Missile defence cannot provide protection against chemical, biological, radiological or nuclear weapons smuggled in US or assembled on its soil. It provides no defence against new technologies like cyber warfare. Hostile states use other forms of attacks which are cheaper, harder to attribute and retaliate against. The attacks on World Trade Center and Pentagon show that NMD could do more harm than good. It could threaten US allies abroad and create new regional tensions. In this sense, the bipolar 'delicate balance of terror' that shaped the Cold War, would be replaced by a 'multipolar delicate balance of deterrence'.[37] The problem is that even if missile defences can be developed and pass operationally realistic testing, foes can always counter by building sufficient numbers of offensive ballistic missiles to overwhelm a system.[38]

Technologically also, BMD does not provide foolproof guarantee against missile attacks. Technologically, it is not perfect and imperfect defences may reduce the risks of missile attacks but will not eliminate the risks posed by missile attacks armed with WMD warheads. Therefore, even if missile defences are deployed, the US will remain vulnerable to missile attacks. It is well known that defences are readily negated by cheap and feasible decoys and the result will be the vulnerability of the US deterrence. Also, by placing so much of emphasis on development and deployment of missile defence, the US has shown to its adversaries that it is deterred by the missile and WMD capabilities of the adversaries. Adversaries are also well aware of the fact that the US cannot develop foolproof technology against missile defence and missiles will effectively deter the US. In such circumstance, adversaries will be encouraged for development of more ballistic missiles.[39]

A similar type of relationship is expressed between first-strike capability and BMD. First-strike capability is an important part of deterrence. However, deployment of ABM system would degrade first-strike capability. The reason is that one side may strike first if it feels that BMD can degrade effectiveness of retaliatory strikes. If the combination of the offensive and defensive capabilities of the US put the first-strike capability of its opponents in danger, they might adopt offsetting actions that cause their weapons to be fired accidentally or prematurely. In such case, defence would exacerbate the problem of deterrence. The accidental and unauthorised use of nuclear weapons is the problem of the deterrence stability.[40] Some of the possibilities are:

- A rogue state armed with small number of vulnerable missiles can attempt to improve the chances that these weapons will survive an attack and penetrate the defence.
- These rogue states could position their weapons close to target to circumvent the US defences. For example, these states can deploy missiles on ships in forward positions or could pre-position a nuclear device on the US territory for detonation in future.[41]

To sum up the main arguments:

- Missile defences decrease deterrence. Missile Defences would question the role of deterrence and even negate deterrence as the 'Cold War concept'.
- Missile defences would provoke first-strike by the country which does not possess BMD.
- The efficacy of defences against biological weapons, cruise missiles and suitcase bombs remain low (Delpech 2000: 63).

Russia and China: Fear of First Strike Attack

Deterrence works on the assumption that a nation will not carry out a first strike on its adversary, as it believes its adversary to be capable of retaliation. For deterrence to work effectively, both sides must believe their forces would survive a first-strike attack and be capable of inflicting sufficient retaliatory damage. A country will carry out a nuclear first strike only if it is capable of defeating another nuclear power by destroying its arsenal to the point where the attacking country could survive weak nuclear retaliation while the opposite side is unable to continue in the war.[42] Russia and China fear that BMD will degrade their second strike capability and will in turn provide the capability to the US to strike first. In turn, they would not be able to retaliate because BMD will intercept and destroy their missiles.

The BMD has raised the risks of a nuclear first strike in two ways. Russia should be kept in mind while considering these situations, as the relationship between Russia and the US has been at its lowest ebb in 2008 since the end of the Cold War. First, politicians and military leaders may begin to think that they could survive a nuclear war due to the existence of BMD. As a result, they may be tempted to strike first to destroy an adversary's weapons. As missile defence becomes powerful enough to deal with second-strike capability, an adversary would not be able to retaliate. Secondly, as Russia is aware that the US is unable to build perfect defences, it may be able to penetrate the deployed BMD of the US by launching vast numbers of its missile force and decoys. In such a case, Russia might adopt a "back-to-MAD" (mutually assured destruction) capability and strike the US first.[43]

This scenario can be explained with an example. If the US deploys BMD systems to protect its cities from ballistic missiles or nuclear attacks, in reaction, Russia may develop anti-satellite weapons (ASATs) capable of destroying US space-based systems. As a result, the US would then develop capabilities to destroy ASATs. If Russia carried out ASAT attacks on the US, it would destroy the US BMD and therefore its capability. On the other hand, if the US first carried out attacks on Russian ASATs, it would destroy Russia's capability of destroying US BMD systems. However, the probability of a Russian attack is lower due to the US's nuclear primacy and Russia is aware that the US would definitely carry out retaliatory strikes in case of such actions. In the present scenario, Russia has threatened Poland

and the Czech Republic with nuclear attacks after they signed nuclear deals with the US. Colonel–General Nikolai Solovtsov, Chief of Russia's Strategic Missile Command has repeatedly stated that missile defence systems in these countries could become potential targets of Russia's nuclear weapons. "We have to take appropriate measures to prevent the weakening of Russia's nuclear deterrence under any circumstances. And I do not rule out that ... some intercontinental ballistic missiles could be aimed at these Polish and Czech facilities". Under such conditions, attacks on Polish and Czech missile defence systems would be regarded as attacks on US facilities. Assuming that the US has already protected its territories by deploying BMD, it would be tempted to strike first on Russian capabilities, before Russia destroys missile defence systems in Eastern Europe. Such an attack would destroy Russia's strategic forces and prevent an attack on the US's allies. Russia would be unable to launch a nuclear strike on the US, as BMD would intercept the remaining Russian missiles. In both cases, deterrence is negatively related to BMD as it leads to fall of deterrence and occurrence of war.[44]

The US already enjoys nuclear supremacy over Russia and China. As of January 2009, the US stockpile consists of approximately 5,200 nuclear warheads; approximately 2,700 operational warheads which compromised of 2,200 strategic and 500 non-strategic warheads and approximately 2,500 additional warheads in reserve. The US ICBMs consist of 450 operational missiles and 14 Ohio class submarines. On the other hand, Russia, has 385 operational missile systems of four different types. Russia's ICBM also consists of 13 strategic missile submarines.[45]

China is much inferior to the US. China is the smallest nuclear weapons country among P-5 nations and could be easily destroyed by the US. Presently, China deploys, approximately 120 land based missiles including DF-3A, DF-4, DF-5A and DF- 21.[46] China's strategic nuclear forces are outdated and based on 1950s and 60s technologies. Its nuclear capability bombers lack sufficient range and are too slow to penetrate modern air defences. Its ICBMs use liquid fuel which corrodes missiles after 24 hours and require lengthy launch preparation times.[47] As the US already enjoys nuclear supremacy, BMD will further enhance its first strike capability while degrading deterrence of Russia and China. This adds to worry of both China and Russia.

It is also argued that the US development of BMD for rogue states is a weird argument. The main reason is to have first strike against Russia and China. The other small nuclear powers are inferior to the US and know well that they cannot win a nuclear war against the US nor they could threaten the survival of the US. Therefore, it very unlikely that the US would use first strike against the states which are inferior to its capabilities and do not intend to threaten the US regime. Such an attack will invite large scale international criticism. While, the US would like to strike first blow on the states with which it faces competition and which could threaten its unipolarity.

However, there are different perceptions of the same problem. The survivors of such state and their allies would retaliate against the first strike of the US by using WMDs. An imperfect first strike or failure of BMD will be a total disaster for the US. Therefore, the US is not willing to go for first strike attack.

Dean Wilkeing has presented a different scenario. He has mentioned that Russia will be left with approximately 800 warheads after the US first strike. He has mentioned that Russia's retaliatory capability on generated alert levels is approximately 240 warheads because this is the number of bomber weapons which are assumed to survive after a first strike and are capable enough to penetrate US air defence systems. They are unaffected by US NMD systems. Further, he has mentioned that by taking 1,428 warhead force as an example, it would take NMD systems with approximately 125 interceptors to degrade Russia's ballistic missile retaliation by 20 percent. In any case, Russia will have bombers that can carry approximately 500 warheads. Therefore, it does not seem that Russia will loose its second strike capability by the US deployment of BMD. In an another study, it was assumed that Russia's nuclear forces were at a level of 3,000 warheads and it was assumed that if the US could preemptively destroy 90 percent of the immobile weapons, 50 percent of the mobile weapons and that BMD is 70 percent effective, 10 percent of Russia's weapons failed or die to friction. Under such circumstances also, Russia would have 539 nuclear warheads left which could destroy the US. Even if BMD is 90 percent effective and there is 50 percent failure due to friction, Russia still have 233 warheads. If Russia's nuclear warheads are reduced to 1000, 78 percent of it will survive and can penetrate the US missile defence system. Scaling down further to 250 warheads, Russia will have at least 20 warheads which could destroy one American city.[48]

Russia rests on the belief that with the advancement of technologies, the US will deploy more and more interceptors which will threaten its deterrence. On the other hand, Chinese allegations are real. China has 20 ICBM warheads in the strategic arsenals and deployment of BMD will certainly threaten its deterrence. China may have 102-190 ballistic missiles capable of targeting the US by 2010-2015 but unlikely to have long range bombers.[49]

Therefore, both the countries will try to strengthen their first strike capability. The first-strike capability could be increased by deployment of decoys. Decoys would increase first-strike capability by spoiling effectiveness of ABM system and thus reduce degradation in first- strike capability caused by missile defence.[50]

Such measures are taken by China and Russia who fear that their deterrence and first- strike capability would be damaged by coming of BMD. Defences would only induce these countries to augment their offensive forces at a cost lower than the cost to the US for augmenting their defences.[51] China has an ICBM force of around 20-silo based weapons. Under such conditions, US system of 100 to 200 interceptors would eliminate its nuclear capability.[52] In order to restore its deterrent value, China is busy in modernising its forces and developing counter-measures. China could use multiple re-entry vehicles with some of them having decoys. Such warheads could be used, which has reduced infrared reflections, thereby limiting effectiveness of kinetic kill vehicle. Such technology could be developed by China to ensure that its warheads penetrate US missile defence.[53]

Similarly, some changes could take place in China's nuclear posture. China has already moved from assured minimum deterrence to limited nuclear deterrence. China could use 'Launch on Warning', which is a defensive response to a confirmed attack. Launch on Warning could be defined as active defence measures taken after the adversary has attacked but before his weapons have wrecked destruction on China. The purpose of such doctrinal changes would be to present credible deterrence and prevent US from using its offensive superiority to threaten while protecting itself with defensive shield.[54]

China would restort to force modernisation. Currently it is building three new mobile, solid propellant Strategic Missiles: DF-31, a land mobile ICBM with range of 8,000 Km, DF-41-longer version of DF-31 with range of 12,000 km, JL-2, a new SLBM system with range of 8,000 km and expects it to be deployed by 2010. China would also put its weapons on high alert. However presently, there is problem for China to keep its weapons on high alert.[55] Russia's successful test of RS-24 also shows that US BMD programme would not guarantee deterrence, as assumed earlier.

Similarly, Russia feels that the US programme to put interceptors and radars in Czech Republic and Poland would degrade its deterrence. According to the plan, the site at Czech Republic deploys midcourse radar while Poland will host battery of ground-based interceptors. These radars and interceptors are mainly deployed to deal with threat of Iran. However, these radars could also detect the Russian missiles launched from bases in Russian European territory.[56] As a result, Russia felt that these interceptors and radars would degrade its deterrence. Russia is engaged in military build up since the US has taken decision to deploy BMD in Czech Republic and Poland.

Russia is busy in developing counter-measures technology since 1960s. According to 1998 NIE, Russia has developed numerous counter-measures. These counter-measures include decoys that stimulate warheads, chaff. These could confuse enemy radars and manoeuvrable warheads that could evade interceptors. Reportedly, Russia SS-18 missiles could hold about 30 decoys in addition to its10 nuclear warheads. Russia is also busy in developing Topol M rocket, which it claims that has the capability to penetrate effectively a potential ABM system of any state.[57] Russia also carried out successful test of RS-24 missile on 29 May 2007, which could carry multiple independent warheads and could penetrate BMD system of the US.[58] In November 2007, Russia said that it could take a decision to deploy the Iskander missile in Beralus in response to the US plans to deploy BMD in Europe. These missiles were not in accordance with Intermediate Range Nuclear force treaty (INF) but Russia has indicated that it could take a decision to withdraw from INF treaty. The actions taken by Russia could be summarised as:

> Russia has resumed long-range nuclear bomber flights, opposes missile defences in Europe, claims the North Pole for Russia and suspends cooperation under the Conventional Forces in Europe (CFE) treaty. Russia also sells air defence missiles to Syria and nuclear technology to Iran, suspends gas and oil shipments to pressure other countries, and threatens both to withdraw from the Intermediate Nuclear forces (INF) treaty and to target NATO countries by basing missiles in Russia's Kaliningrad enclave.[59]

The BMD and Deterrence: Present and Future

The present situation reflects negative relationship between the US deterrence and BMD. Given the present situation, it seems that the US BMD would not help in strengthening the US deterrence. It has presented to the world a kind of situation similar to a 'security dilemma' which could further lead to the offensive-defensive race of weapons. The US looks at the development of missiles by rogue states as a threat to itself and therefore plans to deploy BMD. The US defensive measures are seen as threats by rogue states and by countries like Russia and China. They are further busy in development of missiles so as to strengthen their deterrence and this would further create problems of deterrence for the US. It is important to note that China and Russia have history of proliferation of WMD, including missiles. If they develop counter-measures, it is also possible that they would sell these counter-measures to Middle East countries and to rogue states. This would not only degrade the US interests in the region but also its deterrence against rogue states as terrorists groups will develop other means to harm the US interests like the development of suitcase bombs, cruise missiles or will try to carry out another attack like 9/11. Hence, the US deterrence would not be secure with the development of BMD. The BMD is facing lot of technological and political challenge and thus it does not act as a comprehensive framework to strengthen deterrence of the US.

4

President Obama and New Security Challenges

Introduction

After Presidential Elections, it was hoped that President Barak Obama will give away the plans of having missile defence so as to have the better relationship with Russia and China. As economic recession was also on the table before him, it was hoped that President Obama will need to have better relationship with China[1] and for this he might postpone the US plans for BMD. Also, during his Presidential campaign, President Obama showed his interest in attaining goal of 'global zero' rather than building BMD which is technically not reliable and could lead to offensive-defensive arms race. He mentioned repeatedly that he would not invest further in an unreliable technology. However, the events which soon followed came to manifest that the US had inherited a mess of problems – Taliban in nuclear armed Pakistan, launch of Iran's satellite which could be converted into ballistic missile and debate over its nuclear weapons capability and North Korea's missile test in 2009 which was followed by DPRK's second nuclear test. Although the US did not react to these events, these could provide a trigger for President Obama decision on BMD. It is to be noted that all these threats to the US are coming from Asia- which is the focal point of the US interest. It is also an area where the US forces are deployed.[2]

The question is why these states are developing nuclear weapons despite their technological and financial problems? Realists like Waltz and Mearsheimer argue that a small state obtain security from great power predation by developing a small, invulnerable nuclear arsenal which they can use as an act of retaliation against a large state threatening its survival.[3] It is hard to imagine that the US would have gone for conventional military strike against North Vietnam if they would have nuclear weapons. Similarly, the US would not have attacked Iraq and Afghanistan had they got nuclear weapons. This provides an encouragement to small nuclear powers like Iran and North Korea, to develop their own nuclear weapons. The advanced nuclear weapon small states are well aware that they cannot protect themselves by large military build ups or alliance systems because of large disparity between the US and such states. Most of the states choose to engage themselves with the US rather than forming alliances against it. Therefore, the US adversaries try to protect themselves by developing nuclear weapons.

However, the problem is that the US is not able to play its cards accordingly to maintain its strategic interests in the region. As mentioned by Wohlforth, 'the US must play its cards well if it is to manage its preponderance over the unipolar world successfully.'[4] As a result of this, there is increasing resistance by small states to the US preponderance. Rather than accepting the US leadership small states are seeking regional hegemony, refuse to cooperate on transnational problems, attack American allies and resist and defy the US will. They want to use nuclear weapons as a means to show their resistance against the US. They are fully aware that the US will not attack them with conventional weapons because of their possession of nuclear weapons. They think that the US might be able to go to war against the larger adversary but will not do so against the small nuclear state on the pretext like they did not sell the US oil, harbour terrorists or disturb the global economy. The inability of the US to do so might result into disequilibrium which could be a nightmare for the US foreign policy.[5] There are three kinds of such threats coming from to the US. (1) Rise of Taliban in Pakistan (2) North Korea Nuclear Weapon State (3) Iran's quest for nuclear weapons. What is interesting to note here is that these three states cooperate with each other for the development of nuclear weapons and missiles. These threats are described below.

Growing Instability in Pakistan

The growing Taliban in the nuclear weapon state of Pakistan is not a new thing.[6] The new thing is the reorganisation of this threat by the international community, particularly after 9/11 attacks. Political thinker and activist Iqbal Ahmad wrote that 'Conditions for revolutionary violence have been gathering in Pakistan since the start of 1980 with the internationally sponsored *jihad* in Afghanistan.' He further mentioned that 'revolutionary violence in Pakistan is likely to be employed by religious and right wing organisations which have not set theoretical or practical limit on the use of violence.'[7] He than warned that Pakistan 'is moving perilously towards a critical zone from where it will take the state and society generations to return to a semblance of normal existence. When such a critical point of hard return is reached, the viability of stakeholders depends more on external than internal factors.'[8] Unfortunately, Pakistan government establishment has been ignoring this issue and taking help of Taliban and other extremist groups for fulfilling its own political motives and intentions.[9]

The extremist groups operating in Pakistan can be divided into two parts. The one group belongs to armed Islamist groups such as Lashkar-e-Taoiba (LeT) and its parent organisation Jammat-ud-Dawa (JU) and other similar Pakistani groups originating from Punjab. The aim of these organisations is to turn Pakistan into fundamentalist Islamic State. It was created mainly to have proxy war with India. These organisations are also anti-US and view the US and its allies as a threat to their ambitions. On the other hand, there are Taliban militants in the tribal areas on Pakistan-Afghanistan border. These are essentially local religious warlords who have respective areas of influence.[10] Taliban used to have their rule Afghanistan till 9/11. After 9/11 attacks, the US launched attack on Afghanistan and destroyed Taliban government. However, that does not stop Taliban from achieving their political and religious agenda. Talibans shifted themselves to FATA and NWFP regions of Pakistan and began to expand from there. There are two main reasons for the rise of Taliban in the region. First, the US launched attack on Afghanistan which forced them to regroup in Pakistan gaining support and volunteers from the Wazir and Mehsud tribes in Waziristan. Second, the rise of local militants followed the Afghan's Taliban philosophy. These local militants mainly include those tribesmen who had gone to Afghanistan to fight along with the Taliban against the Northern alliance and foreign forces.[11] As a result, Taliban found safe heavens in Pakistan.

The link between the Taliban and Pakistan is very well known. Pakistan and the US supported Taliban during cold war in the fight against USSR. Since beginning, most of the members of the Taliban originally came from refugee camps in Pakistan and many of them were carrying Pakistani identity cards. In the 1980s, there was a drastic development in the networks of *Madrasa* in Pakistan. Between1960-1983 the number of Talibans studying in Pakistan had increased from 7500 to 78,500. The initial support to Taliban government came from Benzair Bhutto. The coming of Nawaz Sharif did not bring any noticeable change in Pakistan's Afghanistan policy and Taliban remained a cornerstone of Sharif's policy. Pakistan adopted the strategy of waging proxy war with India while trying to maintain friendly government in Afghanistan. After 9/11 General Pervez Musharraf was forced to act against the Taliban when the Bush Administration clearly said that 'either you are with us or you are with them." It was hoped that this would change Pakistan's policy of supporting terrorism. However, a lot has been said but nothing happened. In FATA, Gen Musharraf adopted policy of minimally satisfying American demands, without interfering with the resettlement of militants in Waziristan, and all the while assuring to the JUI led government in Peshawar that the army would not stop their pro-Taliban policies.' The agreement was signed between the army regime and militants in South Waziristan in 2004 which extended amnesty and financial incentives to Pakistan's Taliban and allowing them to have *Sharia law* in the region. Similar agreement was signed in 2006 with militants of North Waziristan. It was agreed to dismantle check posts, release militants who were arrested through counter-terrorism operations and to return weapons and vehicles seized during these operations. Such kind of deals strengthened political base of Taliban in the region without guaranteeing peace to the region.[12] The episode of Red Mosque in 2007 shows the growing influence of Taliban in Pakistan. It showed clearly to the international community that Pakistan *madrasas* are meant to train extremist groups.

After change in the government, speculations were again made about the Pakistan's government policy towards Taliban. As President Zardari is the husband of Benzair Bhutoo who was killed by Taliban, it was hoped that President Zaradari would take immediate steps to end Taliban rule. However, the civilian government proved to be totally incapable in dealing with Taliban and in fact followed the same policy of appeasement with regard to these groups. The Pakistan's government agreed to have peace deal with Taliban in February 2009 under which Sharia law would be implemented in Swat. This was criticised by the international community as it added to the fear of Talibanisation of Pakistan.[13]

The influence of Taliban is not limited just to border areas of Pakistan. The leader of Jaish-e–Mohammad runs a large *Madrasa* in Karachi. Pro-Taliban and anti-Shia sentiments can be seen in Karachi. The PPP coalition partner in the Sindh government and Muttahida Qaumi Movement (MQM) which also runs Karachi district government have expressed their concern about Talibanisation of Karachi. Similarly, Jaish-e-Mohammad and Harkani Mujahiddin have set up bases and transit camps in Rawalpindi for militants who travel from southern Punjab to NWFP.[14] The government has adopted a 'more carrot-less-stick-approach' towards the militants.

In April 2009, Taliban proceeded towards Buner – which is located near Islamabad. The rapidly deteriorating situation in Pakistan was highlighted in a New York Times article on a Sunday that reported the following:

> Initially, Buner was a hard place for the Taliban to crack. When they attacked a police station in the valley district last year, the resistance was fearless. Local people picked up rifles, pistols and dagger, hunted down the militants and killed six of them. But it was not to last. In short order this past week, the Taliban captured Buner, a strategically vital district just 60 miles northwest of the capital, Islamabad.
>
> The militants flooded in by the hundreds, startling Pakistani and American officials with the speed of their advance . . . Today the hopes that those civilian militias inspired are gone, brushed away by the realisation that Pakistanis can do little to stem the Taliban advance if their government and military will not help them . . . The peace deal the military struck with the Taliban in February in neighboring Swat further demoralised people in Buner.[15]

The military operations were carried out in Buner and Pakistan's government claimed that area became free from Taliban. However, it shows the relative ease with which terrorists are operating in the country and trying to take one of the major chunks of Pakistan's territory. It is clear that Taliban are shifting away from Afghanistan and moving towards Pakistan. This is an alarming situation because Pakistan is the nuclear weapon state and these weapons could be passed on to Taliban who are fired with anti-American ideologies. There are two circumstances under which Taliban could get access to Pakistan's nuclear weapons. First, in the event of theft of nuclear weapons by Taliban. Second, Taliban take over of Pakistan which will provide them access to the country's nuclear weapons. Roun Suskind, Pulitzer Prize winner journalist, mentioned in his book *The One Percent Doctrine* that mastermind of 9/11 find 'safe house' of a serving Pakistani military officer having close links with Jammat-i-Islami.'[16] It is often evident that Pakistan's military officers have close links with terrorist organisations like the Jammat-i-Islami, Lashkar-e-Toiba, Hizb-ul-Mujahideen, Harkat-ul-Mujahideen and Jaish-e-Mohammad.[17] The assassination of Benazir Bhutto further raised doubts about the credibility of Pakistan's army. In addition to it, there is ethnic divide among the ranks of Pakistan's army which can easily be exploited by the terrorist groups. Fifteen percent of Pakistan's army consists of Pashtun component. In 2006, these troops were sent to fight with Al-Qaida and Taliban. Surprisingly, large number of Pashtun troops surrendered in the front of Al-Qaida and Taliban fighters. Similarly, Baloch element in Pakistan's army which consists of 9 percent is not ready to fight. They believe that their province and leadership has badly been treated by army commanders who are mostly Punjabi and Mohajir. Similarly, 300 army personnel from Pakistan army and Frontier Constabulary (FC) surrendered to the pro-Taliban militia of Baithullah Mehsud in South Waziristan in August 2007.[18]

Since 2004, one Major General from the Orakzai tribe preferred premature retirement rather than to join army operations against Pashtuns. Some of the other Pashtun colonels have also been posted out of the terrain for expressing their reservations from fighting against Pashtuns militants. According to an estimate provided by Hassan Abbas, the Pastuns constitute 20-25 percent of Pakistan's army and approximately 15-22 percent of army officers belong to this tribe. It was also found that lower ranks continued to have links with the Taliban and this has been overlooked by their officers.[19]

Pakistan army and ISI are not yet ready to give up their links with the terrorist groups and try to differentiate between various elements of militant organisations as per their own wishes. For example, army took action against Al Qaida and radicals like Baituallah Mehsud but ignored the senior leadership of Taliban in Quetta and other key insurgent commanders like Gulbadin Hikmatyar and Jalaluddin Haqqani who operated from Peshawar because of its strategic value vis-a-vis Afghanistan. Instead of fighting and tackling the problem, Pakistan opted for peace deals with them. As a result, the frontier's borders with Afghanistan became a secure heaven for these terrorists group.[20] These groups are waging war against Afghanistan, India, America and even against Pakistan's government for supporting the US in 'war against terror.' This situation is particularly alarming because Pakistan is a nuclear weapon state and its nuclear weapons are in army's hands. Under such condition, the links between terrorist groups and army involves a potential risk for the US.

Beside this, Pakistan's nuclear scientist AQ Khan admitted of providing nuclear weapon technology to Iran, Libya and North Korea. This creates serious doubts about the security of Islamic Bomb. In fact, AQ Khan was not the only scientist who proliferated nuclear technology. It was revealed that Pakistan's top scientists- Sultan Bushiruddin Mahmood and Chaudhary Abdul Majeed met Al Queda members in 2000 and 2001 and possibly shared some nuclear secrets.[21] Pakistan's government has recently released AQ Khan from house arrest which adds the threat of proliferation of nuclear weapons. Beside this, any war between India and Pakistan will result into jeopardising Pakistan's nuclear weapons. Michel Krepon explained 'escalated war with nuclear forces in the field would increase the probability of accidents, miscalculations and use of nuclear weapons.'[22] This is because

> When tensions rise precipitatediy with India, the readiness level of Pakistan's nuclear deterrent also rises. Because the geographical coordinates of Pakistan's main nuclear weapon storage sites, missile, and air bases can be readily identified from satellites — and therefore targeted by opposing forces — the dictates of deterrence

> mandate some movement of launchers and weapons from fixed locations during crises. Nuclear weapons on the move are inherently less secure than. nuclear weapons at heavily guarded storage sites. Weapons and launchers in motion are also more susceptible to "insider" threats and accidents.[23]

When the focus of Pakistan should be fighting terrorism, it is focusing on development of more nuclear warheads. Congressional Research Service released its report on May 2009 which stated that Pakistan is developing or replacing its current uranium based nuclear weapons with plutonium based nuclear weapons which are more destructive and easily deliverable. Jhon R. Bolton has presented two events where there could be threat to Pakistan's nuclear bomb. First is the event of instability in Pakistan which will result into radical disruptions of weak government and also of military. It is possible as military itself is threatened by the rise of Taliban. Secretary of State, Hilary Clinton, also mentioned that Pakistan had dispersed its nuclear weapons and it is possible that these nuclear weapons slipped into the hands of Al Qaida or any other terrorist organisations. This will definitely have global implications. Second, the internal instabilities will result into constitutional collapse and military fragmentation. This could allow a well-organised, tightly disciplined group to seize control of the entire Pakistani government. Taliban could take advantage of the chaos in the government.[24]

Therefore, there is a growing fear of Taliban take over of Islamic bomb. Currently, Pakistan does not have capability to target the US by ballistic missile or long range aircraft. However, Pakistan's Taliban can target US allies in Asia and could use nuclear weapons as a bargaining chip for fulfillment of their demands. However, never touched upon, the US might like to have BMD and TMD to protect itself and its allies from nuclear threat posed by Taliban.

North Korea's Nuclear and Missile Threats

North Korea is one of the case which demonstrates that how nuclear proliferation help state to develop their nuclear capability. After Rumsfled commission report,[25] North Korea tested nuclear missile which alarmed the US. It was North Korea *Taepo Dong* Tests in 1998, which pushed Japan towards acquisition of TMD. Again, when the Obama Administration decided to cut 15 percent from BMD, North Korea tested *Taepo Dong 2* in April 2009 which again shows that North Korea is willing to develop its nuclear deterrence despite US warnings. On 5 April 2009, North Korea launched a three staged rocket in order to place Kwangmyongsong 2 satellite into orbit. North Korea dealt with protests over its launch by saying that 'Every country has the right, an inalienable right, to use outer space for peaceful purpose' and it is not 'democratic' on the part of UNSC to prevent North Korea from such activities.'[26] However, according to NORAD and the US Northern Command, 'stage one of the missile fell into the Sea of Japan. The remaining stages, along with the payload landed in the Pacific Ocean' and 'no object entered into the orbit.'[27] Therefore, it clearly manifests that test was only for the military purpose, and not for the peaceful purpose as claimed by North Korea. The US responded by saying that North Korea has violated the UNSC resolution meant for its ballistic missiles in 2006 and said that the 'violators should be punished.'[28] However, Russia and China veto such sanctions by claiming that North Korean test was meant for peaceful purpose and therefore does not violate UNSC resolution.

The development of ballistic missiles could play an important role for North Korea. First, Development of ballistic missiles will compensate for qualitative differences between North Korea's weapons and those of the US and South Korea. Missiles offer a cost effective way to DPRK for dealing with its threats. Second, North Korea may sell this missile technology to other states which would provide it foreign exchange and will help its economy to swell. Third, development of missiles will help North Korea to extract economic concessions from international community. Fourth, North Korea will be able to grab international attention towards its problems and needs.[29]

The US President Obama was criticised for financial cuts in missile defence as the danger of missiles are growing because of North Korea's recent missile tests. Riki Ellison, the Chairman and Founder of Missile Defence Advocacy Alliance, said 'One would hope, after the events happened, that every possible part of missile defence be fully funded and resorted. But in the era of limited resources, outstanding national debts and other important needs in other fields that will be a challenging task to accomplish.'[30] However, it was realised that the US is exaggerating the threat posed by the North Korean missile because it could not yet reach the US or Europe. Joseph Cirincione pointed out the technological difficulties in North Korea's missile programmes. First, North Korea has to develop bigger and long range missile. Ted Postal also calculates that the failed satellite appears to weigh 150 to 200 kg and was intended for low earth orbit about 550 km. This is not upto a standard, missile which can reach towards the US. In order to deter the US, North Korea needs to develop bigger missile that can carry more weight over a longer distance. Building such a missile will require major advances in metallurgy, rocket engines, guidance, and propulsion and even require foreign assistance. Second, North Korea needs to miniaturise its nuclear warhead in order to place it on the rocket. The nuclear device which was tested by North Korea in 2006 is estimated to weigh more than 1500 kg which is too heavy to be launched on to the vehicle similar to what was tested in April 2009. This is probably the most difficult task faced by North Korea. Retired Gen. Eugene Habiger who is former head of US Strategic Command, said, "The miniaturisation of a nuclear warhead is probably the most significant challenge that any proliferant would have to face. In fact, the U.S. took six to eight years of intensive engineering and testing to get our warheads down to 1000 kilograms (2,205).' Third, it seems that North Korea has not yet developed the re-entry vehicle which is very important as the warhead returning from atmosphere to its target has to survive harsh conditions.[31] Therefore, North Korea will take some years to develop its capacity to threaten the US and Europe. However, North Korea does have the capability to strike South Korea and Japan, who are important US allies. North Korea could launch hundreds of mid range missiles against Japan and South Korea. Jane Defence Weekly estimated the North Korea could rain 500,000 shells an hour into the Seoul area. Also, North Korea could use chemical and biological weapons against South Korea and Japan which could pose grave risk to their economic centers.[32] This makes an argument for Japan and South Korea for acquiring effective TMD systems from the US to protect them.

North Korea's nuclear programme is also well known. North Korea carried out nuclear tests in October 2006 which points to the failure of six party talks. There are two main reasons for North Korea's nuclear tests. First, it wants to be on a negotiating table with the US on a better footing. Second, North Korea's leaders have repeatedly mentioned in 2006 that they need to have nuclear weapons so as to prevent themselves from preemptive attacks of the US. They mentioned that they do not want 'Iraq' to happen in North Korea. North Korea also threatens to again test nuclear weapon and ICBM unless UNSC immediately apologises for adopting 'President Statement' against it and remove sanctions imposed on three North Korean companies after DPRK missile test in 2009.

An article by Kyle M. Ballard, titled 'Doors of perception: national security politics, threat perceptions and North Korea's pursuit of a credible deterrent' in *The Korean Journal of Defence Analysis* shows how the domestic politics of the US pushed DPRK towards the nuclear and missile programme. After North Korea's nuclear activities were detected, an Agreed Framework was concluded with the US. North Korea regarded Agreed Framework as their biggest diplomatic victory. A North Korea's newspaper mentioned, 'We held the talks independently with the US on an independent footing, not relaying on someone else's sympathy, and the adoption of the DPRK-US Agreed Framework is a fruitation of our independent foreign policy.'[33] However, there was lot of criticism of the Agreed Framework in the US. Gerald Solomon authored a newsletter titled *Appeasement Watch* in which he condemned Clinton's engagement with the North Korea. Later, in October 1996, General Accounting Offce (GAO) released a report titled *Nuclear Nonproliferation-Implications of the US/North Korean Agreement on Nuclear Issues* which mentioned that the Agreed Framework should be declared as 'a non-binding agreement.' North Korea felt that this shows the US commitment towards implementing this agreement which DPRK chief negotiator Kang Sok Ju consider as 'a very important milestone document of historical significance and the biggest diplomatic history.' With this, North Korea's confidence in the US falls.[34]

After that, Oil shipments were a month behind the scheduled funding for KEDO project was in dire straits and LWRs project was also behind schedule. In response, Foreign Minister of North Korea, Kim Yong Nam said 'The US government takes us for granted because they regard us as weak. We are loosing patience. Our generals and atomic industry leaders insist that we must resume our nuclear programme and develop appropriate military capabilities. If you don't act in good faith there will be consequences.'[35] When Bush administration came, it declared North Korea as a state in 'axis of evil.' He also pulled the BMD programme further in order to protect the US and its allies from states forming 'axis of evil.' He came with the idea of New Triad which consists of both offensive and defensive systems. This led DPRK to declare, 'In case the US plan for a nuclear attack on the DPRK turns out to be true, the DPRK will have no option but to take a substantial counter-measure against it, not bound to any DPRK-US agreement.'[36] All these events triggered DPRK to have its own nuclear bomb and delivery vehicles. The DPRK often felt that the US is not serious for its commitment under Agreed Framework and regard the North Korea as a threat. The US attacks on Iraq and Afghanistan made it implicit to DPRK that the US can carry out conventional strike against non nuclear weapon state and strive for achieving regime change.

Further, North Korea also declared its decision to boycott six party talks due to the criticism of the international community about its missile test in April 2009.[37] North Korea again carried out second nuclear tests on 25 May 2009 despite all fears of international isolation. According to US estimates North Korea has extracted enough plutonium to build six to eight nuclear bombs.[38] John Bolton has mentioned the reasons for second nuclear tests as:

> A second nuclear test is by no means simply a propaganda ploy. Most experts believe that the 2006 test was flawed, producing an explosive yield well below even what the North's scientists had predicted. The scientific and military imperatives for a second test have been strong for over two years, and the potential data, experience and other advantage of further testing would be tremendous.
>
> What North Korea had lacked thus far is the political opportunity to test without fatally jeopardising its access to the six party talks and the legitimacy they provide. Despite the State Department's seemingly unbreakable second-term hold over President Bush, another test after 2008 might have just ended the talks.
>
> So far, the North Korea faces no such threat from Obama administration. Despite Pyongyang's aggression, Mr. Bosworth has reiterated that the US is "committed to dialogue" and is "obviously interested in returning to a negotiating table as soon as we can." This is precisely what the North wants: America in a conciliatory mode, eager to bargain just as Mr Bush was after the 2006 tests.

Out of these reasons, it also depicts North Korea's attempt to miniaturise the warhead so that it can be placed on missiles. It is to remember that North Korea is a grave nuclear threat because it shows how proliferation networks have helped the rogue states to acquire nuclear weapons. As North Korea is not quite economically and financially developed, the sophistication in command and control structure cannot be expected from it.

Iran's Nuclear and Missile Programmes: Threat to the US

Iran presents the case of state that wants to have a nuclear and missile capability despite international sanctions besides US efforts to stop it. Iran recogsnised the importance of having missiles in its war against Iraq. Iraq used missiles against Iran which forced it to surrender. Iran also learnt that missiles offer a cheap way to deter an enemy as compared to air force which is costly to maintain and train and it needs frequent upgrading. Therefore, Iran launched its missile programme by development of short range missiles like Fazeat, Fadjr, Zelzal as well as long range missiles like of Shahab series. Iranian officials have usually referred to missiles as intended for deterrence and claimed that they have reserved it for the purpose of deterrence and retaliation.[39] However, Iran also depicted that there missiles are also intended for the defence of fellow Muslims and Arabs. Rafsanjani declared that 'missiles are to be seen in purely defensive framework. We have no hostile intentions towards anyone...We will not use missiles to attack any country. He further added 'if the Arabs and Muslims still consider Israel as their real enemy, as in past, they must view Iran as their strategic backyard and must seek cooperation with us.'[40] As it can be seen that focus of Iran is now on Israel which is a close US ally. The US also fears that Iran, in the meantime, will develop the capability to hit the US with its missiles. This is one of the reasons behind the US decision to develop NMD and TMD in Europe.

The US is well aware of the threat coming from Iran's missile programme. The Rumsfled Commission has clearly mentioned that Iran will be able to develop ICBMs capability by next decade. In a speech at the National Defence University on October 23 2007, President Bush said:

> Our intelligence community assesses that, with continued foreign assistance, Iran could develop an ICBM capable of reaching the US and all of Europe before 2015, if it chooses to do so, and the international community does not take steps to prevent it, it is possible Iran could have this capability. And we may need to take it seriously – now.[41]

The latest surprise came in Feb 2009 when Iran successfully launched its satellite into the orbit so as to monitor earthquakes and to enhance communications. It is well known that the technology used in launching satellites into space can be utilised in developing ICBMs. Apart from this, it seems that Iran is developing a capability to hit targets in Europe and in the US. *The New York Times* recently reported, "The Iranian rocket had two stages. If it were carrying a small warhead, the Iranian missile could fire the weapon about 2,500 kilometers, or slightly more than 1,550 miles. The rocket could send a weapon to targets in Israel, but experts said that Iran had already possessed that capability. That falls short of the range of an intercontinental ballistic missile. For Iran to achieve that technical step, it would have to develop a more powerful basic rocket or move to upper stages — two goals that weapons experts think it is pursuing."[42] The newspaper article added, "Dr. Charles Ferguson of the Council on Foreign Relations said that Iran's technical advance, if translated into a military missile, might put a warhead within range of southern Europe, including Turkey, Greece, and Italy.'[43] It seems that Iran is trying to acquire the capability to hit the US and its allies so that it can achieve better terms at negotiation table. This satellite launch has raised eyebrows in the US and clearly reflects that its policy is not working against Iran.

Consequently, Iran is also trying to develop nuclear weapons and debate about Iran's nuclear weapon is not new. International Atomic Energy Agency (IAEA) admitted in 2009 that they have underestimated Iran's nuclear capability by one-third. According to IAEA, Iran possesses 2,227 Ibs of nuclear material which is sufficient for development of one atomic bomb.

However, it seems that the US itself is not very clear about the nuclear programme of Iran. NIE declared in 2007 'with high confidence' that Iran had halted its nuclear weapon programme four years earlier, in the autumn of 2003, and had not resumed work on nuclear weapons as of mid-2007.' The report also noted that Iranian entities were continuing to develop a range of technical capabilities that could be applied to producing nuclear weapons if a decision to do so was made.' This was highly criticised by Israel and it declared that they have 'clear and solid' intelligence agencies to prove that Iran is pursuing its nuclear weapons programme. The subsequent IAEA report also provided different scenario than what was predicted by NIE.[44] It stated that in 2008, Iran has rapidly improved the operation of its centrifuge cascades moving from 20 percent to 85 percent of claimed capacity. By 7 November 2008, Iran had produced 630kg of LEU and was adding 2Kg a day to this total figure. Under optimal conditions, LEU of 700-800 kg is needed to make approximately 20gk of 93 percent of HEU which is required to develop nuclear weapons. This means that Iran could possess necessary material which is needed for development of the nuclear weapons in coming time.[45]

The justification for Iran nuclear weapon is mainly due to the US threat. Like its missile programme, Iran started its nuclear weapon programme after Iran-Iraq war. However, after 9/11 the focus of Iran shifted from Iraq to the US and Israel. After 9/11, Iran cooperated with the US for destroying Taliban sanctuaries in Afghanistan. Iran provided humanitarian aid, tactical intelligence and other forms of cooperation to assist the US in the early stages of invasion. It was hoped by Iran that its help will be recognised. However, the US included Iran in the 'axis of evil' which has greatly upset Iran. After 9/11, Iran found itself to be encircled by the US. In south, there is a powerful US naval presence patrolling the Persian Gulf, augmented by an impressive string of US military bases in Kuwait, Bahrain, Qatar, Oman and UAE. In west, there are American troops in Iraq. To Iran's north, there is presence of the US troops in Azerbaijan as also in the central Asian republics. To Iran's east is the presence of the US and NATO troops in Afghanistan. This sense of encirclement added to Iran's fear of the US and encouraged it to develop nuclear weapons. Iran felt that if Iraq and Afghanistan emerge as a close ally policing the Gulf on the wishes of the US, Iran will stand marginalised and isolated.[46] Also, Israel has nuclear weapon which also encourages Iran to have its nuclear weapons for preserving its security.

The US and UNSC tried to put pressure on Iran for putting end to its nuclear weapons capability by putting sanctions, economic blockages and business withdrawal. From over 25 years, the US had imposed economic sanctions against Iran, armed Iraq to fight against Iran, supported various opposition groups in Iran, and taken various steps to isolate Iran from the international community including a campaign to keep Iran out of World Trade Organisation (WTO). The problem is that Russia and China are supporting mild sanctions against Iran as they have cordial relationship with Iran. Any move for strong action against Iran will be blocked by Russia and China who are also permanent members of UNSC. There was also a threat of military strikes against Iran, particularly by, Israel. Israel carried out bombing in Syria to destroy nuclear reactor which showed to Iran that Israel has both the will and the capability to destroy adversaries' nuclear weapon complex. However, repeated warnings of military strike and economic pressures did not stop Iran from development of nuclear weapons. The MIT based Jim Walsh said 'there is overwhelming evidence that the policy is not working. Moreover, the policy is unlikely to work within a timeframe that is relevant to the nuclear issues.' The former US Ambassador William Luers and Thomas Pickerin said that 'strategy of containment and sanctions, while irritating Iranian regime, will prove irrelevant to the country's nuclear programme.'[47]

The threats emerging from Iran's acquisition of nuclear weapons are as follows. The first is that Iran might use these weapons. However, Iran is not irrational as assumed by the US and it is well aware of the fact that this will invite national annihilation. But this has raised the fear of miscalculation. There is danger of accidental use and unintended miscalculation. The second fear is that Iran might give nuclear weapons to terrorist groups because it has contacts with Hamas and Hezbollah. The probability of such an action is low because it will act as a 'suicidal act' for Iran itself as it will be held responsible and accountable for use of nuclear weapons by non-state actors. However, it is possible that Iran nuclear weapons might fall in the hands of terrorist groups due to weak command control structure or in the event of domestic instability similar to Iranian revolution. Also, there is no doubt that nuclear weapons will give Iran the capability to threaten its neighbours and force them to give up their basing rights to the US.[48]

Therefore, the US felt that BMD and TMD would be an answer to Iran's nuclear and missile threat. However, what has been ignored is whether missile defence will actually deal with Iran's threat or will provide another chance to Iran to strengthen itself. The BMD will provide an opportunity to Iran for strengthening its relationship with Russia and China. After the conclusion of missile defence deal between the US and Czech Republic, Russia indicated its plans to sell SS 300 to Iran. Iran can also focus on non conventional weapons with credible delivery systems. This would provide a well structured deterrent and even a possible counter-measure to the US.[49] As Iran lacks technological and economical capacity to modernise its weapons, it may look towards Russia and China for help which will further enhance their relationship. As a result, the US must craft its missile defence policies very carefully.

Proliferation Nexus: China link and Further Cooperation Among Pakistan-Iran and North Korea

As depicted in Table 4.1, China is a part of problem which the US faces from Pakistan, North Korea and Iran. China's policy is to proliferate nuclear weapons technology or missile technology to the US states of concern so as to undermine the US security interests.

Table 4.1 : China's Nuclear and Missile Proliferation Matrix

	Risk Profile of Countries	PRC Strategic Interests	Nuclear Weapon Technology	Missile Technology
Pakistan	Danger: secondary proliferation is very high, Islamic takeover of the nuclear weapon state.	Counter India with indirect nuclear threat; undermine the US power in South Asia; seen as a nuclear benefactor to Sunni Muslim World; provide indirect aid to Saudi Arbia.	Direct Aid: sold vintage nuclear bomb designs in 1960s and 1980s; provided engineering and material assistance with nuclear manufacturing	Direct/indirect aid: sold Pakistan the means to make Shaheen 1 and Shaheen 2 solid fuel ballistic missiles, sold M-11 SRBMs; likely help with Babur cruise missiles; aided North Korean transfer of liquid fuel missiles.

Iran	Danger: secondary proliferation is high. It has provided cruise missile technology to Hezbollah.	Attain greater influence in Shitte Muslim world; increase energy relations; undermine US power in Middle East.	Direct/indirect aid: nuclear reprocessing technology; nuclear training; continued sale of precursors and dual use technologies that contribute to weapons program; possible access to PRC nuclear weapon design from Pakistan; diplomatic protection.	Direct/indirect aid: Missile technology and training; cruise missile manufacturing technology sale; some PRC technology in North Korean No Dong missiles, Asia Pacific Space Cooperation
North Korea	Danger: secondary proliferation is very high.	Keep Communist regime in power; undermine US influence, create indirect threat to Japan.	Direct/indirect aid: training of nuclear scientists in 1970s; allowed Pakistan to transfer uranium reprocessing technology in late 1990s, diplomatic protection	Direct/indirect aid: technical help with SCUD and No Dong missiles; aided staging on Taepodong; potential for solid fuel aid from Pakistan

Source: Fisher, Richer D (2008), *China's Military Modernisation: Building Regional and Global Reach*, pp 48-49, Praeger Security International: US

Therefore, China stands at the centre of the nuclear programme of Pakistan, North Korea and Iran. As mentioned earlier, these three states (Iran, North Korea and Pakistan) are cooperating with each other in the field of nuclear weapons and ballistic missiles.

Pakistan Link with North Korea

North Korea and Pakistan relationship dated back to Iran-Iraq war when North Korea and Pakistan came together for providing military assistance to Iran. This also proved to be a meeting ground of Pakistan and DPRK for working together on Iran's missile programme.[50] Later, Benzair Bhutoo approached North Korea for obtaining critical weapons. An agreement was quickly reached between the both countries and arms shipments from North Korea started arriving in Pakistan. After withdrawing from SEATO, Pakistan announced establishment of formal alliance with North Korea.[51] There is some information available in open literature that Pakistan obtains missiles from North Korea for exchange of the information on the nuclear weapon technology. The reason is that Pakistan needs missiles against India but lacks proper infrastructure and technological support for the development of missiles. As a result, Pakistan moves towards China who provided short range missiles. China was reluctant to sell long range missiles to Pakistan due to Missile Technology Control Regime (MTCR) commitments and the US pressure. Therefore, Pakistan moved towards North Korea for long range missiles.[52] *New York Times* reported in October 2002 that Pakistan is the source for North Korea gas centrifuge uranium enrichment programme. Such kind of trade begins in 1997 and continued till 2002.[53] In 1999, Indian customs officials detained a North Korea freighter, *Ku Wol-San*, at the Indian port city of Kandla which was carrying precision machine tools used for missile production. This machine was indeed for the construction of a missile production facility at Fatehjung in Pakistan.[54] In early 2000 South Korean intelligence agencies detected North Korean efforts to purchase components for a uranium enrichment programme whose technology bore similarities to the gas centrifuge enrichment process used by Pakistan's Khan Lab.[55]

Pakistan Link with Iran

Pakistan assisted Iran's nuclear programmes probably to ease tension of both states over the issue of Afghanistan and Sunni-Shia violence. By assisting Iran's nuclear weapons programme, Pakistan also wants to depict that its nuclear programme is directed against India only and Iran does not face any threat from it. In 1986-87 a secret agreement was signed between the two countries for their cooperation in the field of nuclear energy. This deal also made a provision that six Iranians should be trained at a nuclear science and technology facility in Islamabad and at another Nuclear Studies Institute. Iranian scientists might have received training at KRL. In 1988, Iranian scientists are suspected to receive training in Pakistan. Through 1995, AQ Khan is reported to have shipped over 2000 components and sub components for P-1 and later P-2 centrifuge to Iran.[56]

The hard evidence of Pakistan and Iran links came up in public domain when IAEA pressurised Iran and got access of its nuclear facilities. The advanced centrifuge programme that was discovered was clearly based on Urenco designs that were stolen by Dr Khan nearly three decades ago.[57]

North Korea-Iran Link

There is littlie evidence for North Korea-Iran link in nuclear weapon programme because North Korea's plutonium based nuclear weapons programme did not match with Iran's programme which stresses on uranium enrichment and fissile production. Both the countries cooperated with each other in the area of missile production.[58] North Korean assistance to Iran's missile programme was started during Iran-Iraq war when it supplied 200 Scud B missiles to Iran. After the war, both the countries entered into series of bilateral agreements under which DPRK assisted Iran with the industrial and technical infrastructure which help it to indigenously produce Scud B missiles.[59] Iran also helped fund and development of North Korea's *No-Dong 1* missile and in mid 1990s it purchased *No Dong* components. In 2005, *Sunday Telegraph* reported that North Korea provided Iran with *Taepo dong* production facilities, diagrams, operating instructions and liquid propellant through Russian intermediators. Again in 2004, National Council of Resistance of Iran (NCRI) claimed that North Korean scientists are helping Iran in development of two long range missiles called as Ghadr 101 and Ghadr 110. Therefore, North Korea and Iran cooperated with each other in development of missiles.[60]

The missile defence alone cannot work because of the proliferation groupings exist between these countries with China at its centre. In fact the US came up with the idea of BMD because it is unable to stop proliferation of missiles through MTCR. It is unfortunate that one of the P-5 members is associated with the proliferation activities. China could be an important player in curbing proliferation but it chooses to become one of the country involved in the proliferation activity. China is well capable to produce decoys and other counter-measures to the US BMD. It may be possible that China will also transfer these technologies to these three countries so as to make the US deterrence vulnerable and to harm its strategic interests. President Obama needs to deal with the proliferation problem along with the development of BMD so as to secure its deterrence.

Risks to the US

There are three main dangers emanating from the proliferation of nuclear weapons and delivery vehicles for the US. First, with the US forces deployed or sent overseas and the security forces of allies like Japan and Israel could be in danger. Second, the danger of nuclear weapons in the hands of the terrorist organisations which are mainly anti-US and could inflict unacceptable damage to the US mainland. Third, nuclear weapon could be smuggled into the US by unconventional means and could be used as a tool for blackmailing the US. It is because of these stated clearly dangers; the US wants to have NMD and TMD.

President Obama on BMD, Goal of Global Zero and Deterrence

Since his campaign, President Obama indicated that his policies are more towards nuclear non-proliferation and disarmament and is against unproovable systems of BMD. He has inherited the deteriorating relations with Russia on the issue of missile defence. As soon as he assumed office in Jan 2009, Russia threatened the US by saying that they would deploy missiles in Kalingarh in a response to interceptors and radars in Czech Republic and Poland. Soon after coming to office, President Obama mentioned that nuclear and missile developments by dangerous states like Iran and North Korea make it necessary for the US to have BMD. He further mentioned that BMD would be an important component for preserving the security of the US and European States but he is against the deployment of 'premature' BMD systems. He said that he will support BMD only if their technologies are proved by rigorous testing. He also indicated that he is well aware of the consequences by mentioning that 'such a plan would certainly produce highly undesirable implications on the entire international security regime with the American public bearing enormous financial costs for an experimental project whose capability remains far from able to guarantee Americans and its allies security from missile attacks.'[61]

After the missile tests of Iran and North Korea, President Obama mentioned 'As long as the threat from Iran persists, we will go forward with a missile defence system that is cost-effective and proven. If the Iranian threat is eliminated, we will have a stronger basis for security, and the driving force for missile defence construction in Europe will be removed.'[62] At the same time, the US Defence Secretary Robert Gates announced a radical overhaul of the DoD budget which saw a $1.4 billion cut to the Missile Defence Agency. In his speech, he proposed restructuring "the programme to focus on the rogue state and theatre missile threat" and to stabilise the number of interceptors in Alaska at their current level. Gates proposed cancelling of the second airborne laser (ABL) prototype aircraft. The ABL consists of a Boeing 747 modified to hold a giant chemical laser that is designed to shoot down missiles from a distance of 600 nautical miles. This has invited criticism from various analysts and the US senators like Sen. Joe Lieberman who mentioned that missile defence cuts will weaken the US and its allies. Representative Trent Franks, R-Ariz also mentioned , 'North Korea's launch of a long-range ballistic missile should be a clarion wake-up call to the whole world that this is not the time to diminish our missile-defence budget, as proposed by the Obama administration.'[63] However, the current administration does not want to limit the BMD programme but wants to balance investments in missile defence capabilities to deal with today's threats with investments in research and development to deal with next generation threats.

It is very clear that the US could not give up BMD programme due to large number of its supporters both in public and among governmental committees and offices. The final report released by the Congressional Committee on Strategic Posture has mentioned about the importance of BMD, as mentioned below:

> Ballistic Missile Defence capabilities can play a useful role in support of the basic objectives of deterrence, broadly defined, and damage limitation against limited threats. These capabilities may contribute to deterrence by raising doubts in a potential aggressor's mind about the prospects of success in attempts to coerce or attack others. They may contribute to assurance of allies, by increasing their protection and also reducing the risks that the United States

> would face in protecting them against a regional aggressor. Defences against short- and medium-range ballistic missiles are seen by some US allies as increasingly important to their security. Israel and Japan have demonstrated the value they ascribe to missile defence by joining in cooperative programmes with the United States. The Commission strongly supports continued missile defence cooperation with allies. It lowers costs for all and strengthens the potential for collective defence.[64]

However, President Obama is likely to change the policy of BMD due to various reasons. He is suspicious of the BMD because effectiveness of the system is yet to be proven despite the huge economic investment made by the George Bush administration. The new administration is particularly conscious about the missile defences because of huge dollars have been spent in Iraq and Afghanistan and global recession has been on its way. Also missile defence has strained the relationship between the US and Russia. Russia has in fact challenged the rationale behind European missile defence as no Iranian missile can reach near the US. In addition to this, the focus of President Obama is not on missile defence but more on global nuclear disarmament which can be achieved only if the major nuclear powers are taken into confidence. However, President Obama cannot scrap the entire missile defence programme because then it will be charged with bowing to the Russian pressures and this will degrade his image. Also, the US has invested lot of money for the development of BMD and they cannot afford to give up this plan.

President Obama declared change in its policy on Ballistic Missile Defence in September 2009. The Obama Administration has called upon the formulation of a four-phase missile defence programme, as mentioned below:

Phase One (in the 2011 time frame) – Deploy current and proven missile defence systems available in the next two years, including the sea-based Aegis Weapon System, the SM-3 interceptor (Block IA), and sensors such as the forward-based Army Navy/Transportable Radar Surveillance system (AN/TPY-2), to address regional ballistic missile threats to Europe and to the US deployed forces.

Phase Two (in the 2015 time frame) – After appropriate testing, deploy a more capable version of the SM-3 interceptor (Block IB) in both sea and land-based configurations, and more advanced sensors, to expand the defended area against short and medium-range missile threats. **Phase Three** (in the 2018 time frame) – After development and testing are complete, deploy the more advanced SM-3 Block IIA variant currently under development, to counter short, medium, and intermediate-range missile threats. **Phase Four** (in the 2020 time frame) – After development and testings are complete, deploy the SM-3 Block IIB to cope with the medium and intermediate-range missiles and the potential future ICBM threat to the United States in a better way.

The Obama administration gave away the plans to deploy missile defence systems in Czech Republic and Poland. There are various reasons for the formulation of such proposal. The main reason given by the Obama Administration was that Iran is developing short-range missiles more quickly as compared to long-range missiles, and therefore, there is need to shift the BMD policies. This proposal has been welcomed, as this is considered a more survivable system and offers a high degree of flexibility and adaptability as compared to the previous system. The reason being that it would allow the US to deploy potentially hundreds of SM-3 missiles to sites in the European and American ships in nearby waterways, and, thus, intercepting more than the planned 10 interceptors in Poland in previous programme. Secondly, this system offers the flexibility to adjust and technologically upgrade the architecture according to the current threat situation, thus leaving room for the deployment of long range interceptors.[65] Another reason for deployment for such system is that the previous systems were technically unproven to protect Poland and Czech Republic from the missile threats. As a result, the US was worsening its relationship with Russia without any concrete reasons. The Obama Administration hopes to receive support of Russia against Iran's nuclear programme by appeasing them from their changed missile defence programme. However, it is very doubtful that Russians will cooperate with Obama's administration in opposing tougher sanctions against Iran. The reason is that Russia has often said that it has benefited a lot by the continued tussle between western countries and Iran. The main reason for this is that, economically, Russia benifitted from missile and nuclear transfers to Iran. Medvedev said that Moscow would not engage in 'primitive compromises or exchanges'. Putin said that the US decision is only one step in improving relationship with Moscow and should be "followed up by the full cancellation of all restrictions on cooperation with Russia and high technology transfer to Russia as well as a boost to expand the [World Trade Organization] to embrace Russia, Belarus and Kazakhstan." Even after scrapping of Bush's BMD programme, Russia has maintained that it still preferred to have incentives to halt Iran's nuclear weapon program rather than sanctions. This position has been maintained by Russia even before Obama's shift in policy.[66] This shows lot more needs to be done for improvement of relationship with Russia.

The Non-Proliferation 2009 has also recommended some steps for the new administration and it seems that President Obama has followed them. A report has mentions that in order to minimise the embarrassment of selling unworkable systems to Poland and Czech Republic and to scuttle criticism that new administration has been bowing to Russian pressure, the President should undertake a sequence of scientific and budgetary reviews. President Obama has cut the missile defence budget on the pretext of budgetary reviews.[67] Second, President Obama is also trying to take Russia into confidence. A controversy was created regarding the US-Russia Iranian deal published by N*ew York Times*. It mentioned that President Obama has written a secret letter to Russia's President that he is willing to give up its plans of missile defence in Europe provided Russia cooperates with the US on the issue of eliminating nuclear and missile threat to the US.[68] However, later both the presidents denied existence of any such deal. President Obama has indicated in his statements that he is willing to give up missile defence programmes provided Iranian threat is eliminated. Defence Secretary Robert Gates also said during a NATO meeting in Poland that he'd "told the Russians a year ago that if there were no Iranian missile programme there would be no need for the missile sites...My hope is that now, with the new administration, the prospects for that kind of cooperation might have improved."[69] Both countries also agree on reduction of their missile programmes under SALT treaty. Therefore, the current policy of the US seems to be focus on global disarmament while taking Russia into confidence. However, whether the goal of global zero is idealistic or realistic is another debate. The question here is whether nuclear deterrence and nuclear abolition can go hand-in-hand? Tom Saucer has presented various schools under this debate, as mentioned below:

- The Nudists: They believe that nuclear elimination does not require nuclear deterrence. In fact, the goal of pursuing nuclear disarmament will be complex if the US continues to have BMD. In fact, they argue that ABM treaty must be resorted.
- The Monokinis: They touch the topic of missile defence more critically than the Nudists and are also critical of the deployment of BMD.
- The Coldies: They did not make mention of the missile defence but from their writings and speeches it is clear that they support the idea of BMD. Schultz, Kissinger & co stated in 2007 that 'Achieving the goal of world free of nuclear weapons will also require effective measures to impede or counter any nuclear related conduct that is potentially threatening to the security of states and peoples.' Their second op-ed concludes that nuclear elimination and missile defences are complementary. They also rejected 'unilateral missile defence' and stand for 'global ballistic missile defence' which will include Russia and other global powers.[70]

Given the present circumstances, the US is pursuing the 'unilateral missile defence' which has created the problem of 'security dilemma' paradox and is not contributing to the development of effective deterrence. Even if nuclear weapons are diminished in numbers, the strategic balance will be in the favour of the US. As a result, Russia and China will definitely feel suspicious of the US and will not cooperate with the US for achieving the aim of nuclear disarmament. The idea presented above about the global ballistic missile defence is more conducive to security. There were proposals like establishment of 'joint missile defence' and sharing of joint radar, but they did not work out due to political reasons. In the previous proposals, it was felt that countries are not comfortable with the idea of sharing technologies with each other. As Haralod Muller said, 'It would require the US to share and transfer cutting edge technologies with the countries its military elites still regards as rivals and potential adversaries. Over the last years, the American inclination to transfer sensitive technologies has diminished rather than grown, even within western alliance.'[71] Also, what is to be noted is that the US has taken initiative to have missile defence talk with Russia on several occasions. On the other hand, no such initiative has been taken to engage China. There is need to engage not only friendly powers, but also adversaries and this has so far been neglected by the US. As mentioned above, there is threat coming from the proliferation nexus of these three countries and China is at the centre of such proliferation nexus. This nexus needs to be broken down so as to secure the US from nuclear and missile threat. This is what has totally been ignored by the Bush administration. For this, there are various problems inherited in the bilateral relationships which the new President needs to deal first.

5

The US Relationship with China and Russia: Hope for the Future and BMD

Introduction

The US faces wide range of nuclear and missile threats mainly due the fact that it has failed to develop such strategies which would discourage states from turning against the US. The US has followed a muscular foreign policy and failed to realise that this would create more enemies than friends and thus will endanger its deterrence. In the past few years, the US has depicted itself as a state which is against the Muslim population by attacking Iraq and Afghanistan. As mentioned in the previous chapter, that the US attacks on Iraq and Afghanistan encouraged countries like Iran and North Korea to have their own nuclear weapons. It depicted itself as a country which wants to maintain its supremacy and uniploarity in the international affairs. This policy has turned China and Russia against the US and they began to proliferate nuclear weapons so as to counter the interests of the US. Without the help of Russia and China it would not have been possible for Iran and North korea to evade from international sanctions and to develop their own nuclear weapons and ballistic missiles. Therefore, it is important for the US to take China and Russia into confidence and to develop a good strategic relationship with them.

It is important to consider these two countries for following reasons. First, these two countries have history of mistrust and conflict with the US. Second, Russia and China are two main countries which hold permanent seat in the UNSC. Third, these two countries are the only states that have the capability to target the US by their nuclear weapons and ballistic missiles. Fourth, they have opposed the US BMD programme repeatedly and have given rise to the fear of offensive-defensive race of weapons. Fifth, Russia and China are the main countries responsible for proliferation of nuclear weapons technology and missiles to Pakistan, Iran and North Korea. The US regards Russia and China as a threat the way they regard the US a threat. Therefore, it is important to understand the relationships between these three countries.

United States and China

The relationship of China and the US is the relationship between the challenger and a hegemonic state. One of the hegemonic theories holds that war results from the rise and fall of hegemony. The challenging powers or the rising powers may seek to change the status quo of international order and the conflicts between the challenger and hegemon is unavoidable. Here, China is a rising power who is willing to take the place of the US in the international affairs. As Robert Gilpin said that a weaker challenger gets stronger while the dominant hegemonic power gets weaker. The cycle of power transition is complete when the challenger surpasses the power of the former hegemon.[1] China is going from such a transition of power by accelerating its economic growth and military modernisation. Soon after the cold war, China began to assume that there would be a multipolar world. As argued by Liu Xuecheng, a senior research fellow at the China Institute of International Relations, 'After the end of the cold war, the multipolar trend accelerated in the Asia Pacific region. A new system with five mutually balancing powers (China, the US, Japan, Russia and European Union) is gradually emerging. More specifically, this is a world of multiple power centers.'[2] Similarly, Hu Fan said 'Today's world is in the process of great historical transformation. The bipolar system has come to an end. Various forces are going through new process of reconfiguration of power. The world is moving in the direction of multipolarity.'[3] Soon, it was realised by China that the US is not going to decline in a near future. Wang Jisi said in 2004, 'Even though the emergence of a multipolar system and the decline of the US are inevitable in the long term, in the short term, it is difficult to identify signs that American power is on decline.

The US superiority is comprehensive, covering the entire spectrum of national power.'[4]

After realising this, China began to complain about the US hegemonic intentions. China began to point towards the various signals of the US hegemonism which include the large and growing US defence budget; a strong tendency to use coercive measures in US foreign policy; allegedly wanton disregard of international institutions and rules when deemed inconvenient, an aggressive liberal agenda in promoting Western values; endeavouring to restrict high technology information to China and other nations; alliances in Europe and Asia and determination to contain emerging powers notably China. China also accused the US regarding its attempt to dominate and control international organisations and regimes in order to legitimise US aggressive acts against other countries. When such efforts are met with resistance, the US disregards international bodies and norms in seeking ad hoc coalitions so as to pursue coercion and to use of military force in accordance with the US interests. China stresses on new security interests based on the five principles of peaceful coexistence as opposed to the 'power politics' and 'cold war thinking' of the US. On the other hand, the US regards the rise of China as a challenge to its international status.[5] All the official documents of the US like National Military Strategy, Quadrennial Defence Review, Nuclear Posture Review and National Strategy to Combat WMD mentioned that China is a potential threat to the US. The US is aware that China's war doctrine mentioned about defeating major powers by taking advantages of their military gaps. The US-China Economic and Security Review Report says, 'China aspires to be a major international power and the dominant power in Asia and China believes that the US is a declining power with important military vulnerabilities which can be exploited.'[6] The US wants to protect its power at all the costs and China wants to break this power so as to take seat of the US in the international affairs. This is the main cause of all conflict between the US and China.

In order to gain predominance, both the countries are competing with each other for their domination in Asia. The US growing domination in South East Asia is of particular concern to China due to the issue of Taiwan. China often stated that there is no need of the US military presence in South East Asia as the cold war conditions are not present. South East Asia is a very important region for the US and it has both economical and security significance. South East Asia is a home to almost 600 million people having GDP of greater than $ 880 million. South East Asia is the US fourth largest trading partner. It is very important from a strategic viewpoint because the region hosts some of the world's most critical sea lanes, most importantly the Strait of Malacca through which nearly a quarter of the world trade pass. This also includes 80 percent of East Asia's oil shipments.[7] Therefore, this region is important for both the US and China. The US currently maintains 100,000 forward deployed military forces in East Asia. The US has also strengthened its military alliance with Japan, South Korea and Australia and has also strengthened military cooperation with the other countries like Singapore, Malaysia and Philippines.[8] The table 5.1 explains the growing threat these countries felt from China which will explain reason behind their alliances with the US.

Table 5.1: China's Threat

Name of the Country	Possible threats emerging from China
Australia	Australia began to recognize 'China's threat' in 1990s which resulted into an agreement between Australia and Indonesia called as 'Agreement on Maintaining Security" which was spurred due to their different perception. Australia considers that China has potential to threaten and dominate region in the years to come. As a result, it chooses to hedge with the US. After 1996 Taiwan Strait incident, Australia was most vocal about its opposition to China and supported dispatch of the US aircraft carriers. Australia also mentioned that it would provide its support to the US and said that it will do everything to defend Taiwan.

Japan	During Cold War, Japan and China had good economic relations and Japan also opposed international sanctions on China after Tiananmen crisis. However, Japan became upset with China when it passed a territorial law which included the Senkakus. Later China tried to occupy Philippine and claimed Mischief Reef. China also began to behave provocatively over Taiwan. As a result, Japan chooses to align itself with the US. Japan clearly mentioned about 'China factor' as a main justification for its alliance with the US.
Philippines	Philippine began to recognise China's threat when China occupied Mischief Reed which was claimed by Philippine. This incident was also combined with other factors like increased Naval presence of China and fishermen in its claimed waters. This forced Philippine to have closer relationship with the US.
South Korea	South Korea is mainly upset with China due to its cooperation with North Korea in development of nuclear and missile technology. It felt need to have TMD systems and thus choose to be an ally of the US

The US has in fact taken advantage of China's regional conflicts with countries in East Asia and develops its own relations with these countries. China believes that such kind of presence of the US has one aim only, i.e., to counter China's growth. The further events like bombing of Chinese embassy in Belgrade by American B-2 bombers during Kosovo conflict, the Cox report accusations that China had stolen US nuclear and missile secrets and US continued military assistance to Taiwan has raised reasons for the China's dissatisfaction with the US. The US valued its relationship with Japan and considers it as an important mechanism for maintaining regional stability. Under the new security alliance arrangement, Japan agreed to provide necessary support and bases to the US troops which allow the US greater flexibility and assistance in facing the military conflicts.

According to New Guidelines, 'the US will help in any situation having a significant influence on Japan's peace and security.'[9] This has greatly upset China and made it suspicious about the US intentions.

Out of all these, Taiwan is the only country which can result into military conflict between the US and China. Chinese leader repeatedly stressed that Taiwan is an 'integral part of China' and often declared that 'reunification' with Taiwan is a 'sacred mission' for Chinese people. The PRC leaders always stressed that Taiwan is the first and foremost strategic target that must soon be subjected if China has to realise its goal of becoming Asia's dominant and unchallenged power. The conquest of Taiwan will shift geo-strategic power in the favor of China. It will provide PLA an 'unsinkable aircraft' carrier astride by the sea lanes which are vital for the economic security of South Korea, Japan, Australia, and India. The conquest of Taiwan will also result into immediate access to China of the deep waters for patrolling of nuclear ballistic missiles. Further more missiles and bombers will be placed in Taiwan which are much closer to the US forces in Guam and can monitor and interdict Japanese and the US forces in Japan.[10] The *Science of Military Strategy* explains further:

> The reunification of China's mainland and Taiwan not only is something that concerns China's national sovereignty and territorial integrity...but also will exert impact upon the survival and development of the Chinese nation and the rejuvenation of the great nation of China in this century...if Taiwan should be alienated from the mainland, not only our maritime defence system would lose its depth, opening a sea gateway to the outside forces, but also a large water area and rich reserves of ocean resources will fall into the hands of others. What's more, our line of foreign trade and transportation, which is vital to China's opening up and economic development will be exposed to the surveillance threats of separatist and enemy forces, and China will be forever locked on the west side of the first chain of islands of the West Pacific... "The independence of Taiwan" means the start of war...Although this is something undesirable for China, we must have to face it. The Taiwan issue is the largest and the last obstacle which we must conquer in the Chinese people's path to rejuvenation in the 21st century.[11]

On the other hand, the people of Taiwan stand for independence since the beginning. In Taiwan, there is a growing sense of separate identity which gave rise to the fear in the China's mind about Taiwan's independence.[12] In such case, China has mentioned the use of force. The problem is that if the US chooses not to act, it will loose its footing in East Asia and will earn misgivings of its allies in East Asia. The US also views this as an opportunity to deplete China's capacity.[13] The US passed Taiwan Relations Act (TRA) which has greatly upset China. The TRA has stated that a military conflict in the Taiwan Straits would have a profound impact on the peace and stability of the entire Western Pacific; therefore, defensive weapons must be sold to Taiwan in order to maintain Taiwan's relative ability to ward off and defend itself against a large military attack by China.[14] The Congress stated that the enactment of this act is necessary:

> To make clear that the US decision to establish diplomatic relations with the People's Republic of China rests upon the expectation that the future of Taiwan will be determined by peaceful means;
> To consider any effort to determine the future of Taiwan by other than peaceful means, including boycotts or embargoes, a threat to the peace and security of the Western Pacific area and of grave concern to the US.[15]

The transfer of weapons to Taiwan by the US upset China. China feels that this will embolden Taiwan and will make its reunification with China problematic. China feels that such an act of the US also makes the peaceful resolution of dispute difficult. China has mentioned several circumstances in which it could use force against Taiwan. It includes formal declaration of independence, an indefinite delay in settlement of the issue, internal unrest on the island and foreign intervention which include establishment of foreign alliance or stationing of foreign forces.[16]

Taiwan is also an issue over which the US and China could have nuclear conflict. Although, China has no first use policy, it has mentioned that no such policy is applicable in case of Taiwan. As mentioned by Sha Zukang, 'the Chinese promise of 'no first use' is not applicable to Taiwan as Taiwan is a national territory of China.'[17] A source from Taiwan stress:

> If Taiwan attempts to become independent and there is intervention from abroad, China would not be reluctant to use tactical nuclear weapons for the sake of defending 'territorial integrity.' The Chinese journal *Guo Fang Bao* (National Defence) has continuously recommended use of nuclear weapons against Taiwan. If the PLA deems it necessary to attack Taiwan by military means, its past commitment on the basic strategy of 'no first use' or 'not using nuclear weapons or threatening to use nuclear weapons against non-nuclear states' would thus be modified...This should be the most threatening action at the psychological level as well as on our political, economic and military facilities.[18]

China has not hesitated to mention that it could use nuclear weapons even against the US, if it intervenes in the issue. In 1996, when the US sent two aircraft carriers in the region, General Xiong Guangkai, deputy chief of staff of the PLA, explicitly asked whether the US really want to protect Taiwan in exchange of loss of Loss Angles.[19] In May 2000, China mentioned that if the US continues military help to Taiwan, it will not hesitate in using nuclear weapons even if it invites disastrous retaliation by the US.[20] The US has also mentioned that it will not hesitate to use limited nuclear weapons in case of Taiwan conflict.[21] Beside this, China often complains of the growing US influence in the world after 9/11 attacks and in the areas surrounding China. During the war against terrorism, US established temporary military presence in Central Asian nations on china's western border.[22]

Beside Taiwan, China has lot of unresolved maritime and territorial disputes, including claims to the Spartle Islands, disputes with Japan over the Senkaku/Diaoyu Islands and the East China Sea and disputes with Vietnam over Paracel Islands. One thing worth taking note is that these areas have considerable natural gas and possible oil resources which are also important to the US. China's increasing population with increasing demand for energy to fuel its economic growth has raised concerns that China might defend its maritime claims more aggressively and seek to develop a 'blue water navy' to protect its sea limes of communications to the Middle East.[23] China's willingness to control South China sea was apparent when its SSBNs were detected in Hainan Islands in 2008 by satellite pictures. It becomes clear that

Hainan Islands would host some of the most important naval bases. In such a situation, it is possible that the Paracel and Sprately bases will eventually serve as links in a chain of sensors to secure the South China Sea as a "bastion" for PLAN SSBN patrols. There is a possibility that China's tolerance to US and Japanese naval activities in this region may diminish.[24]

It is this struggle of the primacy which has given rise to the differences between the US and China on the issue of BMD. Under such conditions, the adversary will often feel that the US BMD programme is targeted against it. It is under this prism that China sees the US programme of NMD and TMD. China regards it as another move by the US to establish sphere of its hegemonic power in world. By giving TMD to Japan and Taiwan, the US is strengthening its military relationship with them which will be harmful for its strategic interests. China has also stated that sale of TMD to Taiwan will embolden Taiwan's independence movement. China believes that the US will interfere in the issue of Taiwan against the interests of China and China will be unable to retaliate due to the US BMD. China also fears that in case it uses force against Taiwan, the US will carry out limited first strike against it. Again, China will be unable to retaliate with its left over nuclear arsenal as the BMD system will intercept the Chinese missiles carrying WMD.

Therefore, it is the relations between the two countries which need to be considered first. Both the countries need to recognise common threats and interests. The 9/11 presented one of such opportunity to both the countries. The following Chinese commentary is illustrative of this shift:

> With the dawning of the 21st century, especially considering the 9/11 attack, the world entered a new post-cold war age. International relations in this age will perhaps be featured by the mixture of cooperation and confrontation but with cooperation as the main theme. Although missile defence will affect the strategic balance among the big powers, they can try to find out and make various compromises and reach a new balance for they need cooperation more than they need confrontation. So the problems caused by missile defence can be solved more easily than at any other time under the new international circumstances...Another important

factor is that there does exist the threat of missile proliferation and one cannot exclude the possibility of future nuclear weapon attack by terrorists. So the US is justified in inventing and deploying limited missile defence. The world perhaps will come to the new terms and consensus with the US on this over time.[25]

However, the events show different things. China is still busy in modernisation of its nuclear weapons and delivery vehicles. China has conducted anti-satellite weapon test in 2007 which could pose a threat to the US. As mentioned above, satellite images show SSBNs in Hainan Islands which are again considered as a Chinese response to the US BMD.

Russia and the US: Cold War is Still On?

After the end of Cold war and disintegration of Soviet Union, it was felt that the relationship between Soviet Union and US will transform drastically and old enmity between them will be removed. In Sept 1990, President George HW Bush echoed Wilosian sentiments of 'New World Order' and believed that the end of cold war will give rise to new and positive perceptions about international relations and security cooperation. In his words:

> As you know, I've just returned from a very productive meeting with Soviet President Gorbachev. And I am pleased that we are working together to build a new relationship. In Helinski, our joint statement affirmed to the world our shared resolve to counter Iraq's threat to peace. Let me quote 'We are united in the belief that Iraq aggression must not be tolerated. No peaceful international order is possible if large states can devour their small neighbours." Clearly, no longer can a dictator count on East-West confrontation to stymie concerted UN action against aggression. A new partnership of nations has begun.[26]

The relationship between the two countries moved in a positive direction like establishment of Cooperative Threat initiative (CTR) and other arms control. However, the issue of NATO enlargement has always haunted the relationship of both the countries. After the end of cold war, there were various theories and viewpoints which talked about the end of NATO alliance as Warsaw pact does not exist. David Calleo rejected the viability of NATO alliance as structured at that time. Similarly, Ronald Steel spoke of 'NATO last mission.' John Mearsheimer argued in 1990 that end of Soviet threat might dictate the end of an alliance. He said 'Take away that offensive threat and US is likely to abandon the continent whereupon the defensive alliance that is headed for 40 years might disintegrate.'[27] This did not happen and NATO in fact chooses the mission of enlargement. The relationship of Russia and the US are affected directly by NATO mission of its enlargement in Europe because US has headed and dominated NATO since its formation. Other scholars have also mentioned the importance of NATO as John Ikenberry said, "Institutions like NATO have helped to do this in an effective way, going back to the post World War II European dictum that NATO was to keep the Soviets out, US in and Germany down.'[28] This further strengthens the Russian viewpoint that the US is still keeping the NATO so as to prevent it from growing.

Valentin Kuin felt that even after the cold war is officially ended the situation that obtains between USA and Russia is that of cold peace due to policies of the US. He has written:

> Obviously, two factors- the plans of further expansion of NATO in which the US holds the leading position, and the US plans to deploy a national anti-missile defence (NMD) system will have the most tangible influence on the development of Russia-US relations in the next few years. Russia categorically disagreed with NATO's expansion, since it holds the view that this threatens its national security and actually reanimates the situation of the cold war era when the European Continent was divided into two confronting camps. Moscow also rejects the alliance's claims to the role of an organisation which must serve as the pivot of the process of the setting up a new European security. Only the organisation for security and cooperation in Europe can play such a role. The Russian leadership also toughly opposes the Washington plans to create NMD system. The Kermlin has stated that creation of a missile shield over America would inevitably result in undermining of the ABM treaty of 1971-72 and hence in the destruction of the entire system of global security which was built through the past

> few decades, since the Russians will be forced to make adequate changes in response to the American ABM systems. Such plans will hardly help Russian-US relations get out of the not simple period of 'cold peace' in which they, at Washington's will, have been for the past several years.[29]

Here, The Russian writer has mentioned two factors responsible for the strained relationship with the US, i.e., NATO enlargement and BMD systems. However, both reasons are linked to each other. As mentioned in previous chapter also, Russia can penetrate the missile defence system of the US and the radars which will be deployed in Europe. The main reason of Russia's objection is that it regards it as a symbol of the NATO's further expansion in Europe which will undermine its national interests. This also means coming together of Europe and the US which is also not accepted by Russia. This factor has always strained relationship of Russia and US because NATO was made and dominated by the US. Russian opposition is, in fact, based on the fact that NATO was established to counter Warsaw Pact during cold war period which was originally headed by Russia. Russia feels that as there is no Warsaw Pact, there should be no presence of NATO. This different perceptions of the US and Russia have always stained their relationship.

The reason for Russia's opposition to NATO can be divided into the particular reasons and general reasons. The particular set of reasons relate to the strongly held belief that NATO and the West have made serious promises about NATO future and its intended involvement to bring in Russia that has simply been renegade upon. This led to Russia's distrustfulness towards NATO alliance. The more general reason is Russia's own concern about its security. Russia feels that enlargement of NATO is a plan of the US to undermine Russia's capability.[30]

Another problem is that Russia was never integrated properly in NATO despite of several efforts. In 1992-93, Russian foreign minister Andrei Kozgrev formulated a concept of 'Common Europe Home.' For Russia, it means rapid and full integration into European institution. Russia assumed that it will be fully integrated into a European Collective Security system with NATO as an important element. On the other hand, the US and west have different opinion of Common

Europe Home. For them, it means freedom from Central European states and disappearance of threat coming from Russia. As a result, Moscow came to the conclusion that NATO enlargement could be prevented if NATO members are convinced that there is no threat coming from Russia. For a manifestation of this, Russia formed PFP on 1994 but this does not stop NATO from having enlargement .In 1996-97, NATO reaffirmed its commitment for enlargement. Russia raised anti-NATO rhetoric and terminated its participation from PFP.[31]

Again to pacify Russia, western countries invited Russia to join NATO in an established special body called as the Permanent Joint Council. It was said that Russia will be consulted, whenever appropriate, in joint decision making and other joint action. Unlike PFP, it symbolised equal role played by Russia in NATO discussion rather than playing the role of a junior partner. However, soon the differences emerged and Russia described the council as a talking shop with no real decision making power.[32]

After Cold War, Russia made its voice against NATO expansion in Europe in 1993 when Yeltsin paid visit to Warsaw. Yeltsin complained that enlargement of NATO in Europe would be illegal under the terms of international deal that led to German unification in 1990s. Kosovo was the watershed movement as the US led forces intervened in Kosovo in the name of humanitarian intervention. It was the first conflict that emerged after the end of cold war where NATO forces and Russian side came to confront against each other. Russia learned that even through nuclear deterrence continues to work for Russia against NATO, there is possibility that Russia and NATO would came together on opposite side in regional conflicts.[33]

From the last few years, the relationship of Russia with the US deteriorated over the issue of NATO enlargement. In March 2004, Bulgaria, Estonia, Latvia, Lithuania, Romania, Slovakia and Slovenia become members of NATO which promoted large Russian protests, especially against admission of Baltic countries. It was followed by Orange Revolution in Ukraine which further brought down the relationship between the US and Russia. Russia blamed the US for engineering such upheavels and added that these colour revolution are meant to affect the Russia's sovereignty. Russia also tried to intervene heavily in Ukraine Presidential elections so as to take direct advantage of election results. A united west protested such intervention by Russia and Kremlin considered it as US led conspiracy against Russian influence in its close proximity. In his frustration, President Putin said in 2005, 'the collapse of the Soviet Union was the biggest geopolitical disaster of the century.' This statement was regarded as the sign of Russia's aggressive stance against the west.[34]

In 2008, Ukraine and Georgia applied for membership action plans to NATO. Russia protested such measure and threatened to ward off Ukraine's joining NATO, 'This may bring into question Ukraine's existence as a sovereign state.' It was soon followed by the war in Georgia which confirmed that even after 20 years, after the fall of the Berlin Wall and the end of cold war, Russia has not successfully integrated into European borders.[35] The main aim of this war was to restore Russian influence in its neighbourhood and to roll back the American and European presence in Eurasia. The goals of such a war were very much clear: restoration of Russia's sphere of influence or 'privileged interests.' President Medvev himself pointed out in the aftermath of the war that there should be an end to NATO's eastward expansion and recognition on the part of the West that Russia is a great power and has to be treated as an equal power. It was also said that this war has put the relationship between the US and Russia back into to the cold war period.[36]

The NATO's enlargement and increasing emphasis on out of area cooperation have only reinforced the perception that NATO alliance is still militarily in essence, anti Russian in its purpose and potentially threatening overall. Russians are convinced that if NATO remains the dominant body for European decision making on security matters, their country will find itself isolated. Instead, Russia wants to develop multilateral institutions for maintaining peace and security like Organisation for Security and Cooperation in Europe (OSCE) and Commonwealth of Independence (CIS). For Russia, NATO is not an organisation that takes decisions objectively on the ways of maintenance of peace and security in a conflict situation. Russia repeatedly argues that with the dissolution of Warsaw Pact and post cold war period, NATO had lost its *raison d'être*. The logic for the existence of NATO becomes more questionable with the disintegration of the Soviet Union. However, the leadership of the US was not interested in dissolving NATO because it believed in the perpetuity of NATO would not only guarantee European Security but could also provide internal, political and economic stability.[37]

It is under this prism that Russia views the US decision to deploy interceptors and radars in Europe. With NATO Expansion in Europe, Russia is the only country which is left over from this arrangement. Under such conditions, the only possible enemy implied by the alliance's "defensive" is considered to be Russia. Every defence policy statement from Central Europe makes perfectly clear that defence against Russia is the main *raison d'être* of NATO. Russia does not want itself to be left alone. This has been reflected by the Putin proposal of having joint cooperation on missile defence with the US in July 2007. Russian President proposed to have modernisation of the radar in Azerbaijan and missile warning and detection system in Southern Russia. He has also recommended having 'an open ABM information exchange centre in a European capital city, for instance, Brussels.' This reflects Putin's wish to be a part of NATO Europe and the US. However, the proposal was rejected by the US. Rejection of this proposal further raised Russian concerns. Russia felt that even after end of cold war, it is not regarded as a partner in the European Security area but as a potential threat against which the US and Europe are building alliance. Russia maintains that since it has given away Warsaw arrangement after the end of cold war then why west cannot give up NATO. Russia maintains that at least west should give up the policy of NATO expansion in Europe.

Russia-China Strategic Alliance: Countering the US?

Li Peng said on 25th Feb 1994 that, "China and Russia share long borders which should be peaceful and friendly ones...The economies of the two countries are strongly complement and their economic and trade relations have experienced rapid development in recent years...Both China and Russia should proceed from reality to explore new ways for further cooperation."[38] Besides this, there are various other common interests that bring both the countries closer to each other. Both nations stand against the unilateralism and promote multilateralism. Both states are opposed to the practise of strong bullying the small power. Both countries are against power politics which allows one country alone having the final say on international issues and frequently use of force. Both states stressed on the importance of UNSC to establish international order and norms of security. Both countries also feel that the face of international set up is badly unbalanced with one superpower having the final say and all the domination.[39] General Leonid Ivas, head of Russian Defence Ministry International Cooperation Department claimed that China is Russia's "ideological ally' with common interest in rejecting "military diktat in international relations" and two are now coordinating their defence doctrines and strategic joint military exercise. He further notes that in the wake of attack on Bosnia, "NATO is being turned into a global organisation and they see no alternative but to draw together to oppose US hegemonic intervention and protested American bombing campaigns in Iraq and Yugoslavia."[40] Russia and China also signed Treaty of Friendship and Cooperation at Shanghai in 2001. The leaders of Russia and China tried to assert before the US that this treaty does not mean to threaten any third party. However, this is only a diplomatic declaration. The China's policy is to find and engage "third power" in the obvious confrontation between the two parties.[41]

There are other reasons also for the development of alliance between Russia and China. After 9/11 attacks, Russia helped the US in the war against Afghanistan. Russia allowed the US military presence at its own backyard and also provided all necessary information which they gathered since their decade long war in Afghanistan. Russia used this as an opportunity to improve its relations with the US. After Russian consent for the US military troops in Central Asia, Uzbekistan emerged as a main strategic partner of the US and received lot of economic aid from the US. This did upset both Russia and China.[42] As a result, both countries built SCO to win the confidence of the Central Asian states.

Both the countries also created Shanghai Cooperation Organisation (SCO) in 2001 so as to counter-balance the US. The organisation was set to resolve border disputes, to struggle against terrorism and illegal drug trafficking in Central Asia and to maintain regional security. The problem for the US is that SCO could create China-Russia-Iran axis which will be harmful to the US. It may later convert into large scale military alliance by the countries who are dissatisfied with the current order of international relations.[43] However, there are some important provisions which deserve consideration. These are principle of not targeting nuclear weapons against the other (art 2) and adhering to the "one China" stance. (art 5). This treaty maintains that each country should refrain from developing and conducting any foreign and defence policy that would jeopardise the interests of the other. Specifically, Russia and China will not enter into any alliance that could threaten or undermine the sovereignty, security and territorial integrity of other signatory. (art 8). It also mentioned that if one of the parties faces a threat of aggression, the two countries should immediately consult each other 'with the aim of removing the threat.' (art 9).[44]

This treaty does represent strengthening of relations between two countries. There are the following advances made in the relationship between Russia and China, besides conclusion of the treaty of friendship:

- Both the leaders of China and Russia have established effective mechanism of summit meetings. In addition to regular meetings held between the Presidents, the PM and Cabinet Ministers of the two governments, the two countries have also started regular meetings at personal level. President Jiang Zemin and Hu Jintao have built personal relationship with President Yeltsin and President Putin which is of great significance.
- Both countries have resolved their historical problems that strained their relationship once. They have solved their border disputes.
- Both countries have conducted cooperation in international area. When President Jiang visited Russia in 1997, both the countries signed Joint Statement on Multipolarisation in the world for establishment of New International Order. They showed their consensus on the opposition to group politics and strengthening UN role. Both have demonstrated identical views on broad range of issues like Kosovo crisis, BMD, ABMT, Arab Israeli conflict, US war on Iraq, Afghanistan, nuclear crisis in Korean Peninsula, Iran and establishment of Nuclear Free Zone in Central Asia.
- The security cooperation between the two countries has been steadily developing and both the countries are continuously holding joint military exercises.[45] A joint military exercise was held in August 2005 as a part of "Peace Mission-2005" which was really very significant in development of Russia-China military relationship and became a background of "Peace Mission 2007" joint military organisation held in 2007 at Russia.

Both the countries have also cooperated with each other in the sphere of armaments. According to Stockholm International Peace Research Institute (SIPRI), China spent almost $ 3 billion on armaments in 2000. According to Western Experts, the major share of those expenses accounted for deliveries of naval vessels and aircraft technologies from Russia. According to the US Ministry of Defence, China's annual expenses on Russian military equipment and technology have increased from $ 1.2 billion in 1990s to $ 2.3 billion in 1999-2003. Presently, about 45 percent of Russian armament and military equipment exports account for China.[46]

This is clear that both the countries are dissatisfied with the international order and try to build an alliance which can be beneficial to the interest of both the countries. It is to be noted that although Russia and China will be dependent on West for economical reasons, they will choose to balance the US and not to bandwagon. The weaker states prefer to bandwagon while stronger states prefer to have alliances. Weak states are well aware that they could not change the outcome of the hegemonic power while strong states can turn the losing coalition into a winning one. Therefore, they promote balancing rather than taking side of the hegemonic power. States will bandwagon when their allies are less in number or totally unavailable.[47] These two reasons are not applicable in case of Russia and China. Both the states are not 'weak states.' After the disintegration, Russia was in a bad shape. However, Putin administration has used oil and energy sector to provide new heights to the Russian economy. On the other hand, China is also developing at a fast pace. Therefore, both the countries will try to balance the US if they continue to have the US policies as opposed to there interest. Both the countries are also not alone while forming alliance. This has been manifested by the formation of SCO. Also, China and Russia have helped North Korea and Iran so as to win their confidence and to use their anti-US feelings in their own interest.

Understanding Trilateral Relations

Before we go further, it is important to understand the trilateral relationship between the two countries and to analyse what shape it will take up in the coming decades. According to Gerald Segal and Lowell Dittmer, the concept of the 'strategic triangle' have been applied to the relationship among the US, Soviet Union and China.[48]

Robert S. Ross also mentioned that their triangular relationships were distinguished by a significant degree of strategic interdependence and security of each state was significantly shaped by the nature of the relationship between the two countries.[49]

Huei Ming Mao has explained the theory of strategic triangle with simplicity. According to the theory of strategic triangle, these relationships can be characterised as 'state of amity (positive)' and 'state of enimity' (negative). There can be triple amicable relationship, two bilateral amicable relationships with two enmities or triple enmities. Henry Kissinger has mentioned that the most important role in triangular relationship is that of 'pivot' who maintains amity with the two players (wings) while pitting them against each other. The pivot may develop a delicate balance between its relations with the two 'wings' so as to derive the maximum benefit. The negative relationship will also exclude the possibility of formation of alliance between the two countries against pivot. (Figure 1) In 1970s, the US occupied the position of pivot and there were tensions between the relationship of the USSR and China. Henry Kissinger said, "the hostility between China and the Soviet Union served our purposes best if we maintained closer relations with each side than they did with each other."[50]

Figure 5.1: Pivot and Wings

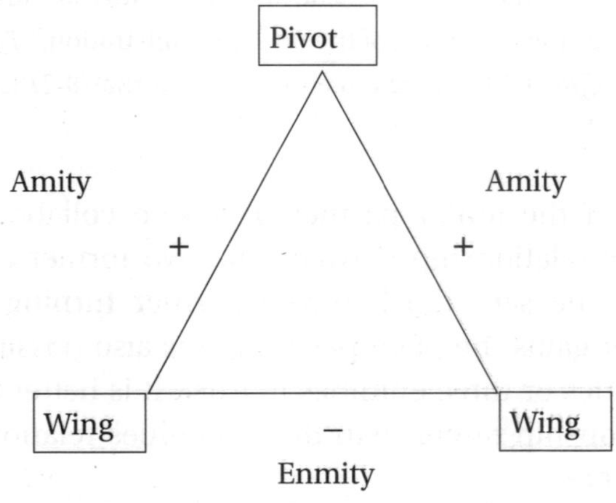

Source: Huei-Ming Mao (2003), "The US-China-Russia Strategic Triangle Relationship Since the beginning of the Bush Administration," *Tamkang Journal of International Affais,* URL: www2.tku.edu.tw/~ti/Journal/8-3/834.pdf, Assessed on 10 May 2009.

In another scenario, if the endogenous elements (i.e the factors exclusively related to the two actors concerned and not to third part) dictate enmity between two players, the best role for either one of them would be to develop positive relationship with the third party. In such a triangle, one find two partners collaborating with each other.[51] (Figure 5.2)

Figure 5.2: Outcast and Partners

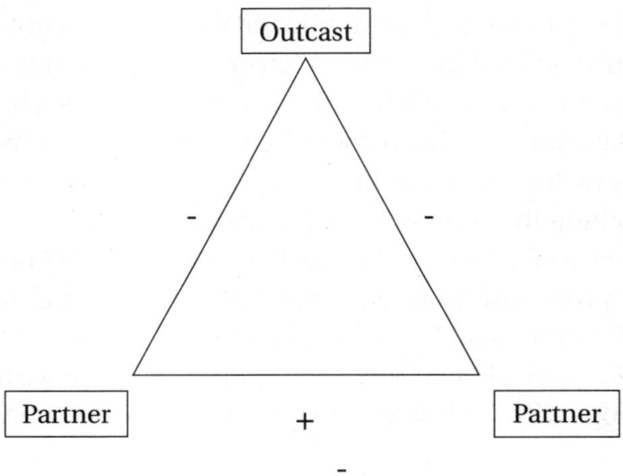

Source: Huei-Ming Mao (2003), "The US-China-Russia Strategic Triangle Relationship-Since the beginning of the Bush Administration," *Tamkang Journal of International Affais,* URL: www2.tku.edu.tw/~ti/Journal/8-3/834.pdf, Assessed on 10 May 2009.

However, if the junior partner begins to collaborate with the adversary, the relationship between the two former allies remains positive and one sees the betrayed partner turning into a wing while betrayer gains the pivot position. It is also possible that there are three amities or three enmities to exist. It is better to have three amities relationship rather than three enmities relationship for the international era.[52]

Lowell Dittmer analysed the concept of strategic triangle in his article in *World Politics* entitled, 'The Strategic Triangle: An elementary Game-Theoretical Analysis.' He described strategic triangle as the sort of transnational game between three players. He mentioned about three types of systematic patterns of relationships: *meanage a trios* which consist of symmetrical amities among all three players; romantic triangle which consists of amity between one pivot player and two wing players but enmity between two wing players and the stable marriage which consists of amity between two of the players and enmity between each and third.[353]

He further explains the complexities involved in each set of relationship. In *meanage a trio* kind of relationship, there is problem of international diplomacy- 'I may be able to ascertain the motives and goals of my immediate negotiating partner, but I can never be sure whether the relationship between second and third parties is in my interest- unless it is visibly negative.' In the 'romantic triangle' kind of relationship, there is deep sense of insecurity. Each wing player is dependent on pivot and is unable to form positive relationship with each other. In such circumstances, each may feel vulnerable to being excluded from a hostile bilateral coalition. In 'stable marriage' it is in the interest of the excluded party to form amity with one of the others and thereby escape further ostracism. However, it is not easy to form such kind of relationship.[54]

He has further explained that the US will play one of the roles out of these three positions. He listed it in an inverse order: outside player in someone else's stable marriage, senior partner in a stable marriage and pivot in a romantic triangle.

Outside Position in Stable Marriage: In such circumstances, player has to cope up with the enmities of other two players. This position requires greater economic self reliance and heavy investment in armaments in order to deter the combined military power of two states, in case they come together. A rational strategy is to build a cluster of patron clients or alliance with the smaller states so as to counter combined strength of both states.

Senior Partnership in a stable marriage: It offers more advantages than the first mentioned position. However, there is risk of cheating or a double cross. A player has to retain the loyalty of its partner by ensuring there is no asymmetry in the relationship.

Pivot Position in a romantic triangle: This is described as a most advantageous position. However, there do have a possibility of uncertainty. The pivot has to maintain the positive relationship with wings and at the same time has to look towards the relationship between the two wings. Each wing has to be cautious of the possibility that other may marry the pivot and thereby will exclude it. However, the problem is that it is very difficult to handle both the wing players as each will have different interests, different bargaining strategies, different capabilities and different offers that will be more or less appealing.[55]

If we analyse, there is always one or other kind of triangular relationship existed between the three countries. As mentioned above, during cold war the US had acquired the role of the pivot. After cold war and present circumstance, it seems that there exist 'stable marriage' between Russia and China while the US stands apart. (Figure below)

Figure 5.3: Present Triangular Relationshp

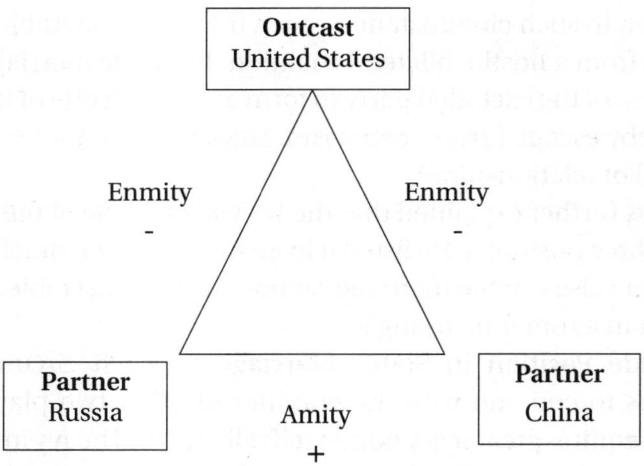

Such kind of relationship presently is not very much visible due to the economic dependence of Russia and China on the US. However, it should not be forgotten that China and Russia are modernising their nuclear structure by keeping the US in mind. Both have jointly collaborated to oppose the US programme of deployment of BMD. Both the countries have also collaborated with each other so as to provide diplomatic shield to Iran and North Korea so as to prevent them from rigorous sanctions of the UNSC. Therefore, such type of relationship is not helpful to the US. Also, it is not possible to have role of pivot which means to maintain positive relationships with both the countries while increasing tensions between them. Russia and China have solved their border issues which were source of contention between them. Also both have same ideologies and it is difficult to create tension between them. Even if tension is created, it will lead to arms race and further proliferation which will be harmful for the US interests. It would be very difficult for the US to keep good relations between them while creating tensions between them. Therefore, presently it is in the US interest to develop triangular amity to preserve its security, to achieve goal of non proliferation and to have globalised BMD systems as discussed above. Even if it is not possible to have globalise BMD systems, the three states should come together to neutralise the threat coming from growing nuclear and missile arsenals. The problem of symmetric amity (as mentioned below) can be solved by having CBMs in place and by having transparency in development of relationship.

The main problem of both the countries is misinterpretation of each other's intentions. As mentioned by 'offensive realists' like John Mearsheimer that since there is no way to know the intentions that drive other states, the only thing a rational state can do is to build up its military capabilities and prepare for the worst.[56] In order to solve such a problem, there is need to establish hot lines between the two countries and have CBMs which will give some insight vis-a-vis relations.

The US should stop labeling 'China' as a threat and China should stop signalling that it is a threat. If China seriously wants to have a permanent solution to the US BMD programme, it should stop its imperialist behavior in the region which is manifested by China's claims over the territory of the other countries in Asia. Also, China has always undermined the interests of the US by its proliferation activities and presently by shielding countries like North Korea and Iran under the veil of its diplomacy. Since North Korea carried out its nuclear weapon test, China has played active role in six party talks. Even before the nuclear test, China has formed Leading Group on North Korean Crisis which was in frequent contacts with North Korea 'at all levels.' However, despite of all warnings and pressure, China failed to stop North Korea's nuclear test. The reason was that North Korea was not ready to give up its core national interests. Even after resumption of Six Party Talks, North Korea is not ready to give up its nuclear weapons and missile programmes. Given the economic relationship between

China and North Korea, China could have pressurised North Korea to give up its nuclear and missile programmes. China-North Korea trade increased by 16.2 percent (US$1.97 billion) in 2007 and accounted for 67 percent of Pyongyang's total external trade. China supplies 80 percent of the state's consumer goods and 87 percent of its crude oil. Given this, China could have exercised economic pressure on North Korea to give up its nuclear and missile programmes.

Therefore, if China wants to change the US policies on BMD, it has to seriously change its own policies on proliferation. China has always used policy of proliferation to impede interests of the US. China should take leading and active role in Asia for halting nuclear and missile ambitions of rogue and unstable states and should take immediate steps to neturalise these threats. This will also result into an improved bilateral relationship between the two countries which can also result into a 'global missile defence,.'

If China seriously engages these countries towards disarmament, especially North Korea, it would remove one of the most significant arguments of the US for the deployment of BMD. A Chinese effort to retard or terminate North Korea's development of nuclear weapons will strengthen China-US talks and will allow China to argue that Missile Defence has no role in East Asia.

Obama administration inherited this mess of complex relationship and he promised to change the existing conditions. Vice President Joseph Biden said on 7 Feb 2009, 'It is time to press the reset button and to revise the many areas where we can and should work .The US and Russia can disagree and still work together where our interests could collide.' The problem is that the previous US administrations failed to clearly articulate the policy for Russia. The Obama administration has to clearly spell out the policy for Russia which should contain at least two policies: to give up idea of Expansion of NATO or to integrate Russia as an equal partner in NATO. As mentioned that China and Russia could play an active part in removal of nuclear and missile threat coming from Iran and North Korea. If Russia is absorbed in NATO as an equal partner, it will definitely help the US in removal of these threats.

Therefore, the problem coming from BMD is actually embedded in the relations between the three countries which need to be solve first. This part is often neglected by the decision makers and they move towards development of military capabilities. Such military capabilities do not solve the problem, especially when the opposite side is also capable to challenge the hegemon. It will further create political problems leading to degradation of deterrence, as mentioned in the next chapter.

6

Assessment of Political and Technical Implications of BMD

The abandoning of the US from the ABM treaty and its decision to build and deploy BMD systems has created debates in the international community, especially in Russia and China. It has presented a situation analogous to the 'security dilemma'. John Hertz described security dilemma as a social state in which individual powers have no authority over them to enforce behavioural norms or to prevent them from attacking one another. The mutual suspicion and fear drive individual states to obtain more security by increasing their powers.[1]

The efforts of the US to strengthen its own security by construction of BMD are considered as a danger to the other countries like Russia and China. Russia and China have regarded construction of BMD as against their deterrence and therefore have intimated the US again and again that they would develop counter-measures technology to deal with the US BMD programme. One of the Chinese diplomats has said:

> The US, like any other country, is entitled to security. But its interfering nature makes it difficult to allow the US the absolute security it seeks. The more secure the US is, the more insecure the rest of the world feels…When the US threatens the security of other countries, than there is need to challenge the US security system which has missile defence as a crucial component.[2]

Following the withdrawal of the US from the ABM treaty, policy makers and disciples mentioned that Russia and China would develop Anti-Satellite Weapon (ASAT) programme so as to engage and destroy US satellites. It was said that Russia and China could not compete with the US effectively in development of conventional and nuclear weapons and therefore would try to respond asymmetrically to American superiority by developing ASAT and posing threat to the US satellites.[3] This concern was certified when China carried out ASAT test in January 2007. Similarly, scholars and diplomats said that withdrawal of the US from the ABM treaty would be followed by Russia's withdrawal from START treaty which will endanger non-proliferation regimes.[4] Although, Russia has not abandoned START treaty, it has suspended its participation from INF treaty and has indicated its intention to withdraw from CFE treaty. Thus, there have been efforts at the international level to penetrate missile defence or alternate means to threaten US deterrence. In this sense, BMD programme of the US does not offer a comprehensive framework for preserving deterrence. Instead, it leads to offensive-defensive arms race.

China's Reactions Against US BMD

China will be more vulnerable to the US BMD and TMD programmes than Russia. The reason being that China possesses only 20 ICBMs which are capable of targeting the US. The US has mentioned again and again that BMD and TMD are aimed against rogue states and not against China or Russia. However, it is difficult for China to believe that the US does not have any master plans in its mind by deploying BMD. Shen Dingli said:

> It is untenable that the US would spend more than ten billions dollars on a system which has only "rogue" states in mind...Only Russia and China currently have the capability to hit US with nuclear warheads on intercontinental missiles...The envisaged NMD cannot stop an all-out Russian nuclear attack, considering the thousands of strategic weapons at Russia's disposal...Given the reported level of China's full range ICBM force, the NMD plans requiring ABM revision would compromise China's strategic capability in two respects. Geographically, it will protect the whole United States from being deterred. Numerically, even interceptors deployed on a single site may be enough to knock out all Chinese CSSS 4s. Hence, China's national security interests are greatly endangered.[5]

Therefore, China regards the BMD programme as against its deterrence policy. China's concerns to BMD could be divided into three parts:

Impact on Global Strategic Stability of Arms Control and Non-Proliferation Efforts

Even before the withdrawal of the US from the ABM treaty, China was opposed to the BMD programme due to concerns of arms control treaties and international strategic stability. Ambassador Sha repeatedly said that missile defence violates both the content and core of the ABM treaty. China has always maintained that the ABM treaty must be preserved as it has served the corner of the strategic stability.[6] While speaking at a Conference of Arms control and disarmament, the Chinese Ambassador said:

> ABM treaty established so called "balance of terror" which can only provide relative security to countries. This might not satisfy some Americans in pursuit of absolute security. Nonetheless, "balance of terror" is better than no balance at all. Between two devils, we have to opt for the lesser evil and this is the best possible choice we can have until the complete elimination of nuclear weapons is achieved. Disturbing such a balance will only lead to greater insecurity for all countries, including the US.[7]

The US focus on BMD further reinforces Chinese perceptions that US wants to achieve absolute security for itself at the cost of others. Ambassador Sha Zukang said, "What the U.S wants is absolute security because it is only from a position of absolute security that it can enjoy complete freedom of action in dealing with other countries.[8]

Under such conditions, it is clear that other countries will not sit idle. Liu Jieyi, Director General of Chinese Foreign Ministers Department of arms control said, "If a country in addition to its offensive power, seeks to develop advanced TMD or NMD, in an attempt to attain absolute security and unilateral strategic advantage for itself, other countries will be forced to develop more advanced missiles."[9] Thus, this will reverse the process of nuclear disarmament. Chinese Ambassador Hu Xiaodi said at a UN Conference of Disarmament:

> NMD is, in essence, a disguised form of unilateral nuclear arms expansion, which will severely hinder the international arms control and disarmament process and even trigger off a new round of arms race...The US possesses the cutting edge nuclear arsenal and the most sophisticated conventional weapons in the world and pursues a policy of nuclear deterrence based on the first- use of nuclear weapons. With that, NMD will become an offensive arms multiplier for that country. It will not only severely impede the US – Russia and the global nuclear disarmament process but also render any initiative on the reduction of offensive nuclear arms meaningless.[10]

Impact on China's Nuclear Deterrence and Credibility

Another major concern for China from the US missile defence programme is its impact on the credibility and deterrence policy of China. Lt Bin mentioned:

> Chinese nuclear deterrence depends directly on American perceptions about Chinese nuclear retaliatory capabilities. Without the backup of NMD, the Americans would worry about Chinese retaliation with the few Chinese nuclear weapons that might survive US first nuclear strike against China. The deployment of NMD system would provide the American public with an illusion that the several surviving retaliatory Chinese ICBM would be intercepted by BMD.[11]

China's nuclear deterrence faces a danger from the US BMD programme because it provides the US deterrence both offensive and defensive forces. On the other hand, China only has the offensive weapons system to preserve its deterrence.[12] China has the smallest nuclear arsenals amongst the P-5 nations and has approximately 20 lands-based ICBMs. The Chinese nuclear and missile forces have a lot of disadvantages: the bulk of Chinese missile force is liquid fuelled, located at fixed sites and requiring heavy time for launch preparation. Chinese nuclear bombs lack sufficient range and are too slow to penetrate air defence system. China's single *Xia*-class submarine is virtually non-operational. With such a small, technologically inferior force, China is concerned that the BMD system would render its second-strike capability impotent and thus enables the US to use nuclear blackmail against China.[13] Chinese arms control specialists have taken the following path:

- The Chinese assumption is that the US would initiate first-strike.
- Chinese possess about two dozens of ICBMs and China assumes that only a small handful of them will survive.
- The handful of ICBM expected to survive the first-strike will be captured by US NMD.
- Thus, NMD would degrade China's retaliatory capabilities.
- This concludes that China's survival is at risk with the deployment of US NMD.[14]

Sha Zukang states that:

> We are against NMD, not because we intend to threaten the security of US with our nuclear weapons. We just hope that the existing mutual deterrence between the two countries can be preserved. As is known to all, China's nuclear arsenal is the smallest and least advanced among the five nuclear weapons states. Yet, China is the first to pursue the policy of no-first use of nuclear weapons. Of course, China will not allow its legitimate means of self defence to be weakened or even taken away by anyone in anyway. This is one of the most important aspects of China's national security.[15]

Impact of TMD on East Asia's Security Relationship with China

China sees deployment of TMD in East Asia as a broader part of the US TMD policy against China in East Asia. These policies become more apparent with the bombing of Chinese assembly in Belgrade, release of Cox report, growing threat of military and political ties between the US and Taiwan.[16] The main allegations laid by China are:

TMD will enable the US to commence undeterrable military operations in East Asia with minimum inhibitions.

US seeks to exploit technical funding, expertise and missile defence in gaining domination in East Asia. By being the part of the US BMD, allies would relay on the US for any security guarantees and become integrated in the US security architecture.

China affirms that determination of the US to have BMD reflects rise of the conservative forces in US government to dominate, defence and foreign policy agenda and to carry out assault on China and North Korea.[17]

The other two considerable concerns for China are deployment of TMD in Japan and Taiwan. Taiwan is always a very sensitive issue for China. China is cautious with the US decision to sell lower tier BMD to Taiwan which they consider it not only as confrontation in its political affairs but also anticipates that TMD systems will embolden Taiwan freedom movement.[18] The Chinese Communist Party (CCP) has addressed the Taiwan issue as its internal matter and rebuffs any attempts by other states to legitimise other states' contacts with Taiwan.[19] Without any TMD, Taiwan is vulnerable to China's short-range missiles. Missile defences in Taiwan would reduce Chinese ability to use missile threats against Taiwan for achieving its political ambitions. If China is unable to use its military power for threatening Taiwan, it will definitely embolden freedom movement. The TMD transfer will strengthen ties between the US and Taiwan which could be harmful to the interests of China.[20] The NMD and TMD would empower the US to intervene freely in the affairs of Taiwan Strait. Besides, the triangular relationship of China, US and Taiwan could cause the fear of escalation of conflict. According to Game Theory, any triad is more susceptible to escalation than any dyad because of exponential increase in interaction.[21]

Similarly, China has concerns regarding TMD in Japan. China feels that deployment of BMD in Japan will promote it to take more aggressive steps against its neighbours. China says that Japan already has a strong military force and has the most advanced weapon systems in Asia. As a result, deployment of TMD will provoke Japan to take a aggressive role in East Asia. Some Chinese analysts also feel that deployment of TMD by Japan has political justifications rather than dealing with threat perceptions coming from North Korea. Japan relies heavily on sea line communications so as to meet its energy needs. Taiwan is located at very important position of this sea line communication. The main aim of Japan is to control Taiwan and South China Sea so as to threaten Chinese interests.[22] China also regards transfer of TMD would lead to remilitarisation of Japan.[23] Therefore, United States' BMD and TMD threaten Chinese nuclear interests and target its nuclear deterrence.

What will China do to Maintain its Deterrence?

Clearly, China will not sit idle and will take steps to enforce its deterrence. The manner in which China will respond depends on whether it will seek to enhance survivability of its nuclear forces or reinforce its nuclear doctrine. China seems to do both these things through the following methods:

Change in Nuclear Doctrine

There have been discussions going on in China to shift from the doctrine of 'minimum deterrence' to the doctrine of 'limited deterrence'. Limited deterrence will provide China the capability to deter conventional, theatre and strategic war and to control escalation in the event of a nuclear war. Under this, China will need to target nuclear installations besides cities and this will require additional deployments. According to Johnson, "a number of Chinese strategists now explicitly annul minimum deterrence as a viable alternative for China as it reduces China's deterrence and therefore increases the country's vulnerability to attack, and offers no means to control arms race."[24] The aim of such doctrinal change is to present credible deterrence and to prevent the US from using its offensive forces against China or threaten to use nuclear weapons against China while protecting itself through the shield. China could also consider changing its doctrine of no-first use to the doctrine of launch on warning (LOW). China said that it is not the violation of NFU but rather a defensive measure taken when launch is confirmed. LOW could be defined as active defensive measures taken after adversary has attacked but before his weapons have wrecked destruction on China, particularly on its retaliatory forces.[25] Therefore, the US BMD programme would lead to change in the nuclear doctrine of China which would lead to more deployments, and continue to pose threat to the US deterrence.

Modernizing Missiles

The second step to be followed by China is to increase its forces, both qualitatively and quantitatively. Quantitatively, China will increase number of nuclear weapons and deployed forces. The CIA predicts that China would increase its nuclear warhead between 75-100 which would be capable to reach to the US. Qualitative increase involves modernisation of nuclear warheads and ability to penetrate missile defence of the US. In fact, the modernisation of missiles and increasing number of missiles deployed is directly linked to the China, limited nuclear deterrence.[26] A Chinese academic mentions:

> China's programme will involve the responses from US missile defence by increasing force level so as to restore to China the minimum deterrence. The problem is this would make China a nuclear force develop into an embryonic limited nuclear deterrent at strategic level....For the purpose of reconstructing minimum deterrence, China is not only required to keep improving the survivability of its nuclear forces through measures such as camouflage of deployment sites, development of solid propellant and acquisition of mobile delivery systems as well as improvements in C4ISR capabilities. More critically, it is required to develop effective means to penetrate missile defence structure so as to strike at least some of the major cities. It is in this connection that China's strategic forces move towards strategic minimum deterrence.[27]

The result for China, modernisation of delivery vehicles would be:

- **ICBMs:** Replacement of DF- 5 and DF-4 with more advanced DF-31 and DF-41. Both these missiles will be solid fuel missiles, thus easier to launch as compared with liquid fuel missiles. DF-31 and DF-41 have a range of 8,000 and 12,000 kms respectively. Some experts have estimated that China could field 50-70 MIRV and solid fuel ICBM by 2010.
- **SLBM:** China plans to deploy four to six generation submarine by 2010. Each submarine will be armed with 12 JL-2 SLBM with a range of 8,000 km and potentially have MIRV capability.[28]

It is said that irrespective of the US BMD programme, China will continue with its modernisation of delivery vehicles. Nevertheless, the BMD programme would accelerate the decision to develop its forces. This makes it clear why the US BMD will not be able to preserve deterrence. Also, China has a history of proliferating weapons to Pakistan and to the Middle East, an area in which the US has a potential interest. Therefore, China could also proliferate counter-measures technology to other states which will not be conductive to US deterrence.

Russia Moves Against BMD

The reasons for Russia's opposition to the US BMD programmes are more or less same as China. Russia is also opposed to BMD programme due to its concerns regarding the ABM treaty. Russia regards this treaty as the basis of strategic stability between Russia and the US. Russian President Putin has mentioned:

> People must realise that the mutual reduction of strategic attack weapons-the most dangerous of all nuclear weapons-is possible only when the ABM treaty continues to hold. Scrapping it would make further reduction of strategic attack weapons according to START I impossible. START II would not come into force either, as it would be impossible to conclude START III, aimed at talking about the radical reduction of nuclear arsenals. This blow would also affect other agreements that are of fundamental global importance: the NPT and the Nuclear Test Ban Treaty…Russia will be forced to look for an alternative to end its commitments not only regarding START, but also the agreement on intermediate-range and short-range missiles, the conclusion of which is linked to the legal and military framework of the START II –ABM process.[29]

On the other hand, Russia accepts the threat coming from proliferation of missiles but maintains that proliferation threat should be dealt with diplomatic measures and multilateral initiatives which will also involve rogue states. President Putin said, "The differences in our approach lies in that we propose to move ahead jointly in preventing ballistic missile threat while preserving the level of trust and balance created by 1972 ABM treaty."[30] In order to deal with proliferation of delivery vehicles, Russia proposed Global Control Systems (GCS).

Secondly, again, the US has repeatedly mentioned that this missile defence is not targeted against Russia or China but both the countries have their doubts.

Thirdly, Russia's deterrence would be in danger with the construction of NMD. Russia affirms that the US is using North

Korea as an excuse and Iran as a threat so as to build BMD. A Russian General said, "US claims that it needs ballistic missile defence to protect itself from North Korea, Iran or Iraq....it is an argument for naïve and stupid. This system will be directed against China and Russia." The events like the US moves to expand NATO, bombing Serbia during Kosovo war and criticism of Russia during Chechnya war demonstrate that US wants to establish "strategic domination."[31] The reasons for Russia's fears of breakdown of deterrence are:

- Russia's nuclear weapons are about to decline sharply over the next few decades, perhaps fewer than 1,500 warheads. The reason behind this reduction is that Russia has old weaponry which will soon become obsolete, and it is not economically sound to acquire new weaponry. On the other hand, the US continues to build larger offensive nuclear weapons, even if it is under arms control agreements.[32]
- Russia is against the deployment of radars and interceptors in the Czech Republic and Poland because these radars and interceptors could detect Russian missiles and therefore, would be harmful for Russia first-strike capability.

Russia's Response to the US BMD Programme

Russia's response to BMD is based on three levels:

- Deploying multiple warheads on New ICBMs and ability to penetrate BMD
- Withdrawal from Arms control treaties
- Building diplomatic allies with Iran and China

Deploying Multiple Warheads on New ICBMs and Ability to Penetrate BMD

Russia has 360 SS-25 missiles and 30 operational SS 27 missiles. The SS-27 missiles were expected to replace SS-25 missiles in the Russian force. Russia is producing 10 missiles per year but expected to increase its production up to 30 missiles per year.[33] Besides, Russia is also working on 'Topol Missiles' which are capable of penetrating the US missile defence system. Russia has carried out successful test of RS-24 and claims that it can penetrate missile defence system. The RS-24 uses a sophisticated navigation system which allows the warheads to lock on to different targets and is capable of penetrating the US ballistic missile defence shield.[34] Russia has also said that it would deploy S-400 Triumph air defence. Therefore, it seems that Russia has started a race of offensive-defensive weapons with the US.

Russia's Withdrawal from Arms Control Treaties

Russia said it would withdraw from the arms control treaties and develop weapons. The INF treaty requires the US and USSR to permanently forswear all their nuclear and conventional ground-launched ballistic missiles with ranges of 500-5,500 miles. On 10 February 2007, during the Russian President's speech at Munich, Russia indicated that it might withdraw from the INF treaty. The international community fears that INF missiles deployed in Russia could pose more of a threat to Europe than to the US. As a result, European states will feel insecure and would deploy corresponding INF missiles in Western Europe. On 14 July 2007, Russia formally suspended its participation from the CFE treaty. This treaty set limits between the NATO group and Warsaw Pact on the specified military equipment known as Treaty Limited Equipment (TLE) in the Atlantic to Urals Zone (ATTU). It was agreed that neither side would have more than 20,000 tanks, 20,000 artillery pieces, 30,000 armored combat vehicles (ACVs), 6,800 combat aircraft, and 2,000 attack helicopters. Russian Foreign Minister Sergei Lavrov at a Russia-NATO council in Oslo said that "None of the NATO members are fulfilling this agreement, and we don't want to look like we're taking part in a theatre of the absurd." He also said that "Relations in the Russia-NATO council are lacking a necessary degree of trust."[35] Russian withdrawal from the CFE treaty has many implications. First, it will allow Russia to deploy additional troops in its southern and northern flanks; and second, it will bring an end to mutual inspections and confidence-building measures, which were part of this treaty. While suspending its participation from the CFE treaty, Russia said that it would not be bound by any limitation on conventional weapons, which indicate that this would have tremendous effect on European security and US-Russian relationship. As a result, it would establish Europe as the battleground between Russia and the US. This situation is very alarming for the US as it does not want to witness the onset of a new Cold War, particularly when it is waging a war on terrorism.[36]

Building Diplomatic Alliance with Iran and China

Russia is building diplomatic alliance with Iran and China so as to counter-balance the US. The relationship between Iran and Russia has been strengthened by the historic visit of the Russian President, Vladimir Putin, to Iran. Russian President Putin has confirmed that Russia will support construction of the Bushehr nuclear power plant at Iran. Moscow also mentioned that it would not back further sanctions against Iran unless the IAEA says Iran is not cooperating or proves it is working on nuclear weapons. Russia has further signed a contract to supply Iran with five Tu-204-100 aircraft. President Putin's visit to Iran could be seen as one of Russia's diplomatic measures to prevent the US from establishing its hegemony in the region and yet another move to demonstrate its opposition of the US' defensive plans. The US has remarked that it wants to establish missile defence so as to counter the ballistic missile threat from Iran; and in this context the Putin visit signifies that Russia would help Iran in making it stronger. Russia and China are coming closer and have conducted war games to show their military power in August 2007. Vladimir Putin, during these war games, ordered the Russian Air Force to resume the Cold War practice of long-range flights by strategic bombers. Observers say the exercise sent signals to Washington and Brussels.[37]

This shows that by building missile defence systems, there does exist a situation of security dilemma in international affairs and countries like Russia and China will respond by various diplomatic and military methods. This will lead to offensive-defensive race of weapons, degradation of arms control regimes and further proliferation of weapons. This would lead to the weakening of deterrence.

Technological Challenges Posed by BMD Programme and Deterrence

The US has combined the strategic and technological perspective so as to achieve complete feasibility of BMD system. Missile Defence Agency (MDA) has proposed five blocks according to which technological programmes of BMD will be framed. These are described below:

Block 1: Defend the US from limited North Korean long range threats.

Block 2: Defend allies and deployed forces from short to medium range threats in one region/theatre.

Block 3: Expand the defence of the US to include limited Iranian long range threats.

Block 4: Defend allies and deployed forces in Europe from limited Iranian long range and intermediate range threats.

Block 5: Expand defence of allies and deployed forces from short to intermediate range threats in two regions/theatres.[38]

These five blocks are then combined with technological aspects so as to provide all US and its allies against threat of ballistic missiles of all the ranges. These are described in the table below:

	Block 1	Block 2	Block 3	Block 4	Block 5
Weapons	GMD: GBI (3 Stage)	Aegis BMD: SM-3 Block 1A SM-2 Block IV THADD: Interceptors	GMD: GBI (3 Stage)	GMD GBI (2 Stage)	Aegis BMD: SM-3 Block 1 A SM-3 Block 1B THADD: Interceptors
Sensors	AN/SPY-1 AN/TPY-2 (FBM) Cobra Dane SBX UEWR-Beale	AN/SPY-1 AN/TPY-2 (FBM)	AN/SPY-1 AN/TPY-2 (FBM) Cobra Dane SBX UEWR-Fylingdales UEWR-Thule	AN/TPY-2 (FBM) EMR	AN/SPY-1 AN/TPY-2 (FBM)
C2BMC	SA/TPY-2	SA	SA/TPY-2	SA/GEM/ TPY-2	SA/GEM

Source: 2008 Assessment of the US Ballistic Missile Defense, URL: http://www.cdi.org/pdfs/FY08BMDSJan09.pdf

Progress made in BMD Capability

In order to accelerate the development of BMD, the US formed Missile Defence Agency (MDA) as a main body within the DOD which is responsible for development of missile defence. They adopted evolutionary approach to the development of BMD. The MDA named this capability-based acquisition as 'spiral development.' Over time, this spiral development approach will integrate all of the segment elements into a layered missile defence system that is capable of defeating ballistic missiles of all ranges and in all phases of flight. The progress made by the US BMD programme is given in the table below.[39]

Summary of Principal US Missile Defence Programmes

Programme	System	Status
Interceptors		
Terminal Phase		
Patriot Advanced Capability-3 (PAC3)	Land-based, air transportable launcher, single stage Extended Range Interceptors (ERINT) miasile armed with explosive warhead, phased array radar and engagement control station (ECS)	Most technologically mature BMD system in the US Army service since 2003.
Terminal High Altitude Area Defence (THADD)	Truck-mounted launchers equipped with hit-to-kill interceptor missiles, mobile X-band radar, and battle management command and control (BMC^2) system	Resumed flight tests in 2005, after major design changes; successful interception tests in Jan and Oct 2007; first unit to be deployed in end of 2009 or in early 2010

Mid Course Phase		
Ground Based Mid Course Defence(GMD)	Long range, multi-stage Ground Based Interceptor (GBI) missile carrying an EKV for intercepting ICBMs; land and sea based tracking radars; and GMD Fire Control and Communications (GFC/C) system	GBI and GMD radar network used in successful interception test in Sept 2007 ;40 GBI missiles to be based at Fort Greely, Alaska, 4 at Vandenberg, AFB, Caifornia and 10 in Poland by 2011
Aegis Ballistic Missile Defence	Aegis ships equipped with AN/SPY-1 radar reconfigured for long range surveillance and track (LRS&T) capability and Block 1A SM-3 hit-to-kill interceptors for engaging short and medium range ballistic missiles	3 Aegis BMD cruisers and 13 destroyers to be in US Navy service at end of 2008 with c.40 SM-3s; the Block 2 SM03 to be fielded in 2013 will have capability to intercept ICBMs
Multiple Kill Vehicle (MKV)	Long range interceptor carrying 8-20 miniaturised EKVs which can independently track and target multiple warheads and mid course counter-measures such as decoys and re-entry vechiles	Control system of payload carrier vehicle tested in 2006; testing of EKVs to begin in 2009; initial operational capability in 2014
Boost Phase		
Airborne Laser (ABL)	Modified Boeing 747 aircraft carrying a modular, megawatt-class chemical oxygen iodine laser (COIL), beam control optics, infrared sensors and target acquisition and tracking laser	Continuing systems-integration problems, successful in-flight test of target tracking laser in 2007

Kinetic Energy Interceptor (KEI)	A fast-burn, high-velocity interceptor missile to be deployed on mobile land launchers or on sea-based platforms near an enemy launch site; may replace ABL as main boost-phase defence system	Land based booster flight tested in 2008; sea based platform selected in 2008; initial operational capability to be determined
Sensors		
Sea-based X-Band (SBX) radar	High resolution radar based on manoeuvrable offshore platform for acquisition, tracking and discrimination of target missiles.	Completed sea trials in 2007; used in successful test of GMD elements in Sept 2007; to be based at Adak Island, Alska.
AN/TPY-2 radar	Transportable high resolution radar for detecting, tracking and discriminating missile threats; designed as part of THADD system.	First radar activated in Oct 2006 by US Army unit at Japanese airbase in Shariki, Japan.
Space Tracking and Surveillance System (STSS)	Constellation of low-earth orbit satellites designed to detect and track missiles in all phases of flight; size of constellation to be determined	
Space-Based Infrared System-High (SBIRS-High)	USAF procurement plan is for 3 satellites in geo-synchronous orbit, and 2 satellites with infrared sensors in highly elliptical orbit, to provide early warning of ballistic missile launches	Programme beset by technical delays and cost overruns; restructured in 2002, 2004 and 2005

Upgraded Early Warning Radar (UEWR)	Modified early-warning radar (EWR) for detection and tracking of post-boost and mid course re-entry vehicles; data transmitted to 2 GMD Fire Control Centres in Alska and Colorado	Upgrade of US EWR at RAF Flyingdales, UK, completed in Aug 2007

The US deployed Initial Defensive Capability that integrates the defence of the US homeland, allies and forward- deployed forces in a global architecture supported by land, allies and forward-deployed forces. This global architecture is supported by a command and control battle management communications (C3BMC) network that can bring online new capabilities as they spiral out of the development programme. Such capability consists of:

- Ground-based midcourse interceptors at two sites, along with supporting sensors and command and control, capable of defeating limited IRBM and ICBM threats;
- Sea-based Aegis/SM-3 systems capable of defeating medium- to intermediate range threats and with the potential to grow in capability against longer range threats;
- Development of terminal high altitude area defence (THADD), a mobile, ground based interceptor and radar system capable of protecting against medium-range threats; and expanded deployment of the PAC-3 hit-to-kill battlefield weapon against shorter range threats in terminal phase of flight.[40]

However, the technological developments of BMD to strengthen US deterrence are in doubt. Despite several successful tests, the certainty of BMD is doubted. Prof. Theodore Postal of MTI charged Ballistic Missile Defence Organisation (BMDO), with elaborate scientific and technological distortions that have been compounded by fraud and misconduct. He has also expressed several misgivings about the 'hit-to-kill' technology. He has been credited with uncovering the massive disinformation and cover up regarding the success rate of Patriot missile fired during Gulf War I so as to counter the Iraqi Scud missile threat and other exaggerated success claims of early missile tests of NMD. Similarly, Union of Concerned Scientists (UCS) has expressed doubts regarding the efficacy of developing systems. They said that the technology has not been developed for realisation of aims. They harbour the reservations about the system to overcome counter-measures.[41] Following are the technological challenges faced by BMD:

Dealing with Counter-Measures Technology

Counter-measures are used to confuse, overwhelm or to defeat the defensive system. According to NIE 1999, counter-measures would be available to the emerging missile states.[42] These counter-measures are easier to build as compared to developing ICBM or a nuclear compact, and are light enough to be delivered by such a missile. Therefore, states which have the capability to build short or medium range ballistic missiles could easily develop counter-measures.[43] There could be variety of counter-measures:

Submutions with biological and chemical warheads

Biological or chemical warheads could be divided into many small warheads, which are called as submutions. An attacker could divide the agent for each missile among hundreds or more submutions that would be released after boost phase. It is very difficult to intercept these numerous submutions. An attacker could readily keep the re-entry vehicle heating of submutions low enough so as to protect the agents from the excessive heat. These submutions would distribute the agent over large areas and disseminate it at lower speeds. This is more effective means of delivering chemical and biological warhead.[44]

Anti-simulation Decoys

Decoys are made to look like missile warhead so as to overwhelm the defence with more targets than it could intercept.[45] In order to mimic the infrared heat signatures of warhead, decoys could be equipped with small heat generators. Decoys could be placed inside the radar effective balloon that would make it impossible to see the interiors of the decoys.[46] Anti-simulation is the technique in which attacker disguises the warhead to make it look like a decoy.[47]

Cooled Shroud

The NMD uses a variety of sensor systems. These sensors can only get the kill vehicle on a trajectory that takes it close to the target. The kill vehicle must itself detect the target, failing which the entire system of NMD fails (Lewis, 2000). The attacker could cover a nuclear warhead with a shroud cooled to a low temperature by Nitrogen Oxide. This cooled shroud would reduce the infrared radiation emitted by warhead by at least one million. This would make detection of warhead impossible.[48]

The problem is that target missile could release 'target cluster' which is made up of closely spaced objects during initial parts of ballistic missile trajectory. Such a cluster could contain warhead, decoys, chaffs, electronic counter-measures, etc. In the diagram below, warhead is surrounded by clusters. The problem of defence under such a condition is to discriminate warhead from other things. As target clusters are released above the earth atmosphere, they will continue to follow same ballistic path unless they re-enter the earth atosphere.[49]

Figure 2: Possible Target Cluster, Source: Mantle J. Peter, "Missile Defence Equation"

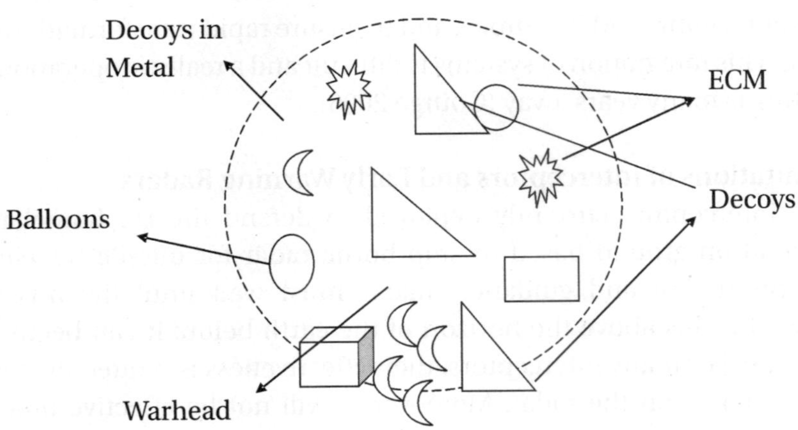

Operational Problems in Ground Based Midcourse Defence (GMD)

In order to have a successful GMD, the following should take place simultaneously:

- The launch of enemy missile must be detected, the heading of missile and information about it must be sent to command and control component.
- The command and control centre must cue the tracking radar so as to track the hostile missile or missiles and to provide immediate high quality data to fire control stations, which then develops a battle plan to engage the incoming missiles.
- Fire control must launch the interceptor's missile or missiles. The exa-atmospheric kill vehicle must then disengage from the booster rocket.
- The in-flight interceptor communication system of the fire control component must relay to the EKV updated target information, including discrimination of objects in the target complex, which it receives from the tracking radar.
- EKV then must acquire the incoming warheads, track it and discriminate between them and decoys, make final target selections and steer itself for hit-to-kill impact. The tracking radar then makes assessment of the success of the intercept.

This requires many systems to integrate together. It must have command and control system, consisting of hardware and communication system so as to provide real time interfaces to integrate entire GMD complex and to ensure rapid transformation of data. This integration of systems is difficult and a realistic operational testing is many years away (Gourge 2006).

Limitations of interceptors and Early Warning Radars

The interceptors currently deployed to defend the US homeland depend on ground based or ship borne radar for missile tracking, discrimination and guidance. Radar must wait until the missile or warhead is above the horizon of the earth before it can begin to operate. For many interceptors, their effectiveness is limited by their dependence on the radar. Moreover, it will not be effective unless the radar is deployed in the right place, looking in right direction and operational at the time when a ballistic missile is launched. To address this problem, MDA is developing Space Tracking and Surveillance System (STSS), which will provide global coverage. However, this technology is yet to be developed. A full constellation of STSS will begin in 2012. Similarly, Early Warning Radars (EW) have their own limitations. The five existing radars belong to the Cold War period and require substantial upgrading to communicate effectively with the national missile defence system. The Cobra Dane EW radar is located at Eareckson Air Station, Alaska, and is pointed towards the East Russian Peninsula and North Pacific Ocean. It is the only EW radar which can detect launches from North Korea; but cannot cover the entire country (Gourge, 2006). Only a portion of Cobra Dane can pick up North Korean missiles.[50]

Failure of BMD to Address the Threat of Cruise Missiles

The Department of Defence (DoD) defines cruise missile as "the guided missile whose flight path to its target is conducted at an approximately constant velocity; depends on the dynamic reaction of air for a lift and propulsion forces to balance drag." Federation of American Scientists (FAS) defines it as, "an unmanned self propelled guided vehicle that sustains flight through aerodynamic lift for most of its flight and whose primary mission is to place an ordnance or special payload on a target." The 2003 Iraq war showed that the US defences could deal with the ballistic missile defence but not with cruise missile. The US and Kuwait batteries Patriot TMD batteries interceptors destroyed all nine Iraqi ballistic missile launched at military targets but they failed to detect and intercept any of the five HY-2/ CSSSC 3 Seersucker missile launched against Kuwait.[51]

Cruise missiles are difficult for current active defences to detect, track and intercept. Defences that exist today protect only small areas or unique, high-value assets. The best defence against a cruise missile would be to destroy the launch platform prior to launch. However, because of its relatively small size and modest launching infrastructure to support a cruise missile, finding and neutralising it with offensive, preemptive counter-force may be problematic for any joint force commander. A number of other factors make cruise missiles attractive to US adversaries. As mentioned earlier, cruise missiles are cheaper to build and buy than ballistic missiles, making them attractive to countries with less advanced militaries and to non-state actors as well. Tracking proliferation of cruise missiles is difficult because the materials and technology involved have multiple uses.[52] There are talks about building of cruise missile defence but no effective step has been taken in this regard.

This analysis shows that though US BMD could deal with some of the missile threats but it is not a compressive framework to strengthen deterrence posture. It has raised political debates in Russia and China about the US real intentions behind development of BMD. As a result, these states are forced to develop counter-measures. The vital point is that benefits of BMD are strongly nullified due to its adversaries (Russia and China) forcing the international community to start a more strategic, competitive, costly and dangerous arms race. Technologically, the BMD is not fully effective. The testing of BMD technology has taken place in pre-determined environment and does not resemble real war like conditions. Therefore, in order to deal with proliferation of missiles, the US should engage with the international community and adopt arms control and disarmament measures. The BMD provides short term benefits while arms control and disarmament measures will be effective in long term.

7

BMD and Deterrence: Way Forward

Reaching Towards Conclusion

From this analysis we can see that there are three main kinds of relationships established between the US nuclear deterrence and BMD:

- BMD could be a substitute to deterrence in cases where deterrence does not function. Such as dealing with rogue states or terrorist groups, which are assessed as 'undeterrable', or dealing with hazards of accidental launch of missiles?
- BMD could complement deterrence when threat is too modest to require nuclear weapons.
- BMD could be considered as a component of 'deterrence by denial'. The potential aggressor could be deterred by the rational calculation that its strikes do not reach the US territory.[1]

However, the questions raised by this research are: how capable is BMD to deal with contemporary threats, and what is the solution to the offensive-defensive race of weapons? The answer is that there are no concrete measures taken by the US to deal with the offensive-defensive race of weapons. It is engaged with the following:

Declining Ballistic Missile Threat

There has been literature published by Joseph Cirincione, the Director of the Carnegie Endowment for International Peace, which has demonstrated that ballistic missile threat has been on the decline since the end of the Cold War. The following prove the fact:

- By 2005, the total number of ballistic missiles in the world had decreased by 51percent. The total number of missiles deployed by the time of Soviet Union to its becoming Russia for threatening the US has decreased from 2400 to 943.

- IRBM arsenals have declined from 778 in 1987 to 20. This represents 97 percent reduction from the Cold War period (Cirincione 2005 : 5-6).
- The US has recognised threat from missiles from countries in the Middle East and South Asia, but the reality is that the number of ballistic missile programmes has decreased since the end of the Cold War. By 2005, Brazil, South Africa and most recently, Libya, have abandoned their missile programmes.
- Nations pursuing ballistic missile programmes are smaller, with fewer resources and limited technology at their command. Therefore, the possibility of their success is limited.[2]

Fig 2: Overview of Missile Arsenals

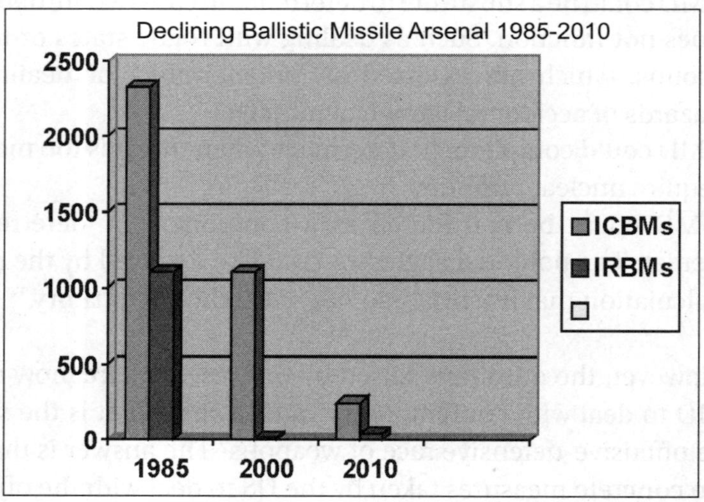

Source: The Exaggerated ballistic missile threat by Joseph Cirincione, 2001 http://www.mi.infn.it/~landnet/NMD/cirincione.pdf

Joseph Cirincione said that the reports of the US assessing the missile threat incorporate 50 states while the ratio is that 48 states possess missiles or have missile programmes. The missile threat was advanced by at least 5 years of the possible date of rogue states long range deployment.[3] The National Intelligence Council (NIC) said:

> Our assessments of future missile developments are inexact and subjective because they are based on often fragmentary information. States with emerging missile programmes inevitably will run into problems that will delay and frustrate their desired development timelines. The impact of these problems increases with the lack of maturity of the programme and depends on foreign assistance at this stage of their development efforts. Most emerging missile states are highly dependent on foreign assistance at this stage of their development efforts, and disturbance of the technology and information flow to their programmes will have discernible short term effects.[4]

Let us examine factual positions. Iran has acquired assistance from North Korea for developing the Shahab series of missiles. North Korea carried out an unsuccessful test of the No-Dong missile in 1998. It was discovered that the No-Dong could carry a payload of 100-200 kg, which means that this payload is considerably less than the amount needed to carry nuclear weapons. This also proves that this missile could carry only small amounts of chemical and biological weapons, which are not adequate to inflict a large mass-casualties. As Iran has obtained the technology of Shahab-3 from North Korea's No-Dong, the reliability of this missile is not very high. It seems neither Iran nor North Korea have been able to develop this technology. Besides, there are several technological limitations of Iran's ballistic missile programme, such as:

- Iran has still to develop a successful stage separation technology. Iran has developed the Shahab-3 single-stage missile but has not carried out the multi-stage rocket test. Shahab-3D consists of liquid fuel in the first stage and solid fuel in the second stage but the test of Shahab-3 D failed in September 2000.
- Iran needs to develop the propulsion system for an ICBM. The current propulsion system of Iran's Shahab-3 and Shahab-4 is not satisfactory for an ICBM.
- Iran does not have the re-entry vehicle and guidance systems to conduct successful attacks on enemy targets. It also does not have the capability to carry out missile attacks.
- Iran's liquid fuel missile programme is such that it takes a long time to prepare before launch. As a result, this increases the vulnerability of missiles and slows down the reaction time.[5]

Therefore, Iran itself is exaggerating its missile threat so as to threaten its adversaries. It will take a longer period of time for development of efficient ballistic missile systems.[6] This shows that the basis on which missile defenceis being built is doubted. Ted Postal says:

> If the purpose of a NMD is to protect the US from North Korea missiles, why is the world most advanced tracking and missile radar about to go online at the Northern tip of Norway instead of Northern Japan? Russia and China will be constantly concerned that the US will evaluate, expand and modify their missile kill interceptors. Both Russia and China are under no illusions about the US agenda but America is lying to the rest of the world, including its own population on using North Korea as a camouflage to disregard its true intentions.[7]

The question arises whether missile proliferation threat to the US or its allies is real? Table 7.1 mentions about the threat coming from various actors. As mentioned below, Russia and China are the only countries which have the capability to hit the US with ICBMs. However, there is no eminent danger from Russia and China as these countries could be deterred by traditional concept of MAD. Presently, no terrorist group claims to have ballistic missiles. Some groups like Hezbollah and Hamas have used small rockets but do not possess ballistic missiles. The countries like North Korea, Iran etc do not yet have ICBMs capability to target the US. They are trying to develop this capability in future. The countries in question have capability to hit the US allies with short range missiles. The genuine danger to the US and to the international community is not from ballistic missiles but from cruise missiles. Cruise missiles are not considered seriously and BMD is unable to detect and intercept them. Therefore, the reason behind building of BMD is tenable. It is unlikely that the US deterrence is in danger due to ballistic missiles. In fact, building of BMD could lead to the development of large-scale offensive weapons, which could put the US deterrence in danger.

Table 7.1: Actors and Threats

	Russia	China	Emerging ICBM Capable States	Emerging Ballistic Missile Capable States	Terrorists	Accidental or Unauthorised launch
Size	Very Large	Medium	Small	Small	Unknown	Small
Long Range Missile Possession	High	High	Small	None	Unknown	Unknown
Short Range Missile Possession	High	High	High	Low-High	Unknown	Unknown
Potential Strategies Against the US	Strategic Deterrence	Strategic Deterrence and Theatre Access Denial	Theatre Access Denial	Theatre Access Denial	Unknown	Unknown
Political Tension	Medium	Medium	High	Low-High	High	Unknown

Further, there are other threats that cannot be dealt with by deployment of BMD. The BMD cannot protect the US or its Allies against the threat of suitcase bombs. The BMD cannot deal with nuclear devices planted inside planes, boats or cars; nor can it protect from threats similar to 9/11; nor it can avert biological and chemical attacks. Although, in theory, it is correct that the post-Cold War threats of missile technology and WMD do strongly warrant effective missile defence systems but the reality is that BMD would become obsolete as soon as it is deployed. The reason is that new technologies advance very quickly. These new technologies will clearly find new mechanisms for inflicting WMD on the US. Also, NMD will encourage the proliferation of nuclear weapons as countries will begin arms race to protect their deterrence.

Threat of Cruise Missiles and Cruise Missile Defence (CMD)

According to Federation of American Scientists (FAS), "Cruise missile is an unmanned, self-propelled guided vehicle that sustains flight through aerodynamic lift for most of its flight path and whose primary mission is to place ordnance or special payload on the target."[8] Cruise missiles are easy to build, easy to maintain and difficult to detect. Therefore, a large number of third world countries are turning towards development of cruise missiles. The NIE-95 19 has mentioned about threats posed by cruise missile proliferation. It was stated that development of ballistic missiles is relatively complicated and involves discrete sequential steps, time and skill. Also, testing of ballistic missiles is difficult and it could be detected by the international community easily. On the other hand, cruise missiles are easier to develop and less detectable because there is no need to test large scale rocket mortars. They are easier to construct and hide because MTCR avoids restrictions on manned aircrafts sales and production. The NIE 95 19 also noted that potential proliferators would use cruise missiles for regional war fighting and could launch them from ships to threaten the US.[9] A report by the US Congressional Research Service states:

> In contrast to ballistic missile proliferation, cruise missiles present a particular challenge for monitoring and control because they exploit technology that is well understood and well established in the civil aviation industry. Missile airframes, navigation systems, jet engines, satellite maps, and mission planning computers and software all can be purchased on the commercial market. Cruise missile technology' hides in plain sight'-making it difficult to identify a military programme.[10]

Another concern is the ability of cruise missiles to carry chemical and biological weapons towards their targets. These kinds of weapons are most effective when disseminated into low stream and at low altitude. Thus, cruise missiles are excellent carriers for disseminating chemical and biological weapons. Cruise missiles can carry conventional high explosive warheads, cluster munitions or fuel air explosives.[11]

Today, 70 countries possess cruise missiles, out of which 40 of them are developing countries.[12] Among them are some rogue states which are considered as direct threats to the US. North Korea has land based SSC-2b, HY-1 Silkworm and HY-2 Silkworm. Iran too has Chinese HY 2 Silkworm and Ji 82. Iranian government also states that cruise missiles like Raad are under development. Above all, China has a bulk of cruise missiles and is also responsible for the proliferation of cruise missiles in the Middle East and Pakistan.[13]

There are two main reasons for proliferation and use of cruise missiles against the US. First, adversaries have seen that the US missile defence programme has a poor performance vis-à-vis cruise missiles. This has been reflected during Gulf War I and II. In 2003, the Patriot missile defence programme faced problems in dealing with cruise missiles and UAVs. Therefore, it encourages the enemy to use cruise missiles as the US has no proper defence against it. Second, the American adversaries are likely to have the operational advantages of combining cruise and ballistic missile launches so as to increase the success probability for even the best of defences of the US. Converting UAV or small airplanes into cruise missiles offer attractive and cost-effective methods to adversaries. When these are combined with more expensive and sophisticated ballistic and cruise missiles, it raises the stakes enormously for American missile defences.[14]

In order to deal with the threat of cruise missile, the US decided to develop CMD. The Defence Department Joint Theatre Air and Missile Defence Office were given the responsibility for CMD. Unfortunately, the US has not given so much importance to CMD as compared to BMD system because cruise missile presents an operational challenge.[15] An effective CMD is required to perform a series of military tasks called the 'kill chain'. The actions to be performed are:

- Surveillance radars must detect manned and unmanned aircraft, including cruise missile.
- CMD must be able to track the aircraft along its course.
- Aircraft should be identified as cruise missile, a friendly or neutral aircraft. This process is called as combat identification.
- The next step is the decision to engage cruise missile either by naval, ground or airborne platforms. This step includes finally intercepting and neutralising the cruise missile with weapons.[16]

However, currently, the US lacks the capacity for tracking and intercepting the cruise missile threat. The reasons are:

- Surveillance systems are ground based, with limited detection against low altitude targets.
- Interception and engagement capabilities are based on widely dispersed fighters, with unrealistically long reaction times against asymmetric threats.
- Alert air defenders use rule of engagement based on visual identification which is extremely insufficient method, especially in bad weather or at night.[17]

Assessment of BMD in 2003 War in Iraq

This war again depicted that engagement between Iraqi ballistic missiles and American Patriot missile defences did not went in the favour of America. All nine Iraqi missiles were detected and destroyed but American and Kuwaiti missile defences and warning systems failed to detect or intercept all five Iraqi low flying cruise missiles. One of the cruise missile came close to the US Marine encampment on the war's first day. Iraq's use of low flying cruise missiles and slow flying air vehicles also resulted into mistaken friendly fire destroying two aircraft leading to death of three crew members. The performance of the US missile defence system is evaluated in the Table 7.21 that follows:

Table 7.21: Threats and Responses in 2003 Iraq War

Date	Threats-Real or Mistaken	Apparent Targets	Response
20 March 0718Z	1 cruise missile-Seersucker	Marine Camp Commando	No detection indicated, not missile interception attempted
20 March 0924Z	1 unknown missile	TAA Thunder	Missile was detected by USS Higgins and intercepted after launch of three PAC 2 GEM missiles.
20 March 1030Z	1 ballistic missile-Ababil 100	Camp Commando and Camp Doha	Missile was detected by Air and Missile Defence Work Station (AMDWS) and intercepted after two PAC-3 missiles were fired.
20 March 2100-2200Z	2 ballistic missiles-Ababil-100, al Samoud		Missiles were not intercepted, fell into Persian Gulf
20 March 2320Z	1 ballistic missile-Ababil-100	Camp Udari	Missile was intercepted after one GEM and one PAC-3 missile were fired

21 March 1001Z	1 ballistic missile-Ababil 100	TAA Fox, Al Jahra	Missile was detected by AMDWS and intercepted after Kuwaiti Patriot battery fired two GEM missiles
23 March 1547Z	Friendly fire-British Tornado GR-4	Somewhere in northern Kuwait	US Patriot PAC-2 battery misidentified friendly aircraft as a missile threat and killed two pilots
23 March	1 ballistic missile-al-Samoud	Camp New Jersey	Missile was intercepted after US Patriot battery fired one PAC-2 and one GEM missile.
24 March 1035Z	1 ballistic missile-al-Samoud	Camp New Jersey	Missile was intercepted after three GEM-Plus missiles were fired.
24 March 1342Z	1 ballistic missile-Ababil 100	Camp Doha	Missile was not intercepted, fell into Kuwait desert
24 March 1248Z	1 ballistic missile-Ababil 100	Camp Commando	Missile was intercepted by Kuwaiti Patriot battery
26 March 1250Z	Friendly fire-US F-16 CJ	Patriot battery forward-deployed to protect 3rd Infantry Division	Mistaking the F-16 for a missile threat, the Patriot's radar "painted" the F-16, which in turn fired on the radar, damaging it. The Patriot battery, reportedly, was operating through automatic mode.
26 March 1658Z	1 ballistic missile-Ababil 100		Missile blew up shortly after launch without causing damage.

27 March, 0831Z	1 ballistic missile-Ababil 100	Coalition Forces Land Component Command Headquarters.	Missile was intercepted by US and Kuwaiti batteries after four GEM missiles were fired.
27 March 2056Z	1 ballistic missile-Ababil 100 or FROG-7	Northern Iraq	Missile was not intercepted, Landed in the desert.
28 March 2250Z	1 cruise missile-Seersucker	Struck shopping mall outside Kuwait City	Press reports indicate no detection and no interception.
28 March	2 manned ultralights	US Army forward encampment south of Baghdad.	No detection until two penetrating aircraft were directly over encampment. Tracked by Avengers, but no interception attempted due to delay in execution by authorities.
29 March 1500Z	1 ballistic missile-FROG-7	Northern Kuwait	Missile was not intercepted, fell into desert.
1 April 0603Z	1 ballistic missile-al-Samound	Forces in LSA Bushmaster	A US Patriot battery intercepted the threatening missile with a PAC-3 interceptor.
1 April	1 unknown missile		Missile was not intercepted.
1 April	3 cruise missiles-Seersucker		Missiles were not intercepted, landed near Iraq-Kuwait border
2 April	Friendly fire-US F/A-18C	Near Karbala	A US Patriot battery misidentified the F/A-18 as a threatening missile and destroyed the aircraft, killing its pilot.

3 April	3 ballistic missiles-FROG-7		Missiles were not intercepted, landed in An Najaf

Source: Gromley, Dennis M (2008), *Missile Contagion: Cruise Missile Proliferation and the Threat to International Security*, Prager Security International

Therefore, the US has no appropriate and reliable defence against cruise missile threat. Cruise missiles are likely to be a weapon used by rogue states or terrorist groups against the US. Thus, the US has to deal with the challenge of cruise missiles proliferation and should look beyond the development of BMD so as to address the real threat in the wake of proliferation. Similarly, the US BMD is unable to deal with unexpected and sudden threats such as 9/11. This will continue to pose threats to the US deterrence in future. As explained earlier, the US BMD would lead to the offensive-defensive race of weapons which would further decrease US deterrence rather than enhancing it. Following are the problems of missile defences which are not conducive to international peace:

- **It would increase the problem of missile proliferation:** If the international community and adversaries are convinced that missiles can penetrate defences, they would increase the proliferation of missiles. The adversaries and competitors of the US will start investing their time and resources into offensive programmes, thus resulting in greater number of sophisticated offensive missile programmes.
- **It would reduce crisis stability:** If the defender is able to make such offensive weapons which could penetrate the missile defences of an opponent, it will increase the incentive for an offender to strike an opponent missile before they are launched. Countries like Russia and China have developed capacities for delivering multiple warheads from a single missile, which have further increased danger for preemptive strikes.
- **It would complicate deterrence:** The development and proliferation of offensive weapons will complicate the deterrence of the US. Further, an enemy would try to deal with the US by development of cruise missiles or suitcase bombs.[18]

Arms Control, Missile Defence and Deterrence

As mentioned in previous chapter that Russia and China fear that the US is enhancing its first strike capability by deployment of BMD. The reason is that the US has not made much change in its nuclear policies and combination of offensive and defensive weapons does give rise to the fear of first strike attack.

The US's nuclear capability is not very different from its level during the Cold War period, during which Robert McNamara estimated that 400 surviving "equivalent megatons" could destroy the Soviet Union's ability to survive as a society. In the present context, various unclassified reports mention that US nuclear plans include approximately 500 nuclear warheads, which are consistent with McNamara's analysis. The US war plans also include a "prompt retaliatory" attack option which means that an attack would be launched within 15–20 minutes of detecting an incoming attack on its territories. This requires a high degree of alertness, thus making the pre-emptive strike option also available to Washington. In addition, the US has repeatedly mentioned that it can launch a nuclear attack to protect European cities.[19]

The US has repeatedly stressed on the reduction of nuclear weapon strategic forces and its commitment to reducing nuclear weapons. However, the actual number of warheads dismantled has been less than that claimed by the US. Only 100 warheads were dismantled in 2006 and approximately 250 in 2007. This is far less than the Pentagon's claim of 1,800 warheads per year. At the current rate, it is estimated that a 50 percent cut in the overall stockpile will only be completed by 2023.[20] China is particularly concerned about the nuclear triad mentioned in the *Nuclear Posture Review* 2001. It includes strategic strikes (conventional and nuclear), strategic defences (active and passive) and dynamic nuclear production facilities.[21] China is also concerned about growing American emphasis on long-range conventional precision strike weapons. China feels that the US could use these weapons to destroy its nuclear warheads. It is also worried about a possible nuclear attack during a Taiwanese crisis, as the US has mentioned that during such a crisis, it would protect Taiwan. The US has stated that the use of nuclear weapons is not its first policy but one cannot rule out the use of limited nuclear capability. As a result, both Russia and China fear that the combination of strategic superiority combined with BMD will give the US "first strike" capability and erode their deterrence.

China also fears that the US ballistic missile submarines stationed in the Pacific Ocean, armed with Trident II D5 SLBMs, could fire at Chinese DF-5A missile silos. The Trident forces are the main element of American nuclear war plans against China. The US may not use long-range bombers based in the Pacific region as they would require a relatively long time to reach their targets and would have to penetrate Chinese airspace. Similarly, the Pentagon will not use its ICBMs, based on silos in the Upper Midwest, as they would have to over-fly Russia and risk triggering its early-warning system. Since the end of the Cold War, US nuclear forces have been shifted to the Pacific in the form of additional Trident SSBNs based at the submarine base at Bangor, Washington. For these reasons, it is believed that Tridents may strike against the DF-5A, which is the sole Chinese nuclear weapon system capable of hitting the American continent and China's primary deterrent against the US.[22] If some strategic forces are preserved by China, they will notbe able to retaliate due to BMD systems.

In order to deal with this issue, the US must first reduce its nuclear weapons and missile capability by conclusion of bilateral and multilateral arms control treaties with Russia and China. The arms control should be real and should not be just in name. If the US wants to deploy BMD, it should keep only small force of nuclear weapons which can deter rogue states and terrorists groups. This will address the fear of Russia and China regarding first strike attacks of the US and move the world towards disarmament. This will also give a chance to these three countries to revise their relationships which is an important part of 'diplomatic deterrence.' As mentioned in previous chapter, the US could only achieve its aim of global nuclear disarmament and deployment of the US BMD, only when it improves its relationship with Russia and China. In fact, arms control agreements and improving relations can go hand in hand.

International Engagement Towards Dealing with the Threat of Missiles

The present situation reflects the multipolar arms race in which the US efforts are towards dominating the scenario by developing BMD while the other states feel left out. This is profoundly dangerous. The absence of any missile control regime has made the situation much worse. Amb. David Smith, speaking on the importance of missile non-proliferation regime said:

> A successful non-proliferation regime could decrease the urgency of more and more advanced defences, offence-defence technological challenge, time to obsolescence, numbers and types of threatening offensive missiles and diversity of likely adversaries."[23]

There could be three main ways to address the proliferation of missiles, both ballistic and cruise missiles, as described below:

Treaty Regime

Control on proliferation of missiles and further restrain on the development of missiles can be attained by the regional and international treaty regime based on the lines of the Non Proliferation Treaty (NPT). This includes global missile Non-proliferation treaty, Global IRBM ban, regional missile ban etc. Although, there has been no such treaty agreed at the international level.[24] It has been said:

> A non-discriminatory and comprehensive treaty prohibiting development, production and acquisition of ballistic missiles would need to be pursued single-mindedly along an incremental time-bound route. Russia, the US , China and perhaps even Pakistan and some other countries may not find a zero ballistic missile regime acceptable. A global anti-missile crusade for a multi-national negotiated treaty may not constitute stray-eyed idealism but be an idea whose time has come.[25]

Such a global non-proliferation regime can be based on the model of Zero ballistic missile programme as anticipated by President Reagan or Global IRBM ban. Zero Ballistic missile consists of four stages:

- **Stage I:** The US and Russia would agree to reduce the number of deployed missile forces beyond START II treaty.
- **Stage II:** An international missile conference which addresses the concerns of all interested countries for missile proliferation, export controls and international space cooperation.

- **Stage III:** Here, ZBM regime would be designed and a ballistic missile free zone would be negotiated.
- **Stage IV:** All states having major missiles, such as the US, Russia, UK and France, would agree to destroy all existing missile arsenals not later than agreed upon year.[26]

Therefore, the ZBM regime would not only deal with the proliferation of missiles but will also provide comprehensive elimination of existing arsenals. Therefore, it is non- discriminatory in nature. Another proposal for the global non-proliferation regime could be Global IRBM ban based on the model of the INF treaty. The INF treaty was signed between the US and the Soviet Union in 1987. This treaty bans all US and Russian land based cruise missiles and ballistic missile systems with a range of 500 to 5,500 kms. Therefore, this treaty covers short range missiles and intermediate range missiles.[27] Such a ban on intermediate range missiles, multiple range systems and new missiles appear feasible not only for P-5 powers, but also for regional missile powers.[28] It would not only eliminate threat of rogue states missiles but will also maintain the status quo regarding large-scale weapons with Russia and China.[29]

Strengthening Export Control Regime: Missile Technology Control Regime (MTCR)

The MTCR was established in 1987 to deal with the problem of proliferation of WMD. It now has 33 members. The aim of MTCR was to set up common export policies so as to control the spread of technology. Such restrictions would enable another country to acquire missiles that could deliver a payload of more than 500 kgs, with a range of more than 300 kms.[30] The MTCR Annexure was divided into two categories. Category I consists of the complete rocket, UAV and their sub systems. The trading of these items is totally restricted. Category II consists of propellant systems, launch and ground support equipments as well as material for construction of missiles.[31] The transfer of these items is less restricted and the following are kept in mind while transferring any such items:

- Whether the intended recipient is pursuing or has ambitions for acquiring WMD

- The purpose and capability of intended recipient missile and space programmes
- The potential contribution the proposed transfer could make to the intended recipient towards development of missiles or WMD
- The credibility shown by the intended recipient towards the purpose of purchase.
- Whether the potential transfer violates any other international treaty.[32]

But there are some limitations of MTCR and therefore it has been unable to deal with the proliferation of missiles. These limitations are mentioned below:

- The MTCR has been unable to deal with the threat of cruise missiles and UAV.
- The MTCR has helped to facilitate missile development and trade among its participants. After becoming a member of MTCR, Ukraine received a concession from that as a participant, it could retain its missiles with a range of 500 kms. South Korea also received the US approval for 300 km-range of missiles and made a case for 500 km-range of missiles for its SLV programme.[33]
- There is lack of transparency and legal mechanisms in MTCR. There are no multilateral mechanisms to check non-compliance and to check the ability and will of members to comply with the agreements of MTCR.
- The MTCR did not offer any incentive to countries to follow the rule of non-proliferation of missile technologies. The countries see no incentive in joining MTCR.[34]
- The MTCR address only the supply-side of the proliferation problem and ignores the demand-side. Missiles are acquired for a variety of reasons such as regional security threats, prestige issues or to maintain deterrence. Unless the demand sides are addressed, the problem of missile proliferation cannot be solved.
- Another problem is that many active missile development states remain outside the MTCR, like, North Korea, Iran, India and Pakistan. Unless all the potential suppliers are part of MTCR, the problem cannot be solved. Also, there are cases of violation, especially by China. China has violated MTCR regime by proliferating M-11 missiles.

- The MTCR is unable to control new technologies like cruise missiles.[35]

Therefore, there are many shortcomings in the present export control regime and there is a need to enforce missile export regime. The MTCR should expand its control regimes and must include small range missiles, scuds and cruise missiles.

MTCR = Demand side controls + Expanding export control to include new technologies + Universal membership + Norm building against missiles.

Confidence Building Measures (CBMs)

The aim of CBMs is to reduce the tensions, anxiety and suspicion among the parties by making the parties' behaviour more predictable.[36] Parties build missiles due to their security concerns. Effective CBMs will reduce such concerns, therefore consequently reducing the incentives for making missiles. Such CBMs could start from measures like launch pre-notification and observations measures and unilaterally, bilateral or multilaterally negotiated no first use policies. This could be followed by de-alerting, de-targeting and establishment of missile free zones. Measures should be taken to build CBMs among bilateral adversaries such as India and Pakistan.[37] Therefore, CBMs can play an important role in addressing the problem of missile proliferation. In fact it has been said that CBMs should be combined with MTCR so as to deal with the problem of proliferation of missiles.

There are two approaches to apply CBMs: Traditionalist and Transformationalist. Traditionalist approach aims to make conflict situations less stable without changing the underlying causes of the conflicts. If this approach is applied to the problem of missile proliferation, it will encourage openness about missile capabilities and launches in order to lessen the danger of surprise attacks and misinterpretations. Transformationalist approach believes that CBMs possess the capacity to change the terms on which states interact rather than to ameliorate them. It aims to build trust and confidence among the members.[38]

Global Control Systems (GCS) and Hague Code of Conduct, which is also known as IcoC, were introduced as CBM measures to control spread of ballistic missiles. GCS was formed to reduce the danger of using missiles in peace times, including the risk of misperception by other states of launches conduct, to develop norms of conduct in the field of missiles and to encourage states to voluntary follow up these norms and to renounce the possession of WMD.[39] Global Control system consists of two important blocks: establishment of non-proliferation regime and transparency.

However, the present proposed CBM measures have several shortcomings. The GCS, although could present a comprehensive approach to address the problem of missile proliferation, it is ambiguous. In view of safeguarding the security interests of states, to halt the development of missiles is neither political nor military feasible. Another criticism of the GCS is that rogue states can legitimise their missile programme by being part of GCS.[40] Under Secretary of State John Bolton said about the Hague Code of Conduct:

> [I]t is no secret that the ICOC has its limitations. For example, in taking on the political commitment pursuant to the ICOC to exercise maximum possible restraint in the development, testing and deployment of ballistic missiles capable of delivering weapons of mass destruction, the United States — like other countries — understands this commitment as not limiting our right to take steps in these areas necessary to meet our national security requirements consistent with U.S. national security strategy.[41]

Countries like India, Pakistan, South Africa, and Brazil were invited to be part of code so as to reap the benefits of the peaceful use of space technologies. But, apart from South Africa, none of these countries have agreed to be part of the Code. The heavy reliance of code on CBMs has also been criticised. Israel said that CBMs could be useful in preventing missile proliferation but should be started at a regional level rather than at a global level. Also, there have been no provisions for incentives for joining the code of conduct to encourage countries like North Korea, Iran etc. These countries see no reason for halting their ballistic missile programmes and to be a part of norm against ballistic missiles.[42]

The objective of the code should be to delegitimise the possession of missiles and thus make ownership of missiles a stigma and breach of the international law. But there has been no such mention in the code. Code mentions that proliferation of missiles is a challenge, and aims to deal with it. It does not make any mention of the reversal and attainment of missile disarmament. This also means that those countries which possess missiles will continue to possess them in the future as well. Under such conditions, other states will continue to fear the missiles developed by other states and would not be prepared to give up their programmes. The other important thing to be noted is that this code or GCS does nothing to deal with new emerging missile threat, i.e., cruise missiles. Cruise missiles are becoming poor men's air force as they are easy to build and develop. Unfortunately, none of the international conducts paid attention to it. Therefore, there is need to strengthen CBM efforts. Some of the CBMs could include ban of flight testing, introduction of ban on flight testing and no-deployment zone etc.[43]

Missile Defence or International Control on Proliferation of Ballistic Missiles?

The reliability of the international community on the existing non-proliferation regimes has been reduced. The recent events show that China is still proliferating missile technology and missile components to Pakistan and North Korea, despite being a part of MTCR. There remain many countries outside the non-proliferation regime that are active in building nuclear weapons and their delivery vehicles. This continues to haunt the security of those countries which are part of arms control or restrict themselves from developing armaments. Many countries refuse to be part of arms control and disarmament process because of their discriminatory nature. For example India has refused to be part of NPT and CTBT because they retain the nuclear weapons of P-5 states without the assurance of nuclear disarmament, and yet prevent other countries from developing nuclear weapons. There is a need for renewed emphasis on the Arms Control and Disarmament efforts and to adopt a non-discriminatory approach.

The US should understand that BMD will neither add to international security nor to its deterrence. It would lead to offensive-defensive race of weapons and more proliferation of ballistic missiles and counter-measures. As mentioned earlier, Russia and China are concerned about the BMD programme of the US and have voiced their apprehensions regularly. China, for example, has threatened that it will not sit silently, but will respond to the US with armament buildup.[44] At the same time, the belief of the US and the Soviet Union that nuclear weapons, ballistic missiles and ABM system add to the deterrence of their respective countries has set an example for other countries to create such systems. Countries like India, Pakistan, North Korea and Iran have either come up with their ballistic missiles and nuclear weapons or are trying to come up with their weapons. Israel has the most advanced nuclear weapons and missile programme outside the P-5 states, but is closely tied to the US. Therefore, there have been no international pressures on Israel for giving up its missile or nuclear weapons programme.[45]

The BMD programme aims to limit only ballistic missiles so as to strengthen US deterrence. But ballistic missiles are not the only means of delivery. There are other platforms used like bombers, aircraft carriers, ships, submarines armed with long-range missiles etc. Besides this, there are suitcase bombs to deliver radiological weapons which could also be used easily by terrorist groups.[46] Therefore, unilateral BMD does not offer a comprehensive framework to deal with proliferation of missiles or WMD. The US should spend its energies in having friendly relationship with other major powers which can further lead to deployment of 'universal BMD' system. Such system, if deployed, would take Russia and China into confidence and would stop them to have proliferation of nuclear weapons. The focus should be on comprehensive treaty regime, norm building, and CBMs to address the problem of missile proliferation. This will not only stop proliferation of missiles but will also protect the US and its allies from missile threats. In view of this, the debate about role of BMD in the US nuclear deterrence needs a completely new approach. The emphasis should be shifted on the Arms Control and Disarmament efforts and to adopt a non-discriminatory approach instead of relying on BMD which in turn escalates international arms race.

Annexure 1

Missile Threat to the US

SRBM Threat

Missile	Propellant	Deployment Mode	Maximum Range
Russia			
SCUD B (SS-1C Mod 1)	Liquid	Road Mobile	185
SS-1c Mod 2	Liquid	Road Mobile	150+
SS-21 Mod 2	Solid	Road Mobile	43
SS-21 Mod 3	Solid	Road Mobile	75
SS-26	Solid	Road Mobile	185+
Iskander E	Solid	Road Mobile	170+
China			
CSS-6 Mod 1	Solid	Road Mobile	370
CSS-6 Mod 2	Solid	Road Mobile	550+
CSS-6 Mod 3	Solid	Road Mobile	450+
CSS7- Mod 1	Solid	Road Mobile	185
CSS7- Mod 2	Solid	Road Mobile	370
CSS8	1st Stage Solid 2nd Stage Liquid	Road Mobile	93
B611	Solid	Road Mobile	93
North Korea			
SCUD B	Liquid	Road Mobile	185
SCUD C	Liquid	Road Mobile	310
Toksa	Solid	Road Mobile	75
ER SCUD	Liquid	Road Mobile	435-625
Pakistan			
Hatf I	Solid	Road Mobile	50
Shaheen 1	Solid	Road Mobile	280 +
Ghaznavi	Solid	Road Mobile	250

Iran			
Fateh 110	Solid	Road Mobile	120+
Shahab 1	Liquid	Road Mobile	185
Shahab II	Liquid	Road Mobile	310
CSS-8	Solid/Liquid	Road Mobile	93

MRBM/IRBM Threat

Missile	Number of Stages	Propellant	Deployment Mode	Maximum Range	Number of Launchers
China					
CSS 2	1	Liquid	Transportable	1,900	5 to 10
CSS 5 Mod 1	2	Solid	Road Mobile	1,100+	Fewer than 50
CSS 5 Mod 2	2	Solid	Road Mobile	1,100+	Fewer than 50
CSS 5 Conventional	2	Solid	Mobile	1,100	Fewer than 30
CSS 5 ASBM	2	Solid	Mobile	900+	Not yet Deployed
North Korea					
No Dong	1	Liquid	Road Mobile	800	Fewer than 50
IRBM	1	Liquid	Mobile	2,000+	Fewer than 50
Pakistan					
Ghauri	1	Liquid	Road Mobile	800	Fewer than 50
Shaheen II	2	Solid	Road Mobile	1,250+	Unknown
Iran					
Shahab 3	1	Liquid	Road Mobile	800	Fewer than 50
Shahab 3 variant	1	Liquid	Road Mobile	1200+	
New MRBM	2	Solid	Road Mobile	1200+	Not yet deployed
IRBM/ICBM	Undetermined	Undetermined	Undetermined	Undetermined	Undetermined

ICBM Threat

Missile	Number of Stages	Warhead per Missile	Propellant	Deployment Mode	Maximum Range	Number of launchers
Russia						
SS-18 Mod 4	2+PBV	10	Liquid	Silo	5,500+	104

SS-18 Mod 5	2+PBV	10	Liquid	Silo	6,000+	(total for Mod 4 and 5)
SS-19 Mod 3	2+PBV	6	Liquid	Silo	5,500+	122
SS 25	3+PBV	1	Solid	Road Mobile	7000	201
SS 27 Mod 1	3+PBV	1	Solid	Silo and Road Mobile	7000	54
SS 27 Mod –X-2	3+PBV	Multiple	Solid	Silo and Road Mobile	7000	Not yet deployed
China						
CSS 3	2	1	Liquid	Silo and Transportable	3,400+	10 to 15
CSS 4 Mod 2	2	1	Liquid	Silo	8000+	About 20
CSS 10 Mod 1	3	1	Solid	Road Mobile	4500+	Fewer than 15
CSS 10 Mod 2	3	1	Solid	Road Mobile	7000+	Fewer than 15
North Korea						
Taepo Dong 2	2	1	Liquid	Undetermined	3,400+	Not yet deployed

SLBM Threat

Missiles	Number of Stages	Warhead per missile	Booster Propellant	Submarine Class	Maximum Range	Number of Launch Tubes
Russia						
SS-N-18	2+PBV	3	Liquid	DELTA III	3,500+	96
SS-N-20	3+PBV	10	Solid	Typhoon	5,500+	40
SS-N-23 / Sineva	3+PBV	4	Liquid	DELTA IV	5,500+	96
Ss-NX-32	3+PBV	6	Solid	DOLGORUKIY (Borey) Typhoon	5500+	16, not yet deployed

China						
CSS-NX-3/ JL-1	2	1	Solid	XIA	1000+	12, Not yet deployed
CSS-NX-14/ JL-2	3	1	Solid	JIN	4500+	Not yet deployed

Source: http://www.fas.org/irp/threat/missile/naic/NASIC2009.pdf

Annexure 2

Relationship Between Deterrence and BMD During the Cold War

Type of Deterrence	Meaning of Deterrence	Relationship between Deterrence and BMD
Massive Retaliation	In case of a war or a conflict, the US is bound to retaliate with nuclear weapons. To maintain this deterrence, the US maintains reliable and credible nuclear weapons.	Both the US and USSR maintain high levels of nuclear weapons and this prevents conflict between the two superpowers. Introduction of BMD would degrade first-strike capability of the other side. As a result, both sides would engage in developing offensive weapons so as to degrade the other's defensive measures.
Flexible Response	Under this doctrine, the US would be open to various options and would respond by using conventional and nuclear weapons, depending on the circumstances. This doctrine was adopted to deal with the USSR's conventional attack.	Flexible Response established positive relationship with deterrence. Mac Namra presents two ways under flexible response: flexible response; offensive and defensive. In case of any military attack by USSR on the US, the US would destroy all the military installations of USSR and would protect its own civilian and industrial population by deployment of BMD.

Mutual Assured Destruction	Both sides would retain high confidence in their retaliatory capacities. The assumption was that attack by one side could lead to escalation of conflict and ultimately to use of nuclear weapons. The use of nuclear weapons would produce catastrophic results for both the US and USSR. This fear prevents war between the two adversaries.	There was a negative relationship between BMD and MAD. BMD would reduce first strike capability of other states. Other states would respond by development of such counter-measures which would penetrate the missile defence of the US. As a result, deployment and testing of BMD was limited with the ABM treaty of 1972.

Annexure 3

Relationship Between Deterrence and BMD in Post-Cold War Period

	Yes	Counter-arguments	No	Counter-arguments
Whether the US BMD programme could enhance deterrence?	It is not possible to deter rogue states like North Korea, Iran and Iraq	Rogue states are not as irrational as the US assumes them to be. North Korea agreed to give up its nuclear and missile programme in exchange for economic and technical help from the US.	States like Russia and China would feel threatened and therefore develop offensive missiles and counter-measures to penetrate BMD.	The US has repeatedly mentioned that BMD is meant to protect the US and its allies from missiles of rogue states and non state actors. It does not aim at Russia and China. Also, 80 percent of Russian Nuclear forces could survive the US first attack and possess the capability to penetrate defences.

	Rogue States are developing ballistic missiles which can threaten the US or its allies.	Rogue states are economically and technically backwards. They do not yet possess the technology to carry out successful missile attacks.	BMD technology is not effective in dealing with counter-measures.	Missile defence proponents addressed the problem of counter-measures by proposing layered missile defence system. Layered BMD system will intercept missile at three stages: boost phase, midcourse phase and terminal phase. It is designed to provide more robust answer to the problem of counter-measures
	If states realise that their attacks will not succeed, they would deter from attacking the US or its allies	States will develop other means to threaten the US such as suitcase bombs, anti-satellite weapons etc.	BMD cannot deal with cruise missiles.	The US is developing cruise missile defence (CMD) so as to address the threat of cruise missiles.

Notes

Chapter 1

1. Jeffrey Record (2004), "Nuclear Deterrence, Preventive War and Counter Proliferation," Policy Analysis paper, accessed on 15 November 2007 URL: http://www.cato.org/pubs/pas/pa519.pdf:1-32
2. There are several cases where nuclear weapons actually prevented war. The most important historical example of this is prevention of conflict between the US and USSR during the Cold War. Even after the Cold War, one cannot dismiss the importance of nuclear deterrence. Soon after the Cold War, the US faced Gulf War I. Iraq was deterred from using chemical and biological weapons mainly because of the US' nuclear capability. Apart from the case of the US, deterrence also worked in the case of India and Pakistan. In the 1998 Kargil War, India deliberately opted not to cross the LOC because of Pakistan's nuclear weapons. Similarly, after the 2001 Parliament attacks, India did not attack Pakistan despite troop mobilisation, mainly because of Pakistan's first use policy. This led states to believe that nuclear weapons could actually prevent war.
3. Ian Kenyon and John Simpson , "Introduction" in Ian Kenyon and John Simpson (eds), *Deterrence and the New Global Security Environment* (London: Routledge Publications, 2006).
4. It is believed that a state which can develop ballistic missiles, can effectively develop counter-measure technology. Developing counter-measures against BMD is less expensive than developing a ballistic missile. Today, almost all states have ballistic missiles. Apart from Russia and China, Iran and North Korea have also shown their ballistic missile capability. Russia and China already have counter-measure technology. It is possible that other states may also develop counter-measure technology or purchase it from Russia and China.
5. DOD Dictionary of Military Terms [Online: web], accessed on 2 August 2007 URL http://www.dtic.mil/doctrine/jel/doddict/
6. Thomas Schelling, *The Strategy of Conflicts* (Cambridge: Harvard University Press,1968).
7. Ibid.

8. Deterrence relies heavily on communication of threats. Miscommunications can, in fact, result in the failure of deterrence. It has to reflect clearly to the adversary message that are unambitiuous. Vague statements must be avoided because this could result in misinterpretation. Effective communication relies on both words and deeds, including moving forces, assembling nuclear weapon warheads and indicating under which circumstances nuclear weapons will be used.
9. Richard Rosecrance, "Strategic Deterrence Reconsidered," *Adelphi Paper No 116* (London: International Institute of Strategic Studies, 1975), p. 2.
10. "The Requirements of Deterrence", Memoranda No 27 (Centre For International Studies, Princeton university, 1954), p. 8.
11. Scott D Sagan, "The Commitment Trap: Why the US Should Not Use Nuclear Threats to Deter Biological and Chemical Weapons Attacks", *International Security*, vol 24, no 4 , 2000, p. 98.
12. Roy E. Jones, Nuclear Deterrence.
13. Glenn H. Synder, "Deterrence and Power," *The Journal of Conflict Resolution*, 4(2):163-178, 1960.
14. Glenn H. Snyder, "Deterrence and Defence" in Art and Waltz (eds), *Use of Force*, p.350.
15. There is always fear of failure of deterrence, particularly, when communication fails or is misinterpreted. Albert Wohlstetter has mentioned that deterrence is not easy to maintain because the potential aggressor must consider not only the risks he accepts if he strikes, but also the risks he takes if he does not strike. If the risks of not striking are very high, deterrence can fail. Also, there is always the fear of accidental attacks. Such questions often led the US policy-makers to think of what will happen if deterrence fails? The fear of failure of deterrence and possibility of huge civilian and infrastructural loss led the US to consider the possibility of development of defence.
16. The security dilemma is a situation where the steps taken by one state to strengthen its security are regarded as a threat to other states. For example, the US is building BMD for the protection of its territories and its allies from the attacks of terrorists and rogue states. While, on the other hand, Russia and China feel that BMD is being developed mainly to degrade their deterrence and to provide the US first strike capability. Therefore, they consider the efforts taken by the US for defence as a threat to their security.
17. Alexander L. George and Richard Smoke, *Deterrence in American Foreign Policy* (London: Columbia University Press, 1974).
18. Ibid.
19. Nirmal Jindal, *War as a Political Weapon in Nuclear Age* (India: Intellectual Publishing House, 1987).

20. Alan J. Parrington (1997), "Mutually Assured Destruction: Revised," *Air Power Journal*, [Online: web], accessed on 18 June 2007, URL: http://www.airpower.maxwell.af.mil/airchronicles/apj/apj97/win97/parrin.html
21. Lawrence Freedman, *Deterrence* (London: Polity Press, 2005).
22. K.S. Triphathi, *Evolution of Nuclear Strategy* (New Delhi: Vikas Publications, 1970).
23. Bernard Brodie, "The Atomic Bomb and American Security" in Philip Bobbitt, Lawrence Freedman and Gregory F. Treverton (ed), *US Nuclear Strategy* (London: MacMillan Press Ltd ,1989).
24. Ibid.
25. Jindal, n.19.
26. Benerad Brodie, *The Absolute Weapon* (London: Harcourt Brace, 1946).
27. Kenneth Waltz, "The Spread of Nuclear Weapons: More May Be Better," *Adelphi Papers*, London: IISS, 1981 URL: http://www.mtholyoke.edu/acad/intrel/waltz1.htm
28. Stuart Mackenzie and Alan Stephens, *Bolt from the Blue: The Ballistic and Cruise Missile Problem*, Air Power Studies Centre, Paper No 20, RAAF, 1994.
29. Aaron Karp, *Ballistic Missile Proliferation: The Politics and Techniques* (London: Oxford University Press, 1996).
30. Glenn H. Synder, "Deterrence and Power," *The Journal of Conflict Resolution*, 4(2):163-178, 1960.
31. Bob Aldridge (2002), "BMD: Boost Phase Interceptors," accessed on 7 July 2007, URL: http://www.plrc.org/docs/010822A.pdf: 1-6.
32. Panskoy and Wiklieng, "Technological Aspects on BMD" in George Bunn and Christopher Chyba (ed.) *U.S. Nuclear Weapons Policy: Confirming Today Threats* (Washington D.C: Brooking Institution Press, 2006).
33. Wilton Park (2002) "Missile Defence, Deterrence and Arms Control," accessed on 20 September 2007, URL: http://www.unidir.ch/pdf/ouvrages/pdf-1-92-9045-002-1-en.pdf: 1-31.
34. James M. Lindsay and Michael O. Halnon, *Defending America: The Case of Limited National Missile Defence* (Washington: Brookings Institution, 2000).
35. Ibid.
36. Bob Aldridge (2002), "BMD: Boost Phase Interceptors," accessed 7 July 2007, URL: http://www.plrc.org/docs/010822A.pdf: 1-6
37. "Basics of Ballistic Missile Defence, [Online:Web], accessed on 10 August 2007, URL: http://pbs.gen.in/wgbh/pages/frontline/shows/missile/technology/basics.html
38. David Martin (2002), "Ballistic Missile Defence," accessed on 9 November 2007,

http://www.nti.org/e_research/official_docs/dos/702DM.DOS.pdf

39. Panskoy and Wiklieng, n.32.
40. James M. Lindsay and Michael O. Halnon, *Defending America: The Case of Limited National Missile Defence* (Washington: Brookings Institution, 2001).
41. Ibid .
42. Panskoy and Wiklieng, n.32.
43. Charles Durr (2002), "Nuclear Deterrence in the Third Millennium," accessed on 15 September 2007 URL: http://www.iwar.org.uk/military/resources/nuclear/Durr_C_W_02.pdf.:
44. Richard A. Paulsen, *The Role of United States Nuclear Weapons in the Post Cold War Era* (United States: Air University Press, 1994).
45. Jindal, n.19.
46. One of the objectives of assured destruction was to limit the defence spending on conventional weapons. The aim of massive retaliation was to reduce the dependence of the US on the ground forces and conventional weapons and to replace it by the nuclear threat. The goal was to achieve "maximum deterrence at a bearable cost."
47. Robert S. McNamara, *The Essence of Security* (New York: Harper and Row, 1968).
48. Record (2004), n.1.
49. McNamara, n.47.
50. Donald M. Snow, *Nuclear Strategy in a Dynamic World: American Policy in the 1980s* (Washington D.C: University of Albama Press, 1981).
51. Lawrence Freedman, *The Evolution of Nuclear Strategy* (New York: St Martin Press, 1989).
52. George and Smoke, n.17.
53. Samuel F. Wells, "The Origins of Massive Retaliation," *Political Science Quarterly*, 1981, 96(1):31-52.
54. Keith Payne, *Strategic Defence: Star Wars in Perspectives* (Lanham: Hamilton Press, 1986).
55. Lynne Davis, "Limited Nuclear Options: Deterrence and New American Doctrine" in Bertarm, Christoph (ed), *Strategic Deterrence in a Changing Environment* (England: Gower Publishing Company Limited, 1982).
56. Ibid.
57. Robert Powell, "Nuclear Deterrence and the Strategy of Limited Retaliation", *The American Political Science Review*, 1989, 83(2): 503-519.
58. Davis, n.55.
59. Morton H. Halperin, "The Evolution of American Military Strategy," in Richard F. Rosser (ed.), *American Defence Policy* (Colorado: US Air Force Academy, 1968).

60. GW Rathjens, "Flexible Response Options", *Orbis*, vol 18, no 3, 1974.
61. J.F. Kennedy, in Allan Nevins (ed.), *The Strategy of Peace* (United States: Harper and Row, 1960).
62. Snow, n.50.
63. Paulsen, n.44.
64. Halperin, n.59.
65. Paulsen, n.44.
66. "Flexible Response and General Purpose Forces 1961-1964," accessed 10 September 2007, UIRL: http://www.usae.army.mil/publications/misc/un19/c-4.pdf:73-113
67. Jane E. Stromseth, *The Origins of Flexible Response: NATO Debate over Strategy in 1960* (New York: St Martin Press, 1988).
68. Snow, n.50.
69. Brainslav L. Slantchev, *National Security Strategy: Flexible Response:1961-1968*, Accessed on 19 September 2007 URL: http://72.14.235.104/search?q=cache:VEkk38JxlgYJ:www.polisci.ucsd.edu/~bslantch/courses/nss/lectures/16-flexible-response.pdf+Flexible+response+in+the+US+deterrence+policy&hl=en&ct=clnk&cd=31&gl=in
70. Freedman, n.51.
71. Slantchev, n.69.
72. Swaran Singh, *Limited War: The Challenge of US Military Strategy* (New Delhi: Lancer Books, 1994).
73. Heman Kahn, *Security in the Nuclear Age* (NJ: Princeton University Press, 1961).
74. Payne, n.54.
75. Keith B. Payne,"The Fallacies of Cold War Deterrence and a New Direction", 2003, Comparative Strategy, Accessed on 21 June 2007 URL: http://www.unm.edu/~gleasong/300/su2006/keith_payne_fallacies.pdf: 411-428
76. Freedman, n.51.
77. Charles L. Glaser, "Why Even Good Defences May be Bad", 1984, *International Security*, 9(2):92-123.
78. The emphasis on conventional forces proved to be expensive and appeared to raise the threshold for the use of nuclear weapons. It has given rise to the fear of conventional war. Also, it raised the fear of conventional attacks on US allies, like the European countries by the Soviet Union.
79. Herbert Scoville, "Flexible Madness?" *Foreign Policy*, 1974, 14: 164-177.
80. Freedman, n.51.
81. Ronald Reagan, "Address to Nation on Defence and National Security", 1983 [Online: web], accessed on 5 July 2007, URL: http://www.cnn.com/SPECIALS/cold.war/episodes/22/documents/starwars.speech/

82. Standord Lakoff, *Strategic Defence in the Nuclear Age* (London: Praeger Security International, 2008).
83. Ibid.
84. Colin Gray, as cited by Robert M. Lawrence, *Strategic Defence Initiative* (1987) (London: Mansell Publishing Limited, 1985).
85. Lawrence Freedman, "The Star Wars Debate: The Western Alliance and Strategic Defence: Part II", in "New Technology and Western Security Policy", *Adelphi Paper No.191* (London: IISS, 1975).
86. Fred Hoffman, *Ballistic Missile Defences and US National Security*, Report prepared by Future Security Strategy, 1985.
87. Freedman, n.85.
88. Lawrence Freedman, "Prevention, Not Preemption", *The Washington Quarterly*, 2003, 26(2):105-114.
89. McGeorge Bundy, "To Cap the Volcano", *Foreign Affairs*, 1969, 48(1):9-12.
90. Keith B. Payne,"The Nuclear Posture Review: Setting the Record Straight", *The Washington Quarterly*, 2005, 28(3):135-149.
91. *Star Wars Debate: The Western Alliance and Strategic Defence*, Part I.

Chapter 2

1. Patrick Hughes, "Global Threats and Challenges to the US and Its Interests Abroad", 1997, [Online: web], accessed on 21 October 2007 URL:http://www.fas.org/irp/congress/1997_hr/s970205d.htm
2. "The National Security Strategy of the United States of America", 2002, accessed on 10 July 2007, URL:http://www.whitehouse.gov/nsc/nss.pdf:1-29.
3. Stuart Mackenzie and Alan Stephens, *Bolt from the Blue: The Ballistic and Cruise Missile Problem*, Air Power Studies Centre, Paper No 20, RAAF, 1994.
4. National Intelligence Estimates 1995, "Emerging Missile Threats to the US in Next 15 Years", [Online: web], accessed on 21 July 2007 URL: http://www.fas.org/spp/starwars/offdocs/nie9519.htm
5. Timothy MaCarthy, "Criteria for Assessing Ballistic Missile Threats", in "International Perspectives on Missile Defences," *Occasional Paper 5*, Centre for Non-Proliferation, 2001.
6. Hughes, n.1.
7. Robert T. Walpole, "The Ballistic Missile Threat to the US", 2000, Statement for record to the Senate Subcommittee on International Security, Proliferation, and Federal Services on the ballistic missile threat to the US, [Online: web], accessed on 20 March 2008, URL: https://www.cia.gov/news-information/speeches-testimony/2000/nio_speech_020900.html

8. Mohammad Said, "Missile Proliferation in the Middle East and Regional Security", 2001, accessed on 2 November 2007 URL: http://www.unidir.ch/pdf/articles/pdf-art75.pdf. : 49-61.
9. Paul H. Nitze and J.H. McCall, "Contemporary Security Deterrence and Precision Guided Munitions" 1997, in *Post Cold War Deterrence Policy* by Naval Studies Board.
10. "NACD: Correlation between Deterrence and Missile Defence," accessed on 28 September 2007 URL: www.dfait.gc.ca/foreign_policy/arms_clf1/isrop/research/hodge_2003/section03-en.asp.
11. John Pike, "The Ballistic Missile Defence Debates," *Current History*, 96(609), 1997.
12. Nitze and McCall, n.9.
13. Richard A. Paulsen, *The Role of United States Nuclear Weapons in the Post Cold War Era* (United States: Air University Press, 1994).
14. Ibid.
15. Michael Klare, *Rogue States and Nuclear Outlaws: America Search for A New Foreign Policy* (New Delhi: Universal Book Traders,1995).
16. Cimbala and Scouras, *New Nuclear Century: Strategic Stability and Arms Control* (Westport: Parage Publication, 2002).
17. Henry F. Cooper, "Active Defence to Help Counter Proliferation" in Peter L. Hays, Vincent J. Jodin and Alan R. Tassel, Primis(ed.), *Countering the Proliferation and Use of Weapons of Mass Destruction* (United States: Custom Publishing, 1999).
18. Ronald Dannreuther, "The Gulf Conflict: A Political and Strategic Analysis", *Adelphi Paper 264*, p. 264.
19. Deterrence in the Post Cold War Era by Jean Louis Gergorin, p. 9.
20. Ibid.
21. Ibid.
22. Cimbala and Scouras, n.16.
23. Stephen A. Cambone (2000), "Threats and Risks Promoting a Commitment to Ballistic Missile Defence," in *Sous la direction de*; Burkard Schmitt and Julian Lindley (eds), "National Missile Defence and Future Nuclear Weapon Policy," accessed on 25 May 2008 URL: http://aei.pitt.edu/713/01/occ18.pdf : 1-73.
24. Ibid.
25. "Executive Summary of the Report of the Commission to Access the Ballistic Missile Threat of the US" (1998), accessed on 22 August 2007 by the "Members of the commission to access the ballistic missile threat of the US" URL: http://www.fas.org/irp/threat/bm-threat.htm
26. Robert Wall (2007), "Pentagon Sees Iran Ashura Missile as Worrying Development,"

Aerospace Daliy and Defence Report, [Online: web], accessed on 4 December 2007, URL: http://www.aviationweek.com/aw/generic/story_channel.jsp?channel=defense&id=news/IRAN113007.xml

27. "The National Security Strategy of the United States of America" (2002), accessed on 10 July 2007, URL: http://www.whitehouse.gov/nsc/nss.pdf:1-29
28. John Newhouse (2001), "The Missile Defence Debate," *Foreign Affairs*, 80(4), pp. 97-109.
29. Masako Ikegami (2003), "Missile Defence and Nuclear Deterrence in Post-Cold War Regional Conflict," accessed on 23 September 2007 URL: www.isodarco.it/courses/candriai03/paper/candriai03-Ikegami.pdf: 1-8.
30. James M. Lindsay and Michael O. Halnon, *Defending America: The Case of Limited National Missile Defence* (Washington: Brooking Institution, 2001).
31. Dean Wilening and Kenneth Watman, *Nuclear Deterrence in a Regional Context* (United States: Rand Publication,1995).
32. Keith B. Payne (1999), "The Case for National Missile Defense," accessed on 18 July 2007, URL: http://fpri.org/americavulnerable/11.CaseforNationalMissileDefense.Payne.pdf: 171-181
33. Ashton B. Carter (2001), "The Architecture of Government in the Face of Terrorism," *International Security*, 26 (3): 5-23.
34. Ibid.
35. Wirtz and Russell (2003), "US Policy on Preventive War and Preemption," *Non-Proliferation Review*, 10(1):113-123.
36. Lawrence Freedman (2005), *Deterrence* (London: Polity Press).
37. Curtis A. Mathis (2005), "United States Missile Defence Policy in the Contempary Strategic Envoirnment," accessed on 5 August 2007, URL: http://www.strategicstudiesinstitute.army/mil/pdffiles/ksil6.pdf: 1-28
38. Stephen M. Walt (2001), "Beyond Bin Laden- Reshaping US Foreign Policy," *International Security*, 26(3):56-78.
39. Gilles Andreani (2004), "The War on Terror: Good Cause, Wrong Concepts" *Survival*, 26(4): pp. 31-50.
40. Wyn Q. Bowen (2004), "Deterrence and Asymmetry: Non-State Actors and Mass Casualty Terrorism," *Contemporary Security Policy*, 25 (1): 54-70.
41. "The National Security Strategy of the United States of America" (2002), accessed on 10 July 2007, URL: http://www.whitehouse.gov/nsc/nss.pdf:1-29
42. Paul K. Davis and Brian Michael Jenkins (2002), "Deterrence and Influence in Counter-Terrorism: A Component in the War of Al Qaeda" RAND.
43. Baker Spring (2001), "Talking Points: Terrorist Attack on America Confirms the Growing Need for Missile Defence", [Online: web], accessed on 2 November 2007,

URL: http://www.heritage.org/Research/MissileDefense/BG1477.cfm

44. *The Military Balance 2004-2005*, International institute of Strategic Studies, 2004.
45. "Annual Report on the Military Power of People Republic of China," US Department of Defence, 2005, accessed on 15 September 2007, URL: www.defenselink.mil/news/Jul2005/d20050719china.pdf: 1-45.
46. Joseph Kahn (2005), "Chinese General Threatens Use of A-bombs if US Intrudes, *New York Times*, 15 July 2005.
47. China Military Power 2009.
48. Statement given by Dr Gary L. Smith, Director of the Johns Hopkings University, URL: http://www.fas.org/spp/starwars/congress/1997_h/h970716s.htm , accessed on 5 June 2009
49. Colin R. Miller (2005), "Electromagnetic Pulse Threat 2010," URL: http://gbppr.dyndns.org/PROJ/mil/herf/bugs_ch12.pdf, accessed on 5 May 2009.
50. Dr Mark Schneider, *The Emerging EMP Threat to the United States* (Fairfax, Virginia: National Institute Press, 2007), p. 4, at *http://www.nipp.org/Adobe/EMP%20Paper%20Final%20November07.pdf* (8 October 2008).
51. Statement given by Dr Lowell Wood, URL: http://www.fas.org/spp/starwars/congress/1997_h/h970716w.htm, accessed on 20 May 2009.
52. Miller, n.49.
53. "Proposed US Missile Defence Assets in Europe" (2007), accessed on 15 November 2007, URL: www.bulgaria.usembassy.gov/uploads/images/uANvQppwr8xiXP9m6A/md706-brochure.pdf: 1-12.
54. Jeffrey Record (2004), "Nuclear Deterrence, Preventive War and Counter-Proliferation," Policy Analysis paper, accessed on 15 November 2007 URL: http://www.cato.org/pubs/pas/pa519.pdf:1-32
55. "National Strategy to Combat Weapons of Mass Destruction (2002)," accessed on 7 March 2008, URL: http://www.whitehouse.gov/news/releases/2002/12/WMDStrategy.pdf:1-6.
56. "US Unveil National Strategy to Combat WMD" (2003), *Disarmament Diplomacy, Issue 69*, [Online: web], accessed on 7 November 2007 URL: http://www.acronym.org.uk/dd/dd69/69ddnr03.htm
57. Mayuka Yamazaki (2006), "Origin, Developments and Prospects for the Proliferation Security Initiative," accessed on 20 July 2007, URL: http://www12.georgetown.edu/sfs/isd/JFD_2006_PSA_Yamazaki.pdf: 1-24.
58. James R. Holmes (2007), "India and the Proliferation Security Initiative: A US Perspective, *Strategic Analysis* 31(2): 315-337.
59. Andrew C. Winner (2005), "The Proliferation Security Initiative: The New Face of

Interdiction," *Washington Quarterly*, 28(2): 129-143.

60. Ibid.
61. Turner Wohlschlegel and Butts (2004), "Maritime Threat Workshop," CSL Issue Paper, accessed on 7 July 2007 URL: http://209.85.175.104/search?q=cache:nF2OtD5CFCMJ:www.stormingmedia.us/24/2487/A248724.pdf+why+Regional+Maritime+Security+Initiative+RMSI&hl=en&ct=clnk&cd=14&gl=in: 1-5
62. Noel M. Morada (2006), "Regional Maritime Security in the Asia Pacific: Problems and Prospects for Maritime Security Cooperation," accessed on 20 January 2008 URL: http://www.swp-berlin.org/de/common/get_document.php?asset_id=3562:1-16
63. Winner, n.59.
64. "UN Security Council Resolution 1540," [Online: web], accessed on 15 November 2007, URL: http://www.state.gov/t/isn/c18943.htm
65. William Walker, *Weapons of Mass Destruction and International Order* (New York: Oxford University Press, 2004).
66. Andrew Prosser and Herbert Scolville (2004), "The Proliferation Security Initiative in Perspectives," accessed on 4 December 2007 URL: http://www.cdi.org/pdfs/psi.pdf: 1-13.
67. Peter Crail (2006), "Implementing UN Security Council Resolution 1540: A Risk Based Approach," accessed on 15 November 2007 URL: http://cns.miis.edu/pubs/npr/vol13/132/132crail.pdf.: 355-388
68. Kerry M. Kartchner, "The Future of the Offence-Defence Relationship" in Jeffrey A. Larsen (ed.), *Arms Control: Cooperative Security in a Changing Environment* (Lyyne Reinner Publisher Inc, 2005).
69. Paul R. Joseph, *Red Atom: Russia's Nuclear Power Programme: From Stalin to Today* (New York: WH Freedman and Company, 2000).
70. Daniel Whiteneck (2005), "Deterring Terrorists: Thoughts on Framework," *Washington Quarterly*, 28(3): 187-199.
71. Record, n.54.
72. Deterring America: Rogue States and the Weapons of Mass Destruction by D. Derek and J. Smith.
73. Scott D. Sagan, and Kenneth N. Waltz, *The Spread of Nuclear Weapons: A Debate Renewed* (New York and London: WW Norton and Company, 2003).
74. "US Quits ABM Treaty" (2001), [Online: web], accessed on 10 July 2007 URL: http://archives.cnn.com/2001/ALLPOLITICS/12/13/rec.bush.abm/
75. Remarks by President Bush on NMD, White House Transcript, 2001, [Online: web], accessed on 10 July 2007, URL: www.whitehouse.gov

76. Robert Grant (2000), "The US View on NMD and Deterrence," in Sous la direction de; Burkard Schmitt and Julian Lindley (eds.), "National Missile Defence and Future Nuclear Weapon Policy," accessed on 10 September 2007 URL: http://aei.pitt.edu/713/01/occ18.pdf : 1-73
77. "National Policy on Ballistic Missile Defence Fact Sheet (2003)", [Online: web], accessed on 14 August 2007, URL: http://www.whitehouse.gov/news/releases/2003/05/20030520-15.html
78. Ibid.
79. Caitlin Talmadge (2007), "Deterring Nuclear 9/11," *Washington Quarterly,* accessed on 7 December 2007 URL: http://www.twq.com/07spring/docs/07spring_talmadge.pdf : 21-34
80. Common Ground Staff (2004), "Ballistic Missile Defence Useless," [Online:web] accessed 20 December 2007, URL: http://commonground.ca/iss/0403152/ballistic.shtml
81. Matthew Yglesias (2006) "Just Add Missile Defence," [Online: web], accessed on 17 August 2007,URL: http://www.prospect.org/cs/articles?articleId=11709
82. Gray Brown (2002), "Walking Away: The US Withdrawal From the Anti-Ballistic Missile Treaty," [Online: web], accessed on15 December 2007, URL: http://www.aph.gov.au/library/Pubs/rn/2001-02/02rn14.htm

Chapter 3

1. "President Bush Remarks at National Defence University" (2007), [Online: web], accessed on 10 January 2008 URL: http://www.whitehouse.gov/news/releases/2007/10/20071023-3.html
2. Glenn H. Snyder (1960), "Deterrence and Power," *The Journal of Conflict Resolution,* 4(2):163-178.
3. Sean Clark (2003), "Determining Trajectory: Defining the BMD Debate," *Journal of Military and Strategic Studies,* 6(2): 1-16.
4. Darryl Howlett (2001), "New Concepts of Deterrence," in "International Perspectives on Missile Proliferation and Defences," *Occasional Paper 5,* Centre for Non-Proliferation.
5. Dean A. Wilkening (2000), "Ballistic Missile Defence and Strategic Stability," *Adelphi Paper No. 334.*
6. "Remarks by President Bush to Students and Faculty at National Defence University (2001)" URL: http://www.whitehouse.gov/news/releases/2001/05/20010501-10.html
7. John Powell (2001), "MAD is Indispensable" *Washington Times,* 21 June 2001.

8. William Walker (2004), "Weapons of Mass Destruction and International Order," *Adelphi Paper No 370.*
9. Ibid.
10. Jean-Louis Gergorin (1991), "Deterrence in the Post Cold War Era," *Adelphi Paper.*
11. Amy F. Wolf (2001), "Missile Defense, Arms Control and Deterrence: A New Strategic Framework," accessed on 3 March 2008, URL http://fpc.state.gov/documents/organization/6254.pdf: 1-6
12. Stephen L. Quackenbush (2006), "National Missile Defence and Deterrence," *Political Research Quarterly,* 59 (4) : 533-541.
13. Ken Jimbo (2000), "Rethinking Japanese Security: New Concepts of Deterrence and Defence," accessed on 21 February 2008 URL: http://www.stimson.org/japan/pdf/JNO-Security_Context.pdf: 24-45
14. Richard Harknett, "Global Stability in a Changing Defence Environment" in James J. Wirtz and Jeffrey A. Larsen (eds), *Rocket's Red Glare: Missile Defence and Future of World Politics* (USA: Westview Press, 2004)
15. Robert Powell (2003), "Nuclear Deterrence Theory, Nuclear Proliferation and Missile Defence," *International Security,* 27(4):86-118.
16. Yoichi Funabashti (2000), "Tokyo Temperance" *Washington Quarterly,* 23(3): 137-139.
17. Remarks by Under Secretary of Defence Walter B. Slocombe to the CSIS. Statesmen's Forum, 5 November 1999.
18. National Policy on Ballistic Missile Defence Fact Sheet (2003), [Online:web], accessed 14 August 2007, URL: http://www.whitehouse.gov/news/re;ease/2002/12/WMDStrategy.pdf: 1-16.
19. David Yost (2006), "Missile Defence on NATO Agenda," NATO Review, Autumn 2006, [Online: web], accessed on 2 September 2007 URL: www.nato.int/docu/review/2006/issue3/english/analysis1.html
20. Panskoy and Wiklieng, "Technological Aspects on BMD" in George Bunn and Christopher Chyba (2006), *US Nuclear Weapons Policy: Conforming Today Threats* (Washington D C: Brookings Institution Press, 2006).
21. Masako Ikegami (2003), "Missile Defence and Nuclear Deterrence in Post-Cold War Regional Conflict," accessed on 23 September 2007 URL: www.isodarco.it/courses/candriai03/paper/candriai03-Ikegami.pdf: 1- 8.
22. James Mulvenon (2002), "Missile Defence and Taiwan Scenario," Report 44, A.Henry Stimson Centre, accessed on 22 February 2008 NMD-China report URL: http://www.stimson.org/china/pdf/mulvenon.pdf: 1-8
23. *Nuclear Posture Review* (Excerpts), Submitted to Congress on 31 December,

"Nuclear Posture Review Report", 8 January 2002, [Online: web], accessed on 30 July 2007, URL: www.globalsecurity.org/wmd/libaray/policy/dod/npr.htm

24. Campbell Craig (2009), "American Power Preponderance and the Nuclear Revolution," *Review of International Studies*, 35 , pp. 27-44.
25. Ikegami(2003), n.21.
26. Stephen J. Cimbala, *Nuclear Weapons and Strategy, US Nuclear Policy for Twenty-First Century* (New York: Routledge Publication, 2005).
27. Walter A. Slocombe (2001), "The Administration Approach," *Washington Quarterly*, 23 (3): 79-85.
28. J.M. Goldgeir and J.M. Lindsay (2001), "Deploying NMD: Not Whether, But How," *Survival*, 42(1):6-28
29. David Krienger (2001), "Nuclear Deterrence, Missile Defence and Global Instability," [Online: web], accessed on 8 Oct 2007 URL: http://www.wagingpeace.org/articles/2001/04/00_krieger_nuclear-deterrence.htm
30 Quackenbush, n.12.
31. P.H. Gordon (2001), "Bush, Missile Defence and Atlantic Alliance," *Survival*, 43(1), 17-36.
32. James H. Lebovic, *Deterring International Terrorism and Rogue States: US National Security Policy after 9/11* (New York: Routledge Publications, 2007)
33. Stephen A. Cambone (2000), "Threats and Risks Promoting a Commitment to Ballistic Missile Defence" in Sous la direction de; Burkard Schmitt and Julian Lindley(eds), "National Missile Defence and Future Nuclear Weapon Policy," accessed on 25 May 2008, URL: http://aei.pitt.edu/713/01/occ18.pdf: 1- 73.
34. Neha Kumar (2007), "Warning Signals for the US: Russia-Iran Relations," *Mainstream*, XLV (45): 9-10
35. Lebovic, n.32.
36. Steven Miller (2001), 'The Flawed Case for Missile Defence,' *Survival* , 43(3).
37. Anthony H. Cordesman, *Strategic Threats and National Missile Defence, Defending US Homeland* (Washington D.C: Praeger Publisher, 2002).
38. Dayrl G. Kimball (2007), "Of Missiles and Missile Defences," *Arms Control Today*, [Online: web], accessed on 1 Nov 2007, URL: http://www.armscontrol.org/act/2007-10/focus.asp
39. Miller, n.36.
40. Lebovic, n.35.
41. Ibid.
42. Stephen Cimbala (2000), *Deterrence and Nuclear Proliferation in the Twenty-First Century* (Westport: Praeger, 2000).
43. Neha Kumar (2008), "Enhancing the United States First Strike Capability with the

Development of Ballistic Missile Defence," *World Affairs*, 12(3): 70-83.

44. Ibid.
45. Robert S. Norris and Hans M. Kristensen (2009), "Nuclear Notebook : US and Soviet/Russian Intercontinental Ballistic Missiles, 1959-2008," URL: http://thebulletin.metapress.com/content/037qk4866n431045/fulltext.pdf
46. Hans M. Kristensen and Robert S. Norris, "Chinese Nuclear Forces 2008," *Bulletin of the Atomic Scientists*, pp. 50–4, July–August 2008.
47. Ibid.
48. Stansfield Turner (1997), *Caging the Nuclear Genie: An America's Challenge for Global Security* (US: Westview Press, 1997).
49. Wilkening, n.5.
50. Frederic S. Nyland (2000), "Russian-American Nuclear Stability Issues: Opportunities and Risks in 21st Century" in Stephen Cimbala (ed), *Deterrence and Nuclear Proliferation in 21st Century* (Washington D.C: Palgrave Publication, 2000).
51. Panskoy and Wiklieng , n.20.
52. Krienger, n.29.
53. Paul H.B. Godwin (2002), "Potential Chinese Response to the US BMD" (Online:web), accessed on 1 March 2008 URL: www.stimson.org
54. Ibid.
55. Peter Dyvad, "China Response to the US Missile Defence Programme: National Options and Regional Implications," in Bertel Heurlin and Sten Rynning (ed), *Missile Defence Regional and International Implication* (London: Routledge Publications, 2002).
56. Pavel Podwig (2007) "Missile Defence: The Russian Reaction," [Online: web], accessed on 18 February 2008, URL: http://www.thebulletin.org/columns/pavel-podvig/20070226.html
57. James M. Lindsay and Michael O. Halnon (2001), *Defending America: The Case of Limited National Missile Defence* (Washington: Brooking Institution, 2001)
58. Huke Harding (2007), "Russia Missile Tests Add to Arms Race Fears," *Guardian*, 30 May 2007
59. James Hackett (2007), "Re-election Strategy or New Cold War," [Online:web], 1 November 2007 URL: http://johnibii.wordpress.com/2007/10/25/re-election-strategy-or-new-cold-war/

Chapter 4

1. During the intial stage of the administration, Secretary Hilary Clinton said that there is no use pressing China on the issue of human rights and the need is to

focus more on issues like climate change and economic insecurity. President Obama and President Hu Jintao of China agreed on a "U.S.-China Strategic and Economic Dialogue." According to the release, the dialogue will focus on addressing the challenges and opportunities that both countries face on a wide range of bilateral, regional and global areas of immediate and long-term strategic interest. This shows interest of the Obama administration in strengthening the relationship with China.

2. The US has deployed its armed forces in Iraq, Japan, South Korea and Israel. Iraq and Israel faced a threat from Iranian missiles while South Korea and Japan faced a threat from North Korea's missiles.
3. John Mearsheimer (1993), "The Case for a Ukrainian Nuclear Deterrence", *Foreign Affairs*, 72(3)
4. William C Wohlforth, Richard Little, Stuart J .Kaufman, David Kang, Charles A. Jones, Victoria Tin Bor Hui; Arthur Eckstein, Daniel Deuneey and William J. Brenner (2007), "Testing Balance of Power Theory in World History," *European Journal of International Relations* URL: http://www.dartmouth.edu/~govt/docs/Testing%20Balance-of-Power%20Theory%20in%20World%20History.pdf
5. Campbell Craig (2009), "America Power Preponderance and the Nuclear Revolution", *Review of International Studies*, 35, pp. 27-44
6. Since the fall of the General Musharraf government began, there have been various reports regarding the possibility of a Taliban takeover in the country due to the political vacuum left. There are also reports about the Pakistan's nuclear command and control structure and fear of possible breakdown.
7. As quoted by A.H. Nayyar and Zia Mian (2009), 'Violence without Limit and Pakistan's Challenge,' *Himal*, pp 35-36
8. Ibid.
9. It needs to be remembered that Pakistan's government has been supporting the Taliban since its origin, for two main motives. The first is to have a friendly government in Afghanistan and the second is to use the Taliban in a proxy war against India with which it has border disputes on Kashmir. After 9/11, Gen Musharraf declared support to the US in its war against terrorism and so against Taliban. However, nothing of this sort happened. Pakistan has taken millions of dollars in aid from the US in the name of eradicating the Taliban and has misused these dollars in building its military against India. Pakistan regards the Taliban as a strategic asset in managing its interests on both sides of borders.
10. Ahmed Rashid (2008), *Descent into Chaos: The United States and a Failure of Nation Building in Pakistan, Afghanistan and Central Asia* (US: Penguin Publishers).

11. Khalid Aziz (2009), "Stability in Pakistan and Afghanistan," *South Asia Journal*, no 23
12. *Pakistan: The Militant Jihadi Challenge*, Asia Report N°164 – 13 March 2009, URL: http://www.crisisgroup.org/library/documents/asia/south_asia/164_pakistan___the_militant_jihadi_challenge.pdf, Accessed 10 April 2009
13. Implementation of the *Sharia* law shows the total incapability of the Pakistan government to deal with Taliban. Instead of eradicating them, the Pakistan government bends on their demands. It was later proved by the Taliban's attack on Buner that the period of peace was used by the Taliban to strengthen their forces and to plan their tactics. This peace deal was criticised internationally.
14. n.12.
15. Jane Perlez and Zubair Shah (2009), "In Pakistan, Guile Helps Taliban Gain," *New York Times*, 25 April 2009.
16. As quoted by Reshmi Kazi (2007), 'Security of Pakistan's Nuclear Weapon,' URL: http://www.idsa.in/publications/stratcomments/ReshmiKazi291107.htm, [Online: Web], accessed on 10 March 2009
17. Ibid.
18. Neha Kumar (2009), "Securing Islamic Bomb," *Asia Defence News*.
19. Ashok Behuria (2007), "The Rise of Pakistan's Taliban and Response of the State," *Strategic Analysis*, 31(5).
20. Ashley Tellis (2008), "Engaging Pakistan-Getting the Balance Right," URL: hf, Accessed on 20 March 2009.
21. David Albright and Holly Higgins (2002), "Pakistan Nuclear Scientists: How Much Assistance to Al Queda?" URL: http://www.exportcontrols.org/pakscientists.html [Online: web], accessed on 19 April 2009.
22. As quoted by Paul Kerr and Merry Nikitin (2008), "Pakistan's Nuclear Weapons: Proliferation and Security Issues," URL: http://www.fas.org/sgp/crs/nuke/RL34248.pdf, Accessed 10 May 2009
23. Ibid.
24. John Bolton (2009), "The Taliban's Atomic Threat," *The Wall Street Journal*, 2 May 2009.
25. The Rumsfeld Commission report was released in 1998 so as to access the ballistic missile threat to the US. It said that North Korea is working on a ballistic missile programme and could pose a threat for the US and its allies. Soon after this report, North Korea tested the Taepo Dong missile. While the test was failure, it showed that North Korea is moving toward the development of missiles. It is not clear whether Rumsfeld calculations proved to be correct or this report triggered the DPRK towards a missile test. It is possible that the DPRK, angry about being

designated as a threat, and responded by carrying out a missile test.

26. "North Korean Diplomat Warns of Strong Step against UN Security Council," *Guardian*, 8 April 2009
27. Jenny Shin (2009), "Chronology of North Korea's Missile Tests," URL: http://www.cdi.org/pdfs/NKmissiletimeline4.14.09.pdf, Accessed 29 April 2009
28. Helene Copper and David Sanger (2009), "Obama Seizes on Missile Launch in Seeking Nuclear Cuts," New York Times, 5 April 2009
29. Jacques Fuqua (2009), "North Korea Launches Another Ballistic Missile- Now What?," URL: http://www.tribstar.com/flashpoint/local_story_108211411.html , [Online: web], Accessed on 14 May 2009
30. Tony Magana (2009), "Half Hearted Missile Defence Won't Do," *American Daily Review*, URL: http://www.americandailyreview.com/home-features-articles-blog/2009/4/10/half-hearted-missile-defense-wont-do.html, [Online: web], Accessed on 12 April 2009
31. Joseph Cirincione (2009), "North Korean Launch Not a Cause for Panic," URL: http://edition.cnn.com/2009/POLITICS/04/05/cirincione.north.korea/, [Online: web], Accessed on 10 April 2009
32. Jon Herskovitz (2009), "What's the Real Programme of North Korea's Nuclear Programme," URL: http://www.reuters.com/article/latestCrisis/idUSSEO279416, [Online: web], Acessed on 30 April 2009
33. Kyle Ballard (2008), "Doors of Perception: National Security Politics, Threat Perceptions and North Korea's Pursuit of a Credible Deterrent," *The Korean Journal of DefenceAnalysis*, 20(3), pp 231-246.
34. Ibid.
35 Ibid.
36. Ibid.
37. "North Korea Says It Has Started Extracting Plutonium," *Reuters*, 25 April 2009
38. avely, Joe (2009), "North Korea's Nuclear Trump Card," URL: http://english.aljazeera.net/news/asia-pacific/2009/05/20095275496115535.html, Assessed on 3 June 2009
39. Shahram Chubin, *Wither Iran? Reform, Domestic Politics and National Security*, (US: International Institute for Strategic Studies, 2002).
40. Ibid.
41. Richard Garwin (2008), "When Could Iran Deliver a Nuclear Weapon?" URL: http://www.thebulletin.org/web-edition/features/when-could-iran-deliver-a-nuclear-weapon, [Online: web], accessed 25 March 2009
42. Nazila Fathi and William J. Broad (2009), "Iran Launches Satellite, Is a Challenge for Obama," *New York Times*, 3 February 2009

43. Ibid.
44. Shannon N. Kile, "Nuclear Arms Control and Non-Proliferation" in *SIPRI Yearbook 2008: Armaments, Disarmament and International Security* (Oxford University Press: UK, 2008)
45. Mark Fitzpatrick (2008), *Iranian Nuclear Crisis: Avoiding Worst Case Outcome, Adelphi Paper No. 398.*
46. Bradley L. Bowman (2008), "The Demand Side : Avioding a Nuclear Armed Iran," *Orbis*, Fall 2008 , pp. 627-642
47 Kile, n.44.
48. Mark Fitzpatrick (2006), "Assessing Iran's Nuclear Programme," *Survival*, 48(3)
49. Anoushiravan Ehteshami (2000), "Tehran's Tocsin," *Washington Quarterly* , 23 (3), pp 171-176
50. Joseph S. Bermudez (2000), "DPRK-Pakistan Ghauri Missile Cooperation", URL: www.fas.org/news/Pakistan/1985/05/ghauri2.htm, [Online: web], accessed on 15 May 2009
51. Arvind Virmani, *Trilateral Nuclear Proliferation: Pakistan's Euro-Chinese Bomb* (IDSA: Delhi, 2006).
52. Gaurav Kampani (2002), "Second Tier Proliferation: The Case of Pakistan and North Korea," *The Non-Proliferation Review.*
53. David Sanger and James Dao (2002), "US Says Pakistan Gave Technology to North Korea," *New York Times*, 17 Oct 2002
54. Shishir Gupta (1999), "India Detains Ship Carrying Tools for Missile Proliferation," *Hindustan Times*, 4 July 1999.
55. Gaurav Kampani (2002), n.52.
56. Virmani, n.51.
57. Arpit Rajan (2004), "Pakistan's Nuclear Black Marketing: North Korea, Iran, Libya," URL: http://www.observerindia.com/cms/export/orfonline/modules/occasionalpaper/attachments/occpaper_1163398195078.pdf, Accessed 13 May 2009
58. *North Korea's Weapons Programmes: A Net Assessment* (2004), International Institute for Strateigc Studies.
59. Ibid.
60. Mark Fitzpatrick (2006), "Iran and North Korea: The Proliferation Nexus," *Survival*, 48(1), pp 61-80
61. Loan C. Pham (2009), "President Obama and the Ballistic Missile Defence System in Europe," URL: http://www.wagingpeace.org/articles/2009/01/30_pham_obama_bmd.php, [Online: web], Accessed 10 May 2009
62. Toby Harnden and Bruno Waterfield (2009), "Barack Obama Goes Ahead With

Missile Defence Shield Despite Disarmament Pledge," URL: http://www.telegraph.co.uk/news/worldnews/northamerica/usa/barackobama/5110918/Barack-Obama-goes-ahead-with-missile-defence-shield-despite-disarmament-pledge.html, Accessed 9 April 2009

63. "House Missile Defence Caucus Remarks on North Korean Missile Launch," URL: http://www.house.gov/apps/list/press/az02_franks/franks_missilekoreastatement_April062009.html. Accessed 3 May 2009

64. "America's Strategic Posture : The Final Report of the Congressional Commission on the Strategic Posture of the US (2009)," URL: http://media.usip.org/reports/strat_posture_report.pdf.

65. Andrien Hauri (2009), "A Better Missile Defense," URL: http://www.isn.ethz.ch/isn/Current-Affairs/Security-Watch/Detail/?lng=en&id=106572, Accessed on 5 October 2009

66. Richard Weitz (2009) "Praising Moscow Iran Policy," URL: http://www.worldpoliticsreview.com/Article.aspx?id=4411, Accessed 12 October 2009

67. *2009NationalSecurityandNonProliferationBriefingBook*, (2008) PreparedbyPeace and Security Initiative, URL: http://www.cdi.org/pdfs/2009NSNPbriefingbook.pdf, accessed on 14 April 2009

68. Peter Baker (2009), "Obama Offered Deal to Russia in Secret Letter," *New York Times*, 2 March 2009

69. "President Obama Signals to Russia Missile Defence Shield Can Vanish If Iran Doesn't Get Nukes," URL: http://blogs.abcnews.com/politicalpunch/2009/03/president-oba-3.html, Accessed 5 April 2009

70. Tom Sauer (2009), "Missile Defence and Nuclear Elimination: Mutually Destroying Each Other"

71. Tom Sauer (2003), "Back to Arms Control: Limiting US National Missile Defence Program," Contemporary Security Policy, 24 (3), pp 91-128

Chapter 5

1. Robert Glipin, *War and Change in World Politics*,New York : W.W. Norton, 1988).
2. Liu Xuecheng (1999), *Zhingguo he Meiguo:duishou haishi huoban* (China and the United States: Foes or Partners), (Beijing: Jingji Kexue chubanshe,1999).
3. Hu Fan (1999), *Daguo di zunyan* (The Dignity of a Great Power), (Beijing: Haitian Chubanshe, 1999).
4. Zhu Feng, "Yilake zhanzheng yu guoiji zhanlue geiju xin taishi" (Iraq War and New Trends in International Security), in Fu Mengmei (ed) *Fankong Beijing xia Meiguo quanqiu zhanlue* (American Global Strategy in the Age of War on Terrorism), (Beijing :Shishi chubanshe, 2000).

5. Robert G. Sutter, *China's Rise in Asia: Promises and Perils* (UK: Rowman and Littlefield Publishers, 2005)
6. Martin Walker (2006), "China Boosts Defence Spending Another 15 Percent," URL: http://www.spacewar.com/reports/China_Boosts_Defense_Spending_Another_15_Percent.html (online: web), Accessed 12 May 2009
7. Elizabeth Economy (2008), "China, the US and Japan: Reconfigurating Relations in Southeast Asia," in Suisheng Zho (ed) *China-US Relations: Transformed Perspectives and Strategic Interactions*, (London: Routledge Publication, 2008).
8. Phillip Yang (2000), "Challenges to the US East Asian Security Policy: Implications for Taiwan's Security," URL: http://taiwansecurity.org/TS/Yang-1000.htm (Online: web), Assessed 12 April 2009
9. Ibid.
10. Richard D. Fisher (2008), *China's Military Modernisation: Building for Regional and Global Reach* (US: Praeger Security International, 2008).
11. Ibid.
12. Phillip C. Saunders, "Managing a Multifaceted Relationship Between the USA and China," in Suisheng Zho (ed), *China-US Relations: Transformed Perspectives and Strategic Interactions* (London: Routledge Publication, 2008).
13. Yang, n.8.
14. Ibid
15. Fisher, n.10.
16. Bates Gill, Nicholas R. Lards and Derk Mitchell, *The Balance Sheet: China*, (New York :Public Affairs, 2006).
17. Ronald Dannreuther (2000), "Escaping the Enlargement Trap in NATO-Russian Relations,." *Survival*, 41(4), pp. 145-164.
18. Ye Jicheng, Chen Meihui and Lu Shijun (2002), "Review and Future Estimation of PLA Force Development," *Journal of National DefenceManagement*, 23(2), pp 55-68
19. Ting Wai, "The Potential Flashpoint: Taiwan" in Paul J. Bolt and Albert Willner (ed), *China's Nuclear Future* (Delhi: Viva Books Pvt Ltd, 2008).
20. Ibid.
21. Neha Kumar (2008), "Enhancing the US First Strike Capability by Deployment of Ballistic Missile Defence," *World Affairs*, 12(3): 70-82.
22. Ivan Eland (2003), "Is Chinese Military Modernisation a Threat to the US?" URL: www.cato.org/pubs/pas/pa465.pdf, Accessed on 14 April 2009
23 Fisher, n.10.
24. Ibid.
25. Zhuang Jianzhong, "Missile Defence and Big Power Relations," conference

paper, Shanghai Center forPacRim Strategic Studies, Shanghai, January 2002 as quoted by Brat Roberts (2003), "China and Ballistic Missile Defense: 1955-2002 and Beyond," URL: http://www.fas.org/nuke/guide/china/doctrine/bmd.pdf, accessed on 20 April 2009

26. Sherman W. Garnett and Norman A. Graham (2007), "From Wary Collaboration to Wary Cooperation? US-Russian Security Cooperation Since the End of Cold War," URL: http://www.isp.msu.edu/cers/occasionalpapers/FromWaryCollaborationtoWaryCompetition.pd f, Accessed on 2 May 2009
27. Ibid.
28. Ibid.
29. Valentin Kunin (2000), "Cold Peace Instead of Cold War," *Ria Novosti*, March 2 2000.
30. Dannreuther, n.17.
31. Oksana Antoneko (2000), "Russia, NATO and European Security after Kosovo," *Survival.*, 41(4), pp. 124-144
32. Ibid.
33. Ibid.
34. Anders Aslund and Andrew Kuchins (2009), "Pressing the Reset Button on US-Russia Relations," URL: http://www.csis.org/media/csis/pubs/090405_policy_briefing_russia_balance.pdf, accessed on 7 May 2009
35. Ibid.
36. Eugene Rumer and Angela Stent (2009), "Russia and the West," *Survival*, 51(2), pp 91-104
37. ON Mehrotra, (1998), "NATO Eastward Expansion and Russian Security," *Strategic Analysis*, pp. 1125-1135
38. Li Peng on Sino-Russian Relations in BBC Summary on World Broadcasts, 25 February 1994.
39. Paradorn Rangsimaporn (2006), "Russia's Debate on Military-Technological Cooperation with China: From Yeltsin to Putin," *Asian Survey*, 46(3): pp. 477-495.
40. Dittmer Lowell, "The Sino-Russian Strategic Partnership: Ghost of Strategic Triangle" in Guoli Liu (ed), *Chinese Foreign Policy in Transition* (New York: Aldine De Gruyter, 2004).
41. Ibid.
42. KO Sangtu (2008), "Russia's Choice of Alliance: Balancing or Bandwagoning," URL: http://src-h.slav.hokudai.ac.jp/coe21/publish/no16_1_ses/08_sangtu.pdf., Accessed 15 May 2009
43. Col. AA. Migunov (2009), "Reorganisation of Chinese Armed Forces and Further

Development of Russo-Chinese Relations," *Military Thought.*

44. Huei-Ming Mao (2003), "The US-China-Russia Strategic Triangle Relationship-Since the beginning of the Bush Administration," *Tamkang Journal of International Affais,* URL: www2.tku.edu.tw/~ti/Journal/8-3/834.pdf , Accessed on 10 May 2009.
45. Pan Guang, "China in the Shanghai Cooperation Organisation," in Wang Gungwu and Zheng Youngnian, *China and the New International Order,* (London: Rouledge Publicatio, 2008).
46. Migunov, n.43.
47. Sangtu, n.42.
48. Lowell Dittmer, "The Strategic Triangle: An Elementary Game Theoretical Analysis," *World Politics,* 33 (4) and Gerald Segal (1982*), The Great Power Triangle,* (New York: St Martin Press, 1981).
49. Robert S. Ross, *China, the United States and the Soviet Union: Tri-Polarity and Policy making in the Cold War* (New York : ME Sharp, 1993).
50. Huei-Ming Mao (2003), "The US-China-Russia Strategic Triangle Relationship-Since the Beginning of the Bush Administration," *Tamkang Journal of International Affais,* URL: www2.tku.edu.tw/~ti/Journal/8-3/834.pdf , accessed on 10 May 2009.
51. Ibid.
52. Ibid.
53. Dittmer, n.48.
54. Ibid.
55. Ibid.
56. John Mearsheimer, *The Tragedy of Great Power Politics,* (New York: W.W Norton and Company, 2001)

Chapter 6

1. Here the problem is that states consider the defencive steps of other states as offensive measures. As a result, states prepare for defensive purposes but these are again taken as offensive steps. Such a situation is visible since the US decided to have BMD systems and do give away with the ABM Treaty. The US builds BMD systems so as to protect itself from the missile attacks of rogue states and terrorist groups. For the US, this is a defensive action but China and Russia consider it as offensive because they believe that this would degrade their deterrence. As a result, they take defensive measures by building more missiles and by changing doctrines, which are regarded as offensive measures by the US. This results in a continuous arms race.

2. Dingli Shen (2000), "Ballistic Missile Defence and China's National Security," *Jane DefenceWeekly*, May 2000.
3. Michel Krepon, (2001), "Lost in Space: The Misguided Drive Toward Anti-Satellite Weapons," *Foreign Affairs*, 80(3):2-8.
4. Ibid.
5. Brad Robers (2003), "China and Ballistic Missile Defence: 1995-2002 and Beyond," *IDA Papers*, accessed 30 January 2008, URL: www.fas.org/nuke/guide/china/doctrine/bmd.pdf: 1-47
6. Jing-Dong Yuan (2000), "MTCR and Missile Proliferation: Moving Towards Next Phase," URL: http://www.dfait-maeci.gc.ca/arms/isrop/research/yuan_2000/menu-en.asp?#toc
7. * Sha Zukang (1999), "Can BMD Really Enhance Security?" Remarks at the Second US-China conference on Arms Control, Disarmament and Non Proliferation, [Online: web], Accessed on 20 Feb 2008, URL: http://www.nti.org/db/china/engdocs/shabmd.htm
8. Ibid.
9. Ibid.
10. *Hu Xiaodi (2001), Statement in 2001of UN Disarmament Commission, by Head of the Chinese Delegation", [Online: web], Accessed on 4 March 2008, URL: http://www.nti.org/db/china/engdocs/hu41001.htm
11. Bin Li (2001), "The Impact of NMD on the Chinese Nuclear Modernisation," accessed on 15 February 2008, URL: www.emergingfromconflict.org/readings/bin.pdf
12. Patrick MO Donogue (2000), "Theater Missile Defence in Japan: Implications for the US-China-Japan Strategic Relationship," accessed on 19 February 2008 URL: http://www.strategicstudiesinstitute.army.mil/pdffiles/pub66.pdf.
13. "China's Opposition to US Missile Defence Programme," [Online: web] accessed 23 February 2008, URL: http: www.nti.org/db/china/mdpos.htm
14. David Finkelstein (2001), "National Missile Defence and China Current Security Perceptions," accessed on 16 Februry 2008 URL: http://www.stimson.org/china/pdf/finkelstein.pdf
15. * Sha Zukang (2001), Speech at NMD briefing "Permanent Mission of the PRC to the UN Mission Geneva," [Online: web], accessed on 2 May 2008, URL: http://www.nti.org/db/china/deterpos.htm
16. Jing-Dong Yuan (2000), "MTCR and Missile Proliferation: Moving Towards Next Phase," URL: http://www.dfait-maeci.gc.ca/arms/isrop/research/yuan_2000/menu-en.asp?#toc
17. Ibid.

18. Roberts Delgado (2005), "What Should be the United States Policy Towards Ballistic Missile Defence in Asia," accessed on 10 August 2007 URL: http://www.strategicstudiesinstitute.army.mil/pdffiles/ksil24.pdf: 1-17
19. Patrick M.O. Donogue (2000), "Theatre Missile Defence in Japan: Implications for the US-China-Japan Strategic Relationship," Accessed on 19 Feb 2008 URL: http://www.strategicstudiesinstitute.army.mil/pdffiles/pub66.pdf.
20 Wade L. Huntley and Robert Brown (2001), "Missile Defence and China," Foreign Policy in focus, 6(3), accessed 5 March 2008 URL: http://www.fpif.org/pdf/vol6/03iftaiwan.pdf
21 James Mulvenon (2002), "Missile Defence and Taiwan Scenario," Report 44, A.Henry Stimson Centre, accessed on 22 February 2008 NMD-China report URL: http://www.stimson.org/china/pdf/mulvenon.pdf: 1-8
22. Arthur S. Ding (1999), "China Concerns About Theatre Missile Defence: A Critique," *Non Proliferation Review,* URL: http://cns.miis.edu/pubs/npr/vol06/64/ding64.pdf
23. Jing-Dong Yuan (2000), "MTCR and Missile Proliferation: Moving Towards Next Phase," URL: http://www.dfait-maeci.gc.ca/arms/isrop/research/yuan_2000/menu-en.asp?#toc
24. *"China Attitude Towards Nuclear Deterrence," [Online: web], Accessed on 17 February 2008, URL: http://www.nti.org/db/china/deterpos.htm
25. Paul H.B Godwin (2002), "Potential Chinese Response to the US BMD" (Online:web), accessed on 1 March 2008 URL: www.stimson.org
26. Brad Roberts (2003), "China and Ballistic Missile Defence: 1955 to 2002 and Beyond," accessed on 30 Jan 2008 IDA Papers URL: http://www.fas.org/nuke/guide/china/doctrine/bmd.pdf :1-47
27. Godwin, n.25.
28. Joseph Cirincione (2000), "China Nuclear Modernisation," Proliferation Brief, 2(8) [Online:web], Accessed on 17 February 2008 URL: http://www.carnegieendowment.org/publications/index.cfm?fa=view&id=93&prog=zgp&proj=znpp
29. Putin (2000), "Russia is Still a Superpower," Interview with Russian President Vladimir Putin, *Hamburg Welt am Sonntag,* June 11, 2000
30. Ibid.
31. James M, Lindsay and Michael O. Halnon, *Defending America: The Case of Limited National Missile Defence* (Washington: Brooking Institution, 2001).
32. Amy F . Wolf (2002), "National Missile Defence: Russia Reaction," accessed on 20 February 2008, URL: http://fpc.state.gov/documents/organization/11635.pdf:

1-20

33. Ibid.
34. Neha Kumar (2007), "Russia Joins Radar Gamble," [Online: web], Accessed on 14 July 2007 URL: http://www.ipcs.org/whatsNewArticle1.jsp?action=showView&kValue=2350&status=article&mod=b
35. Neha Kumar (2007), "Implications of Russia Withdrawal from Arms Control Treaties," [Online: web], Accessed on 23 August 2007 URL: http://www.ipcs.org/whatsNewArticle11.jsp?action=showView&kValue=2376&status=article&mod=b
36. Ibid.
37. Neha Kumar (2007), "US Exaggeration of Iran Ballistic Missile Threat," *Mainstream*, XLVI (1)
38. 2008 Assessment of the Ballistic Missile Defence (2009), URL: http://www.cdi.org/pdfs/FY08BMDSJan09.pdb, accessed on 25 May 2009.
39. Joseph Cirincione, *Bomb Scare: The History and Future of Nuclear Weapons* (New York : Columbia University Press, 2007).
40. Ibid.
41. George Lewis, "The Planned U.S. National Missile Defence: Will it work? [Online: web], accessed on 23 July 2000. www.epsusa.org/publications/newsletter/july2000/lewis.htm
42. Counter-measures, [Online :web], accessed on 15 December 2007 www.ucsusa.org/global_security/missile_defense/countermeasures.html
43. Lewis, n.41.
44. "Counter-measures," [Online :web], accessed on 15 Dec 2007 www.ucsusa.org/global_security/missile_defense/countermeasures.html
45. n.43.
46. Lindsay and Halnon, n.31.
47. n.44.
48. Ibid.
49. Peter J. Mantle, *The Missile Defence Equation* (Virginia: American Institute of Aeronautics and Astronautics, 2004).
50. Michael C. Sirak (2004), "Year of the Missile Shield," *Air Force Magazine*, 25-29.
51. Dennis M. Gormley (2004), "Addressing the Spread of Cruise Missiles and Unmanned Air Vehicles," [Online: web], accessed on 15 December 2007 URL: http://www.nti.org/e_research/e3_39a.html
52. " The Cruise Missile Defence: The Prospect for Homeland"(2008), URL: http://www3.ausa.org/pdfdocs/nsw06-3.pdf, Accessed 3 March 2009

Chapter 7

1. Bruno Tertrais (2001), "US Missile Defence: Strategically Sound, Politically Questionable," accessed on 28 December 2007 URL: http://www.cer.org.uk/pdf/cerwp11.pdf: 4-23
2. Joseph Cirincione (2007), *Bomb Scare: The History and Future of Nuclear Weapons* (New York: Columbia University Press, 2007).
3. Ibid.
4. *"Foreign Missile Developments and Ballistic Missile Threat Through 2015," Unclassified Summary of National Intelligence Estimates 2001, accessed on 22 Aug 2007 URL: http://www.dni.gov/nic/PDF_GIF_otherprod/missilethreat2001.pdf:1-15
5. Neha Kumar (2007), "US Exaggeration of Iran Ballistic Missile Threat," *Mainstream*, XLVI (1)
6. Ibid.
7. Ted Postal (2000), "Missile Defence: The Russian Reaction," [Online: web] Accessed 18 Feb 2008, URL: http:// www.thebulletin.org/columns/pavel-podwig/20070226.html
8. Cruise Missiles, Federation of American Scientist [Online:web], accessed on 15 Dec ember 2007, URL: http://www.fas.org/nuke/intro/cm/
9. *National Intelligence Estimates 1995, "Emerging Missile Threats to the US in next 15 Years," [Online: web] accessed on 21 July 2007 URL: http://www.fas.org/spp/starwars/offdocs/nie9519.htm
10. *Crishtopher Bolacom and Sharon Squassoni (2002), "Cruise Missile Proliferation," URL: http://www.fas.org/spp/starwars/crs/RS21252.pdf.
11. Igor JP Gardner (1999), "Theatre Land Attack Cruise Missiles," Accessed 12 Feb 2008, URL: http://www.intellnet.org/documents/600/070/675.pdf: 1-23
12. DM. Gromley and SK. MacMohan (1996), "Who is Guarding the Backdoor? The Neglected Pillar of US Theatre Missile Defense," *International Defence Review*, 21-24
13. Thomas G. Mahnken (2005), "The Cruise Missile Challenge," accessed on 25 February 2008 URL: http://www.csbaonline.org/4Publications/PubLibrary/R.20050310.CruiseMiss/R.20050310.CruiseMiss.pdf: 1-41
14. Dennis M. Gormley (2004), "Addressing the Spread of Cruise Missiles and Unmanned Air Vehicles," [Online: web], accessed on 15 Dec 2007 URL: http://www.nti.org/e_research/e3_39a.html
15. Missile Defence Update (2006), [Online: web], accessed on 20 September 2007, URL: http://www.unidir.ch/pdf/ouvrages/pdf-1-92-9045-002-1-en.pdf: 1-31
16. *Ravi R. Hichkad and Cristopher Bolkcom (2004), "Cruise Missile Defence," accessed

on 15 December 2007 URL: http://www.fas.org/man/crs/RS21921.pdf.

17. Charles Lambert (2003), "The Cruise Missile Conundrum," Aerospace America, [Online: web], Accessed 15 Dec 2007, URL: http://www.aiaa.org/werospace/Articles.cfm?issuetocid=309&ArchieveIssueID=35
18. Richard Speier (2007), "Missile Non-Proliferation and Missile Defence: Fitting Them Together," *Arms Control Today*, [Online: web], Accessed on 21 Feb 2008, URL: http://www.armscontrol.org/act/2007_11/Speier.asp
19. Hans M. Kristensen and Robert S. Norris (2008), "The US Nuclear Forces 2008," *Bulletin of the Atomic Scientists*, March 2008: 50-54.
20. Ibid.
21. "Rational and Requirments for US Nuclear Arms Forces and Arms Control," Executive Report by National Insitute of Public Policy," accessed 15 September 2008 URL: http://www.carnegieendowment.org/files/nippnukes.pdf
22. Neha Kumar (2008), "Enhancing First Strike Capability by Deployment of Ballistic Missile Defence," World Affairs, 12(3): 70-82
23. Mark Smith (2002), "Stuck on the Launch Pad? The Ballistic Missile Code of Conduct Opens for Business," *Disarmament Diplomacy*, [Online: web], accessed on 10 March 2008, URL: http://www.acronym.org.uk/dd/dd68/68op01.htm
24. Dinshaw Mistry, *Containing Missile Proliferation: Strategic Technology, Security Regimes and International Cooperation in Arms Control*," (London: University of Washington Press, 2004).
25. Kapil Kak (1999), "Missile Proliferation and International Security," *Strategic Analysis*, XXIII (3), [Online: web] Accessed on 21 March 2008 URL: http://www.ciaonet.org/olj/sa/sa_99kak02.html
26. Jerome J. Holton, Lore Lumpe, Jeremy J. Stone (1993), "Proposal for Zero Ballistic Missile Regimes," [Online: web] Acceessed on 20 February 2008 URL: http://www.fas.org/asmp/library/articles/zerobal93.htm
27. Thomas Graham and Dinshaw Mistry (2006), "Two Treaties to Contain Missile Proliferation," [Online: web], accessed on 2 March 2008, *Disarmament Diplomacy* URL: http://www.acronym.org.uk/dd/dd82/82tgdm.htm
28. Mistry, n.24.
29. Graham and Mistry, n.27
30. Keith Payne (1995), "The Missile Technology Control Regime-European involvement and compliance Issue 2," [Online: web], accessed on 12 July 2007, URL: http:// wwww.fas.org/irp/threat/missile/rumsfeld/pt2_payne.htm
31. Daryl G. Kimball, and Wadia Bose (2007), "Of Missiles and Missile Defences," *Arms Control Today*, [Online: web] Accessed 1 Nov 2007, URL: http://www.armscontrol.org/act/2007_10/focus.asp

32. Ibid .
33. Amitav Mallik (2004), *Technology and Security in the 21st Century: A Demand Side Perspectives* (New York :Oxford University Press, 2004).
34. Smith, n.23.
35. Jing-DonYuan (2000), "MTCR and Missile Proliferation: Moving Towards Next Phase," URL: http://www.dfait-maeci.gc.ca/arms/isrop/research/yuan_2000/menu-en.asp?#toc
36. Michelle Maiese (2003), "Confidence Building Measures," [Online: web], Accessed on 14 March 2008 URL: http://www.beyondintractability.org/essay/confidence_building_measures/
37. Yuan, n.35.
38. Mark Smith (2001), "Missile Proliferation, Missile Defences and Arms Control" in "International Perspectives on Missile Control," Occasional Paper 5, Centre for Non-Proliferation
39. Yuri E Fedorov (2002), "The Global Control System and International Code of Conduct: Competition or Cooperation," accessed on 25 February 2008, *Non-Proliferation Review* URL: http://cns.miis.edu/pubs/npr/vol09/92/92fed.pdf: 30-36
40. Victor Mizin (2005), "The Evolution of the Russian Approach to MTCR: The End of Chapter," accessed on 24 Feb 2008, *Journal of Military and Strategic Studies*, 8(1) URL: http://www.jmss.org/2005/fall/articles/mizin.pdf.
41. John Bolton (2002), "International Code of Conduct against Ballistic Missile Proliferation," [Online:Web], accessed on 22 Feb 2008 Annexure 3 URL: http://www.basicint.org/pubs/Notes/2002HagueBM.htm
42. "International Code of Conduct against Ballistic Missile Proliferation," [Online:web], accessed on 24 Feb 2008 URL: http://www.nti.org/db/china/icoc.htm
43. Smith, n. 38.
44. Erik Ekholm, "China Response to the US Missile Defence Program: National Options and Regional Implications," in Heurlin, Bertel and Rynning, Sten (ed), *Missile Defence Regional and International Implication* (London: Roulteldge Publications, 2000)
45. Andrew Lichterman, Zia Mian, MV Ramana and Jurgen Scheffran (2002), "Beyond Missile Defence," accessed on 21 April 2008 URL: http://www.waslweb.org/docs/missilecontrol.pdf: 1-11
46. Ibid.